My first dubbing

I recently had a chance to meet the voice actors for the *Prince of Tennis* anime.
Thank you for taking time out from your busy schedules to help me out. Let's continue working hard together to make *The Prince of Tennis* even more exciting*!!*

– Takeshi Konomi

About Takeshi Konomi

Takeshi Konomi exploded onto the manga scene with the incredible **THE PRINCE OF TENNIS**. His refined art style and sleek character designs proved popular with **Weekly Shonen Jump** readers, and **THE PRINCE OF TENNIS** became the number one sports manga in Japan almost overnight. Its cast of fascinating male tennis players attracted legions of female readers even though it was originally intended to be a boys' comic. The manga continues to be a success in Japan and has inspired a hit anime series, as well as several video games and mountains of merchandise.

THE PRINCE OF TENNIS
VOL. 15
The SHONEN JUMP Manga

**STORY AND ART BY
TAKESHI KONOMI**

English Adaptation/Michelle Pangilinan
Translation/Joe Yamazaki
Touch-up Art & Lettering/Andy Ristaino
Design/Sam Elzway
Editor/Pancha Diaz

Managing Editor/Frances E. Wall
Editorial Director/Elizabeth Kawasaki
VP & Editor in Chief/Yumi Hoashi
Sr. Director of Acquisitions/Rika Inouye
Sr. VP of Marketing/Liza Coppola
Exec. VP of Sales & Marketing/John Easum
Publisher/Hyoe Narita

Printed in the U.S.A.

Published by VIZ Media, LLC
P.O. Box 77010
San Francisco, CA 94107

SHONEN JUMP Manga Edition
10 9 8 7 6 5 4 3 2 1
First printing, September 2006

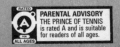

PARENTAL ADVISORY
THE PRINCE OF TENNIS is rated A and is suitable for readers of all ages.

RATED A ALL AGES

THE WORLD'S MOST POPULAR MANGA

www.viz.com

www.shonenjump.com

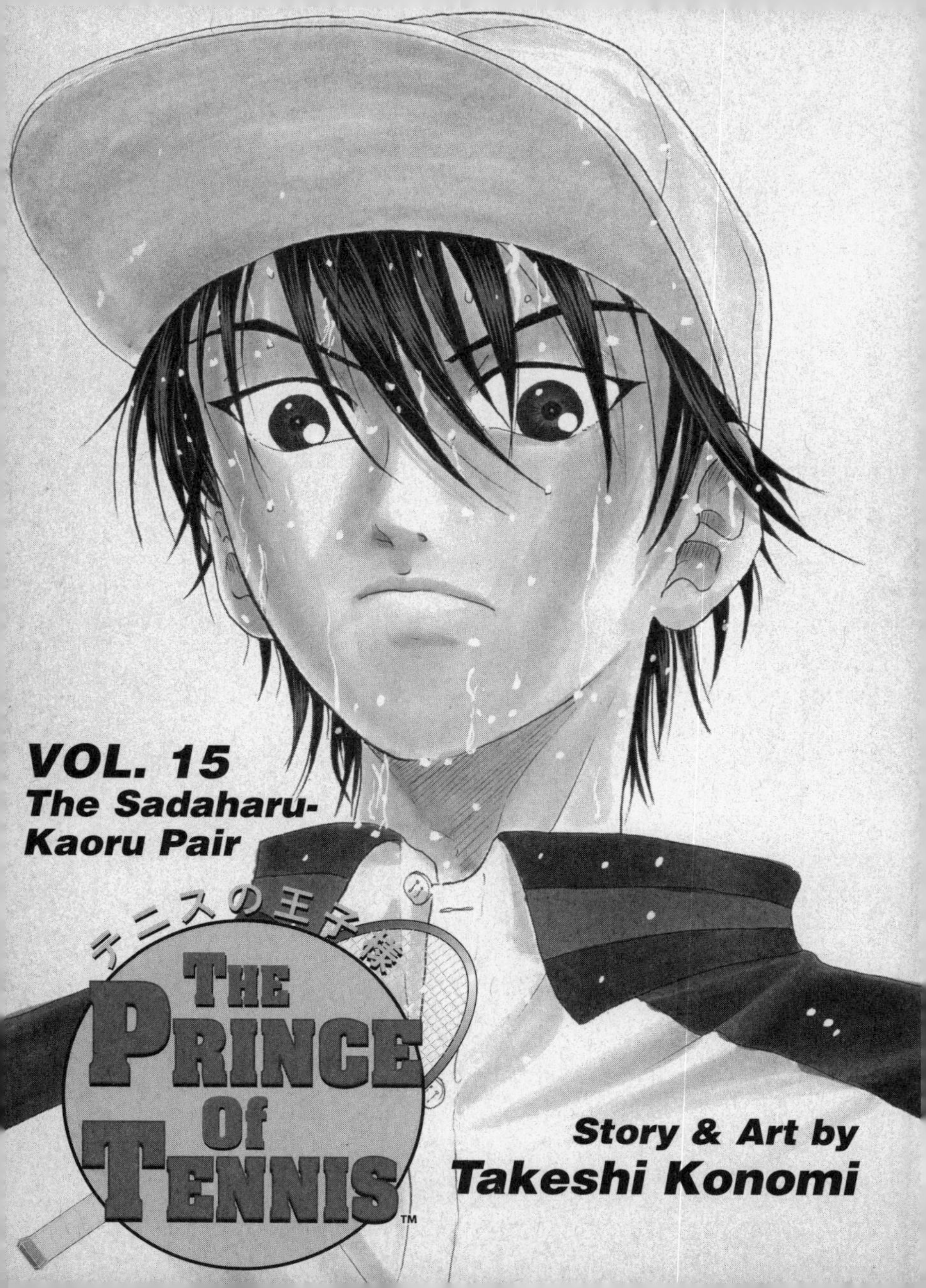

VOL. 15
The Sadaharu-Kaoru Pair

テニスの王子様

THE PRINCE OF TENNIS™

Story & Art by
Takeshi Konomi

ENNIS CLUB

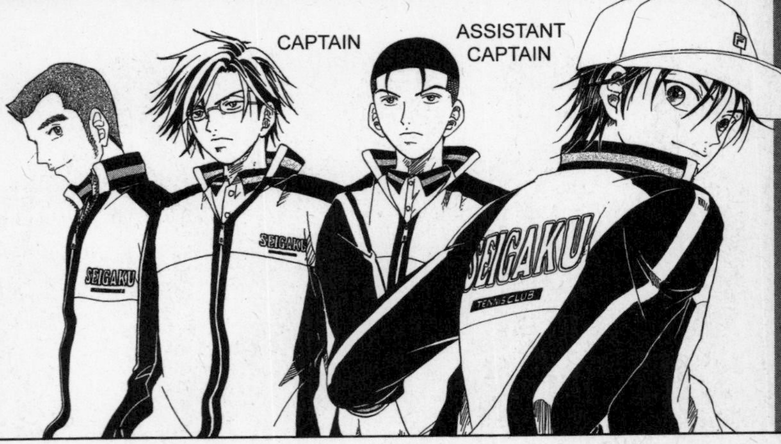
CAPTAIN
ASSISTANT CAPTAIN

●TAKASHI KAWAMURA ●KUNIMITSU TEZUKA ●SHUICHIRO OISHI ● RYOMA ECHIZEN ●

Ryoma Echizen, a student at Seishun Academy, is a tennis prodigy who has won four consecutive U.S. Junior tournaments. This first ever 7th-grade starter has qualified for the District Preliminaries! Despite a few mishaps, Seishun wins the District Prelims and City Tournament and finally earns a ticket to the Kanto Tournament.

Seishun's customary intra-squad ranking matches are held right before the tournament. While the current starters steadily keep their positions, Sadaharu, who has been out of the starting line-up, regains his position on the starting team! Momo, on the other hand, loses his spot.

But Oishi is injured right before his match on the opening day of the Kanto Tournament. As a result, Seishun is forced to use Eiji and Momo as their No. 2 Doubles pair. How will this brand new doubles team fair against Hyotei—last year's runner-up??

STORY &

HARACTERS

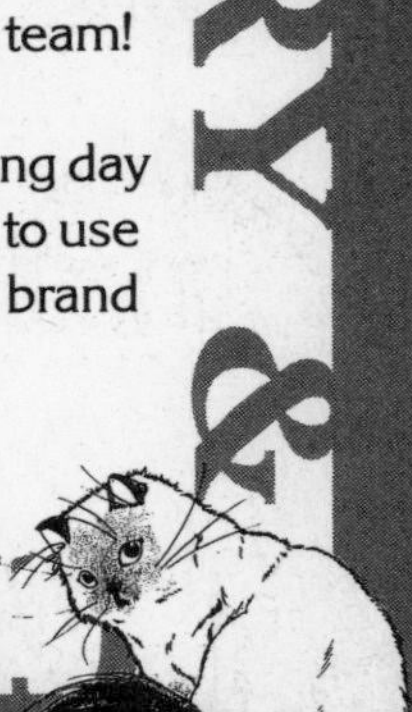

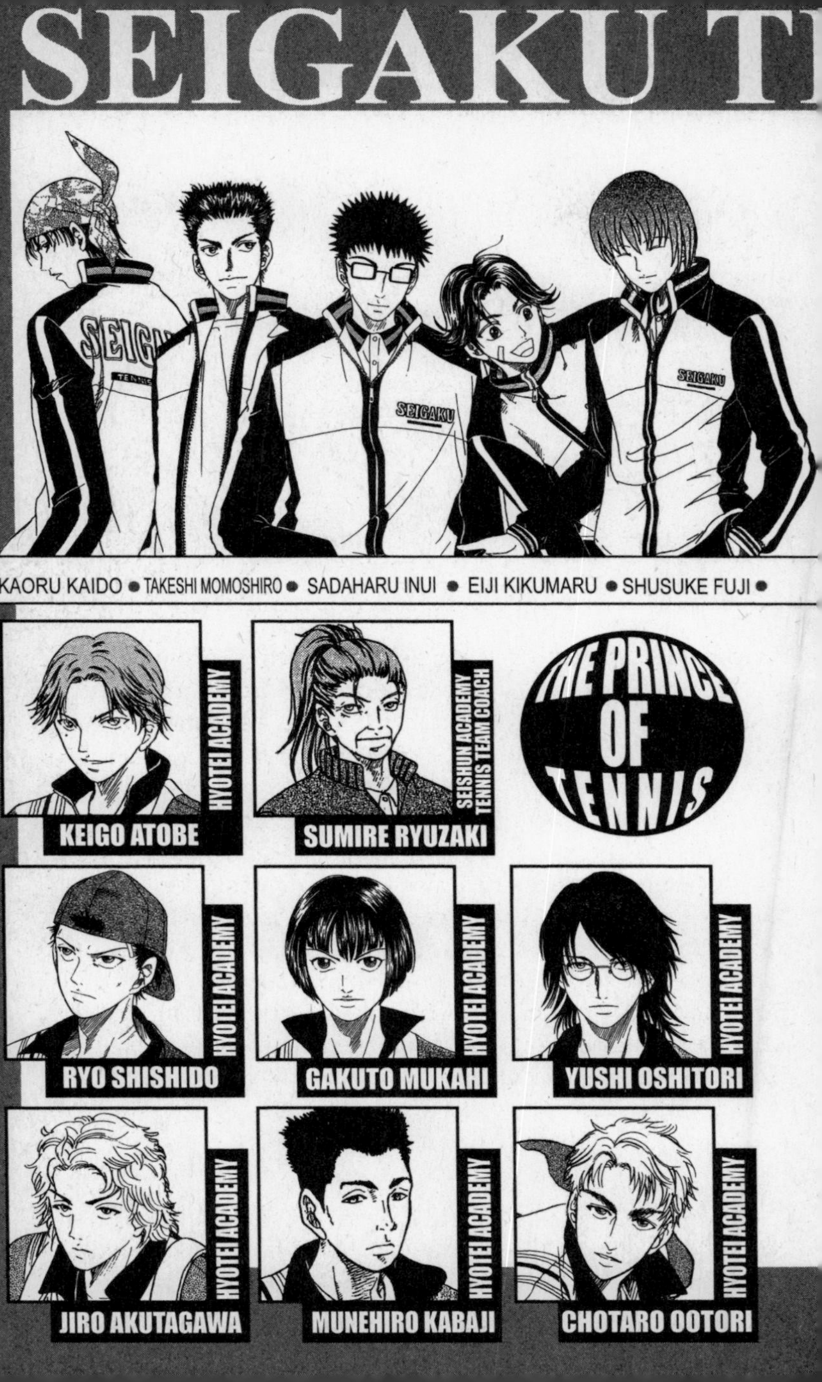
SEIGAKU T
SEIGAKU
SEIGAKU
SEIGAKU
• KAORU KAIDO • TAKESHI MOMOSHIRO • SADAHARU INUI • EIJI KIKUMARU • SHUSUKE FUJI •
THE PRINCE OF TENNIS
KEIGO ATOBE
HYOTEI ACADEMY
SUMIRE RYUZAKI
SEISHUN ACADEMY TENNIS TEAM COACH
RYO SHISHIDO
HYOTEI ACADEMY
GAKUTO MUKAHI
HYOTEI ACADEMY
YUSHI OSHITORI
HYOTEI ACADEMY
JIRO AKUTAGAWA
HYOTEI ACADEMY
MUNEHIRO KABAJI
HYOTEI ACADEMY
CHOTARO OOTORI
HYOTEI ACADEMY

CONTENTS

Vol.15
The Sadaharu-Kaoru Pair

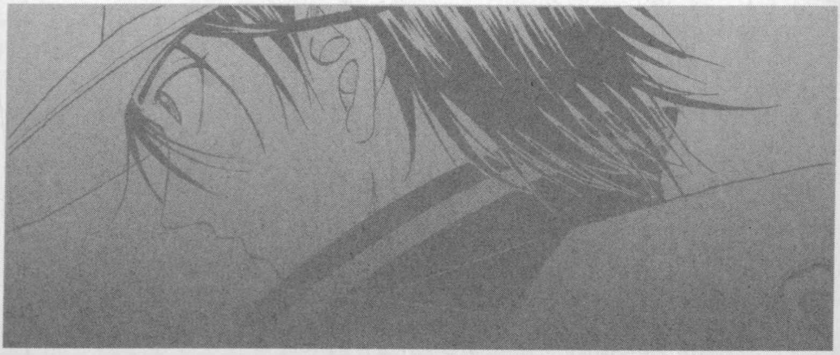

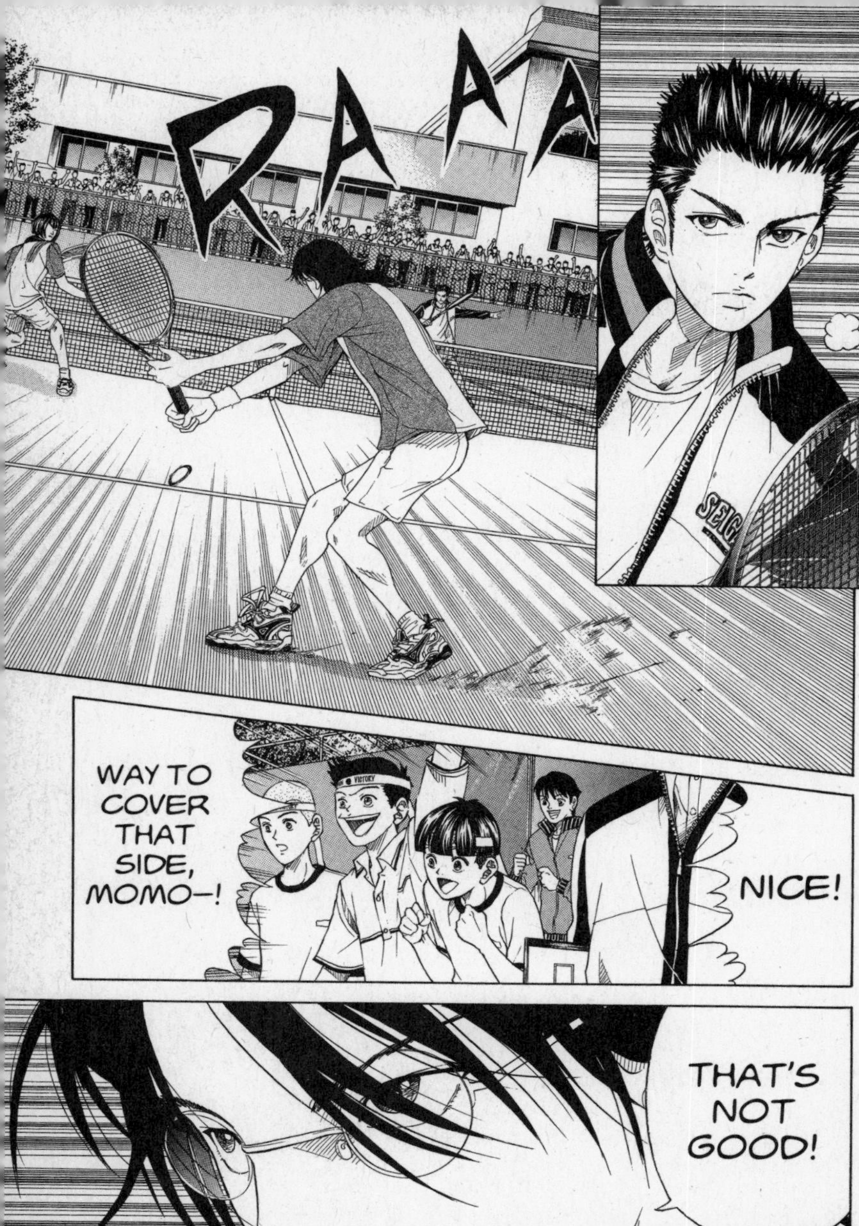
RAAA
NICE!
WAY TO COVER THAT SIDE, MOMO-!
THAT'S NOT GOOD!

GENIUS 124: ACROBATIC BATTLE

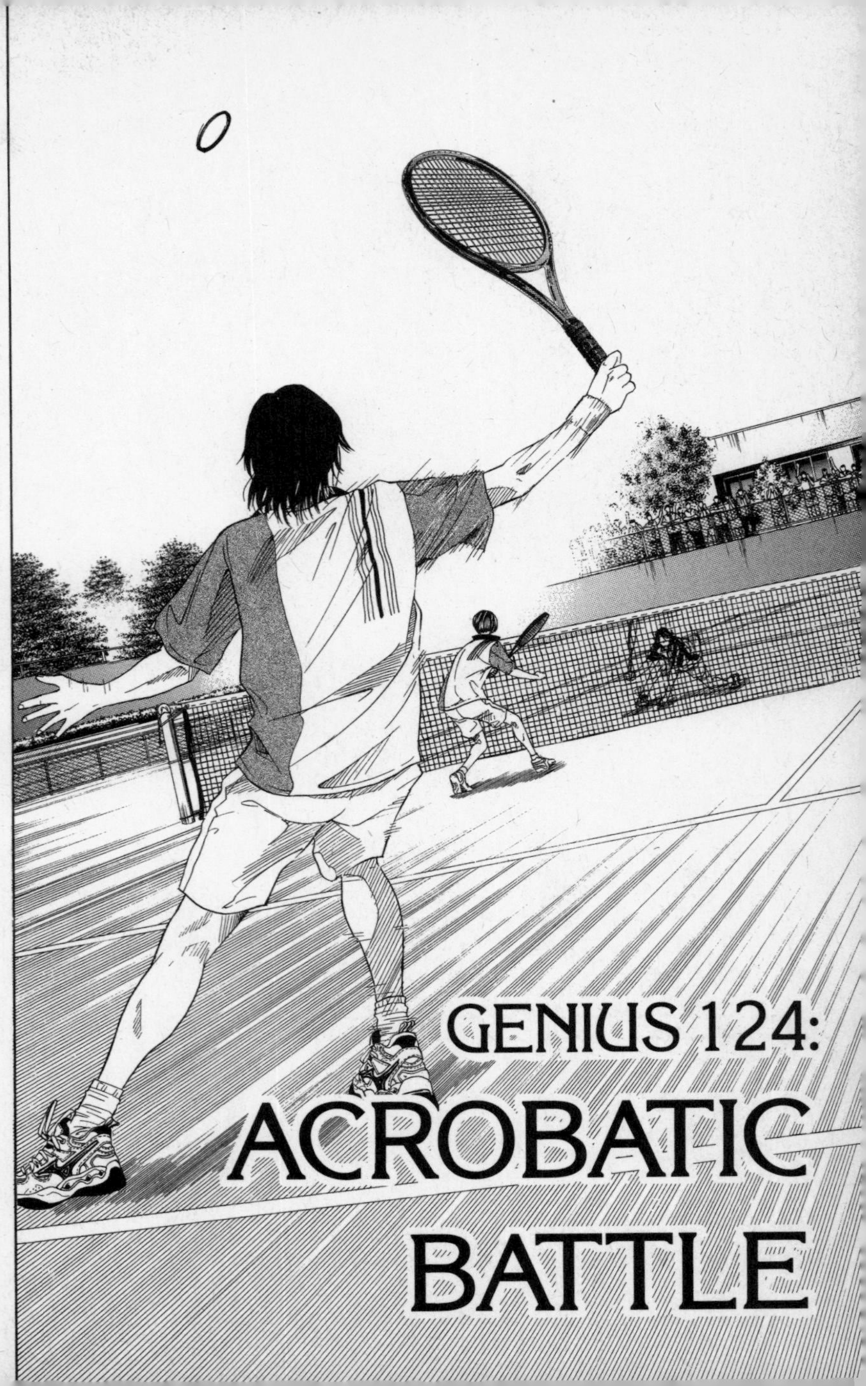
GENIUS 124:
ACROBATIC
BATTLE

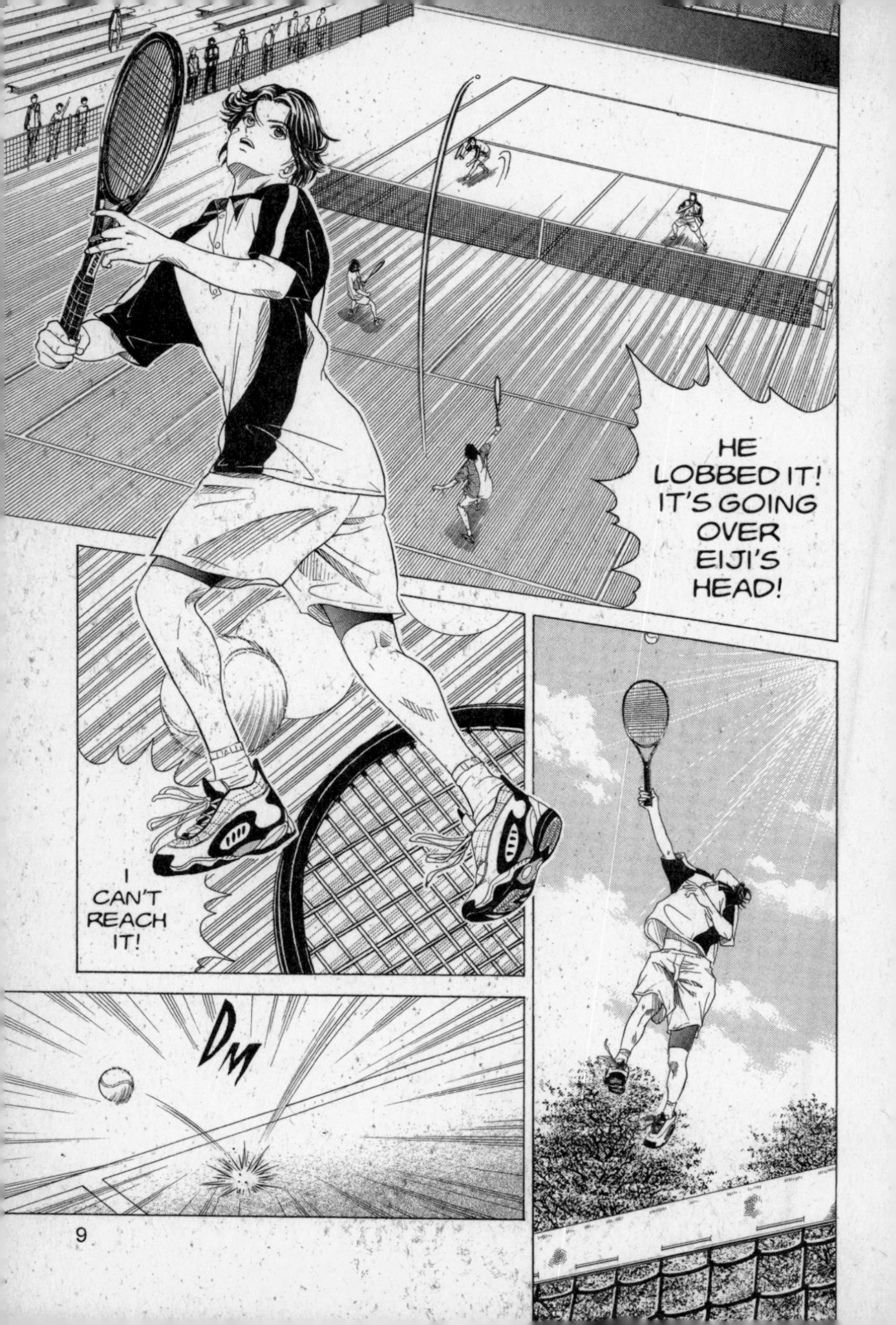
HE LOBBED IT! IT'S GOING OVER EIJI'S HEAD!
I CAN'T REACH IT!
DM

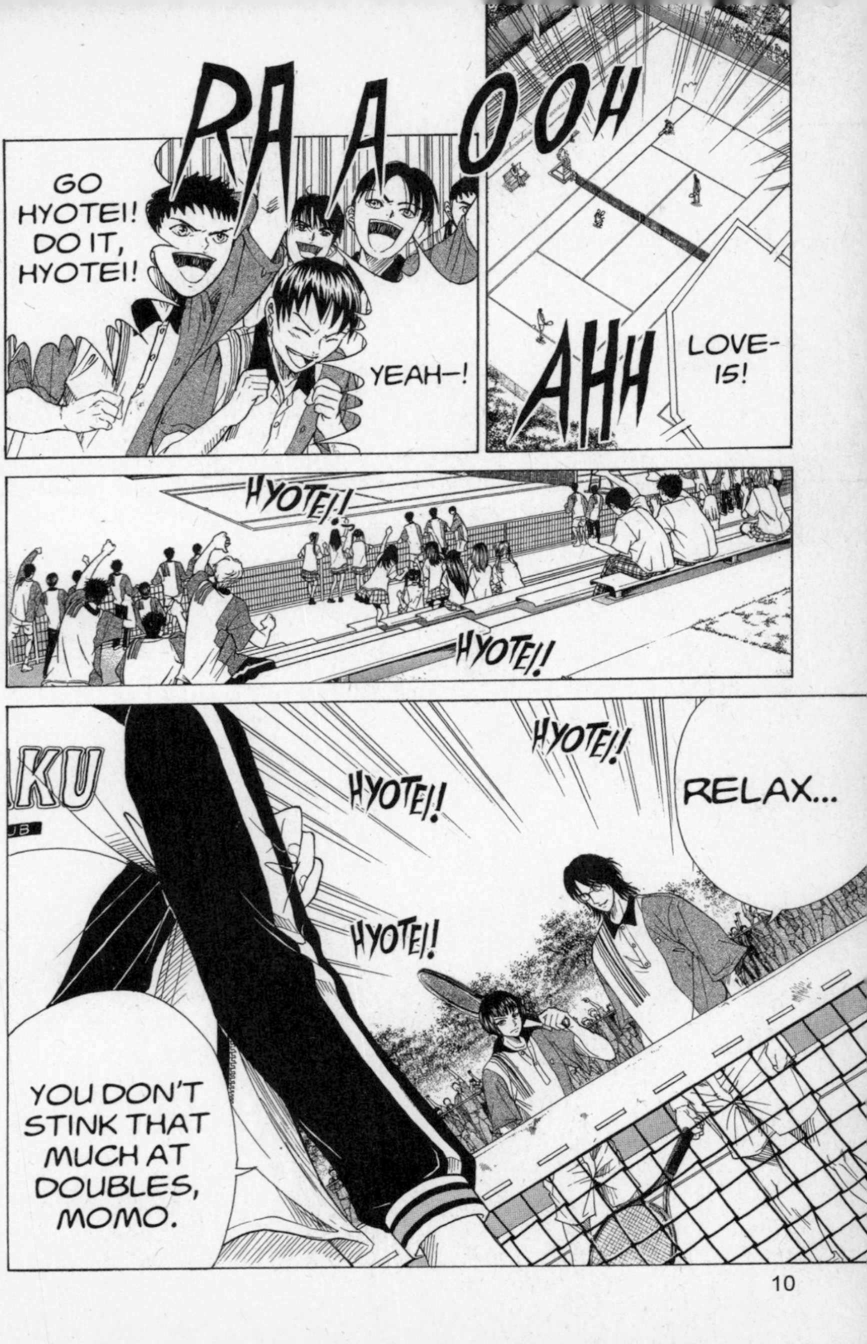
AHH
LOVE-15!
RA A OOH
GO HYOTEI! DO IT, HYOTEI!
YEAH-!
HYOTEI!
HYOTEI!
RELAX...
HYOTEI!
HYOTEI!
HYOTEI!
YOU DON'T STINK THAT MUCH AT DOUBLES, MOMO.

READ THIS WAY

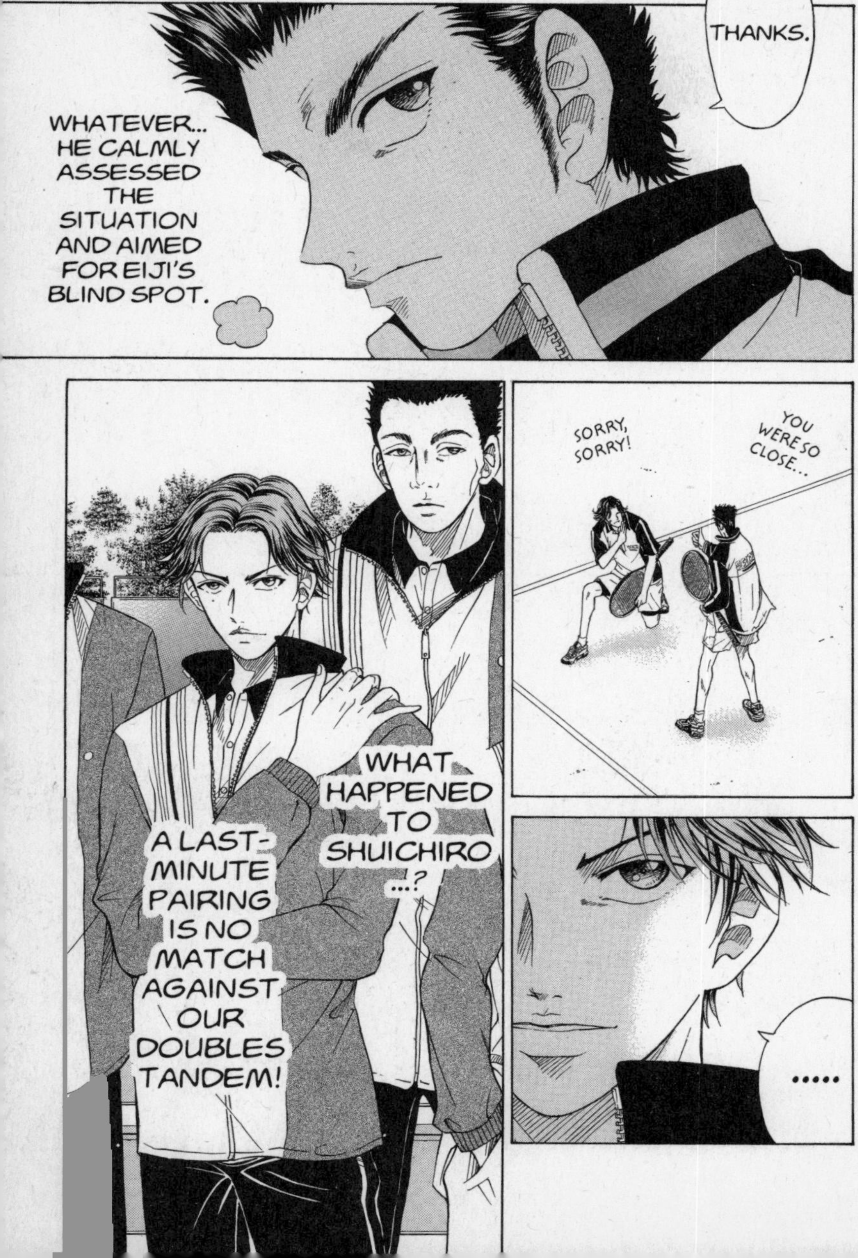

THANKS.
WHATEVER... HE CALMLY ASSESSED THE SITUATION AND AIMED FOR EIJI'S BLIND SPOT.
YOU WERE SO CLOSE...
SORRY, SORRY!
.....
WHAT HAPPENED TO SHUICHIRO ...?
A LAST-MINUTE PAIRING IS NO MATCH AGAINST OUR DOUBLES TANDEM!

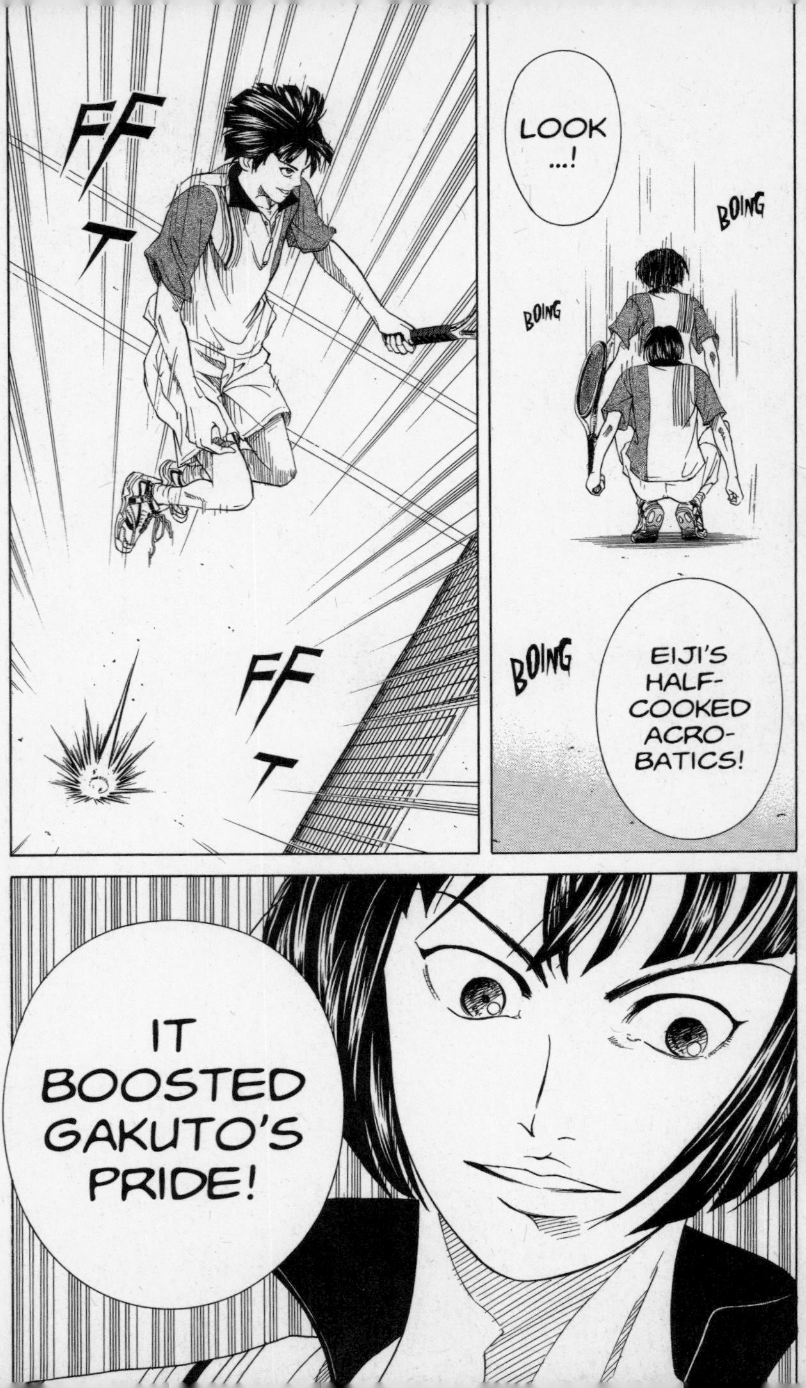
LOOK ...!
BOING
BOING
EIJI'S HALF-COOKED ACRO-BATICS!
BOING
FFT
FFT
IT BOOSTED GAKUTO'S PRIDE!

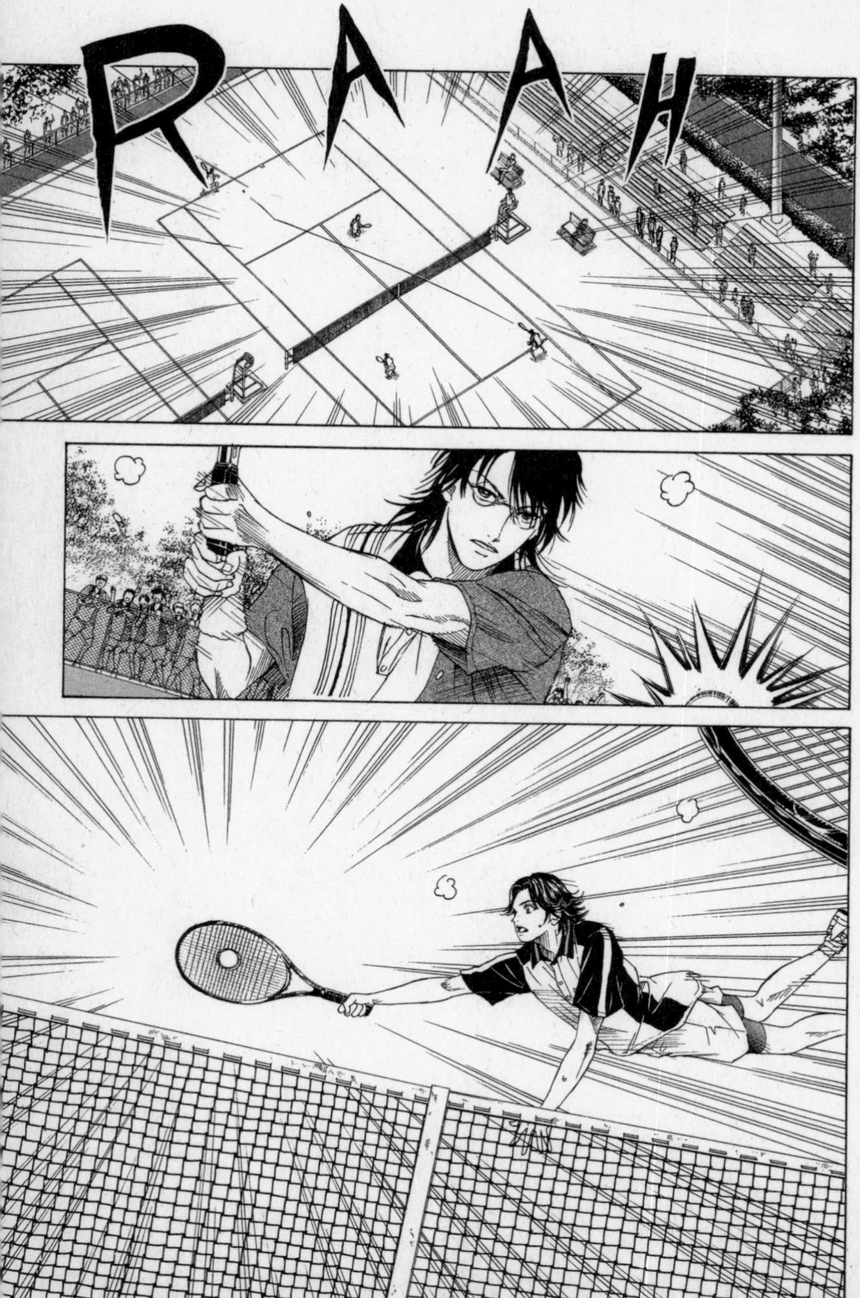
RAAH

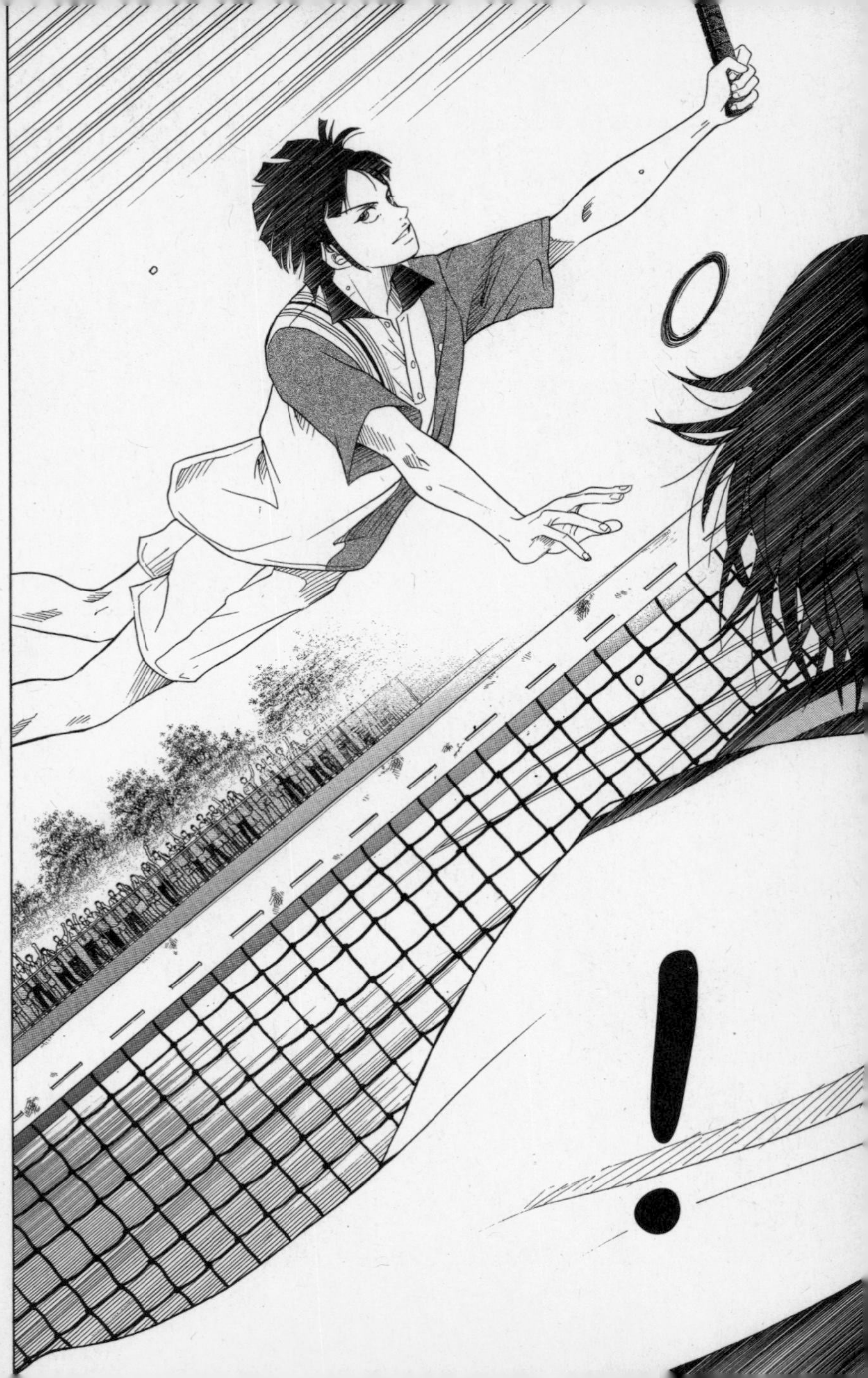
!

READ THIS WAY

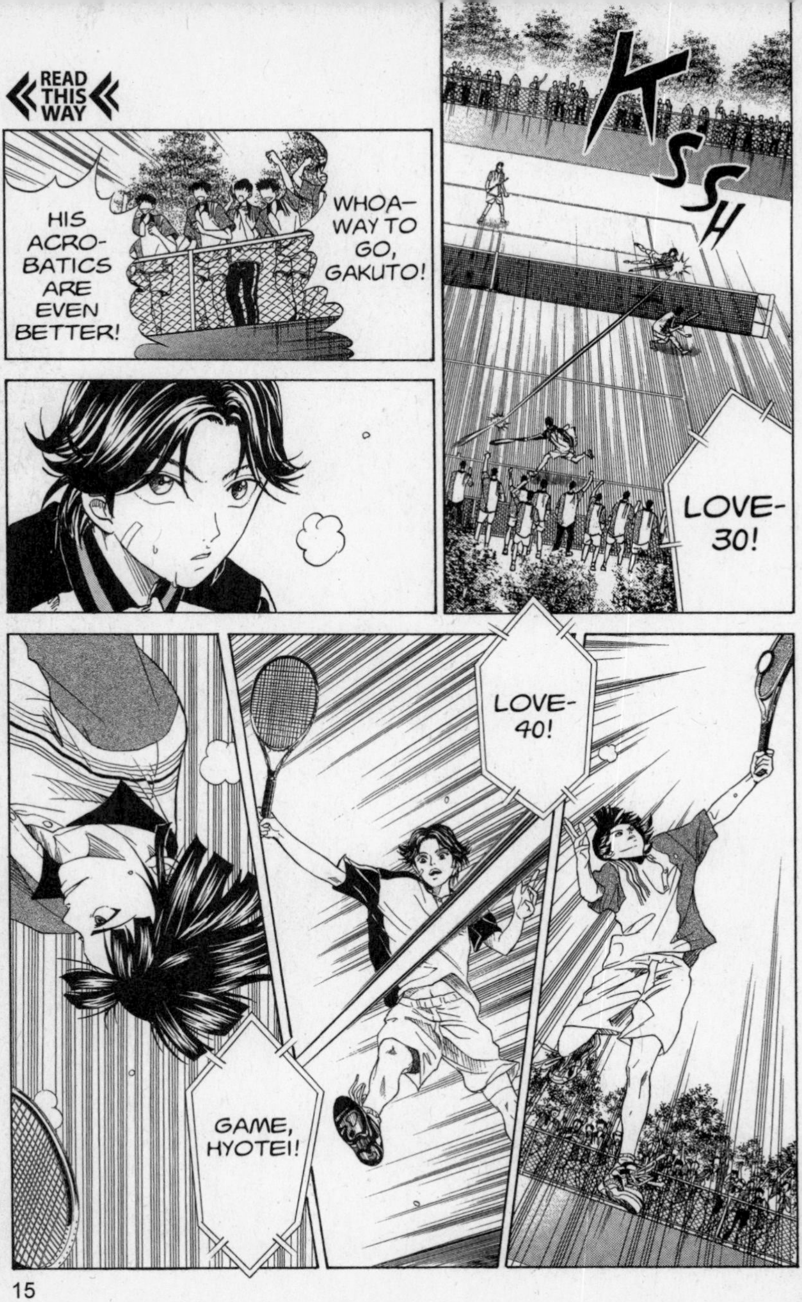

KSSH
LOVE-30!
WHOA—WAY TO GO, GAKUTO!
HIS ACROBATICS ARE EVEN BETTER!
LOVE-40!
GAME, HYOTEI!

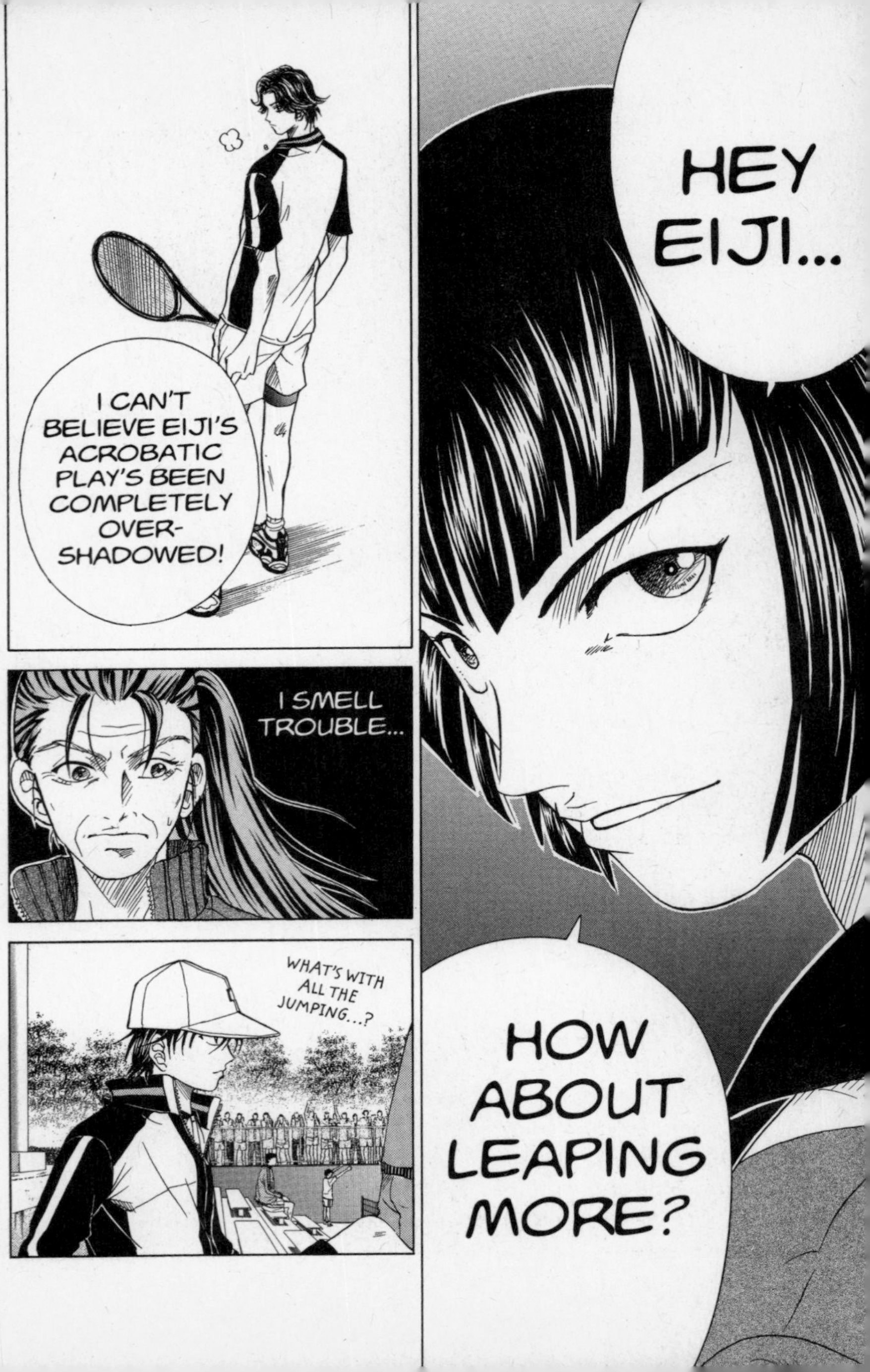
HEY EIJI...
HOW ABOUT LEAPING MORE?
I CAN'T BELIEVE EIJI'S ACROBATIC PLAY'S BEEN COMPLETELY OVER-SHADOWED!
I SMELL TROUBLE...
WHAT'S WITH ALL THE JUMPING...?

READ THIS WAY

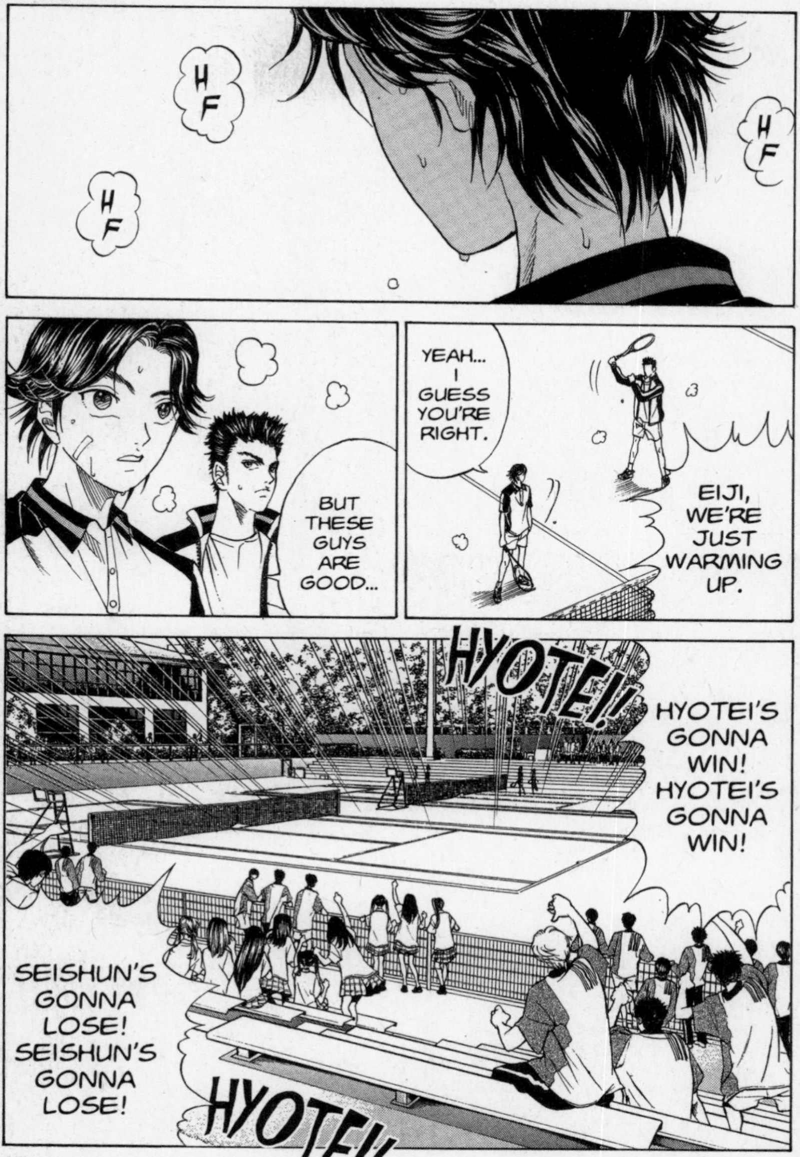
HF
HF
HF
EIJI, WE'RE JUST WARMING UP.
YEAH... I GUESS YOU'RE RIGHT.
BUT THESE GUYS ARE GOOD...
HYOTEI!!
HYOTEI'S GONNA WIN! HYOTEI'S GONNA WIN!
SEISHUN'S GONNA LOSE! SEISHUN'S GONNA LOSE!
HYOTEI!!

THINGS AREN'T LOOKING GOOD—
I GOTTA DO SOME-THING ABOUT THAT GUY...
BOING
BOING
I'LL KEEP HIM FROM DOING HIS MOVES!

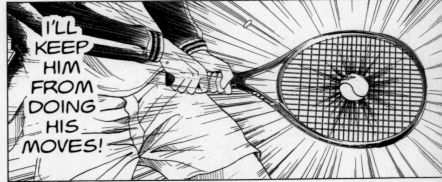

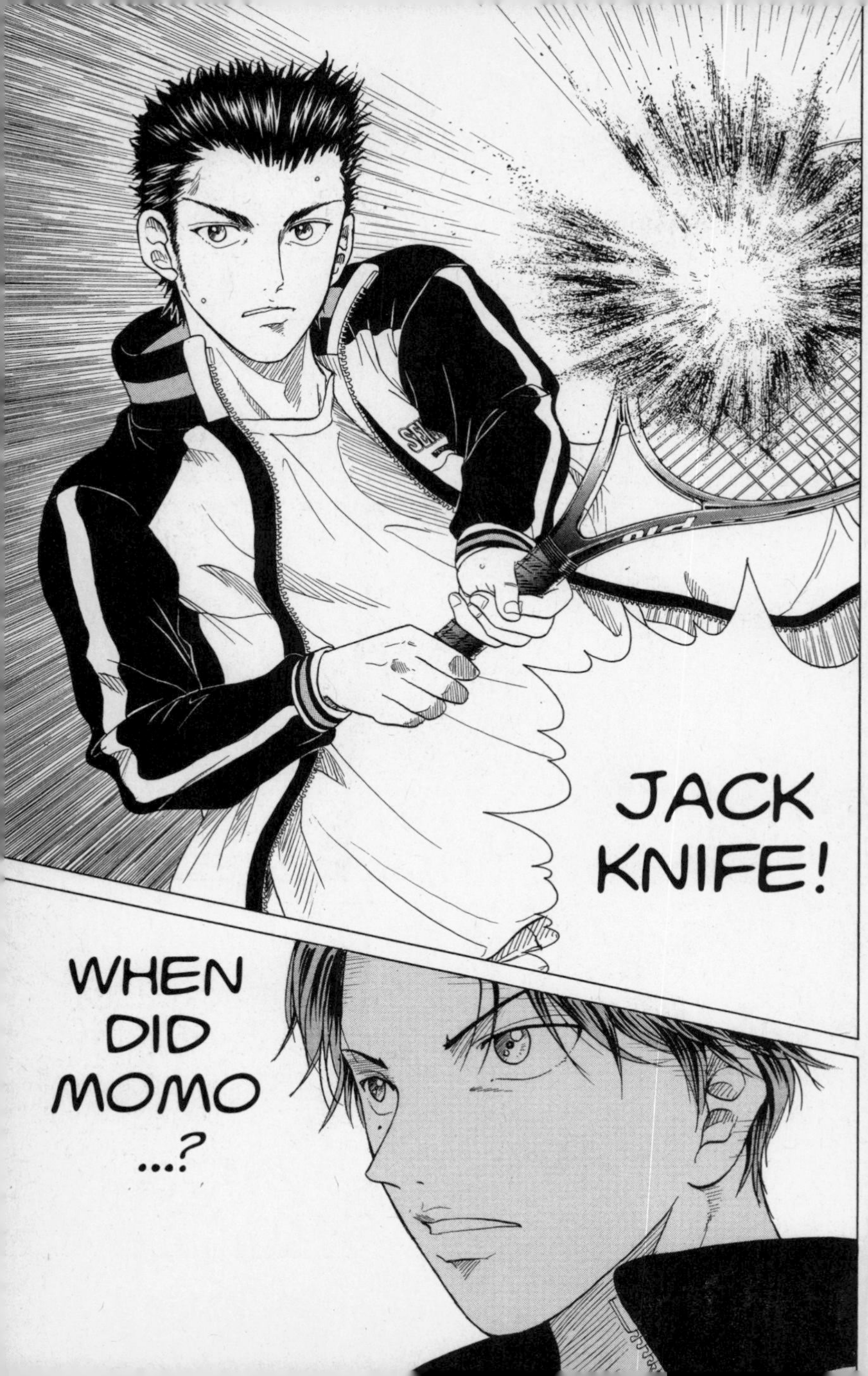
JACK KNIFE!
WHEN DID MOMO ...?

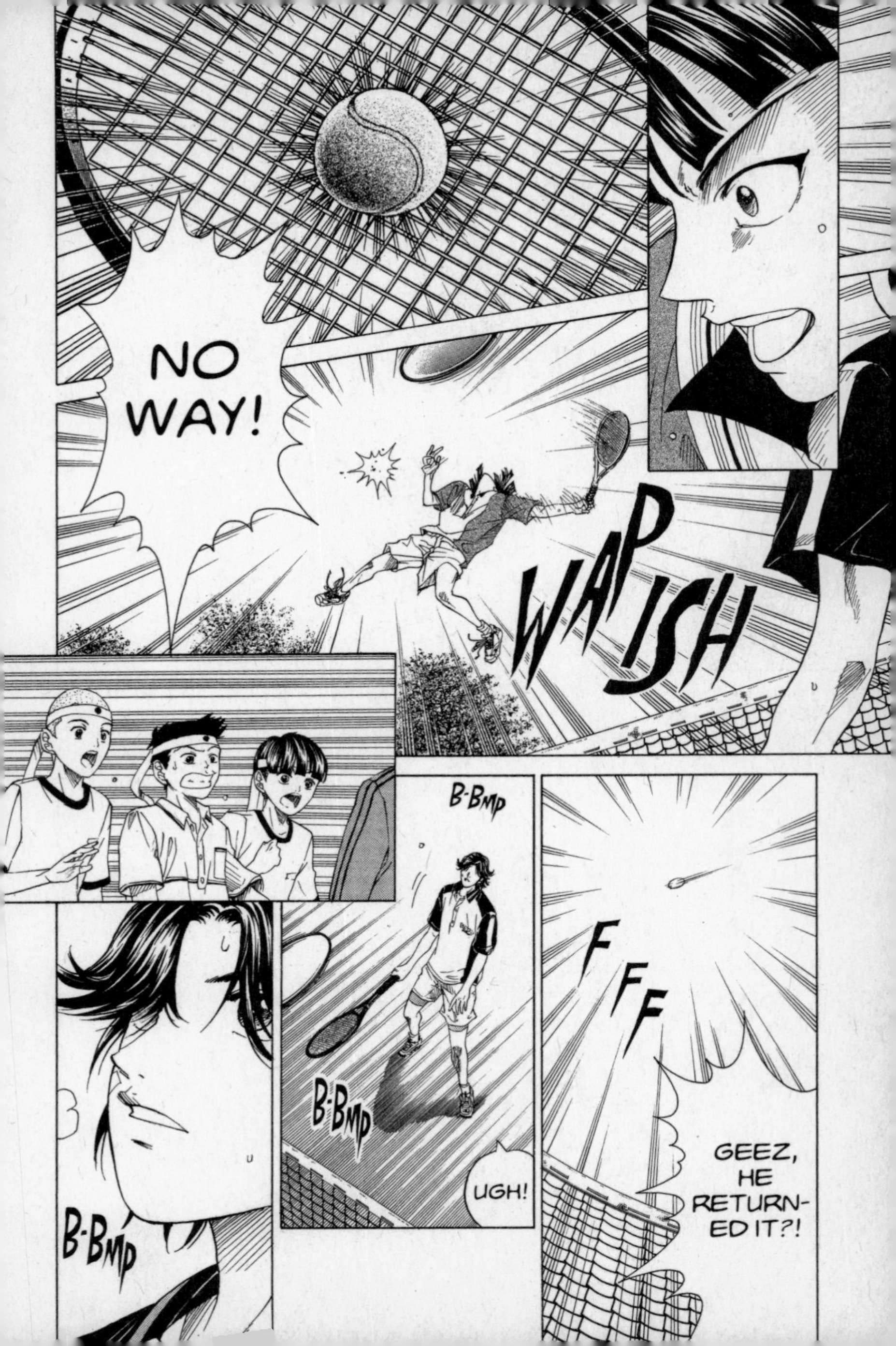
NO WAY!
WAPISH
GEEZ, HE RETURNED IT?!
FFF
B-BMP
UGH!
B-BMP
B-BMP

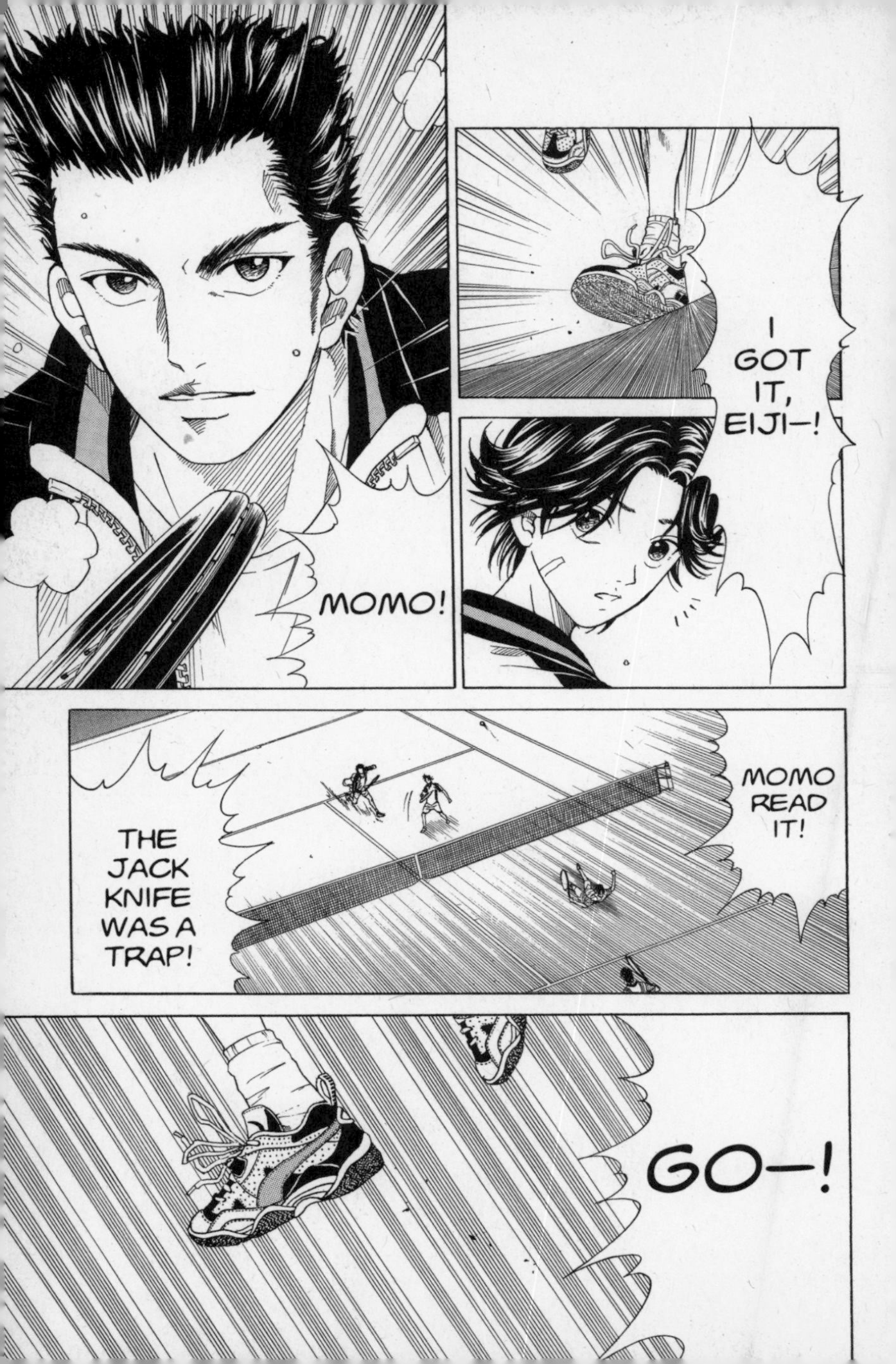
I GOT IT, EIJI—!
MOMO!
MOMO READ IT!
THE JACK KNIFE WAS A TRAP!
GO—!

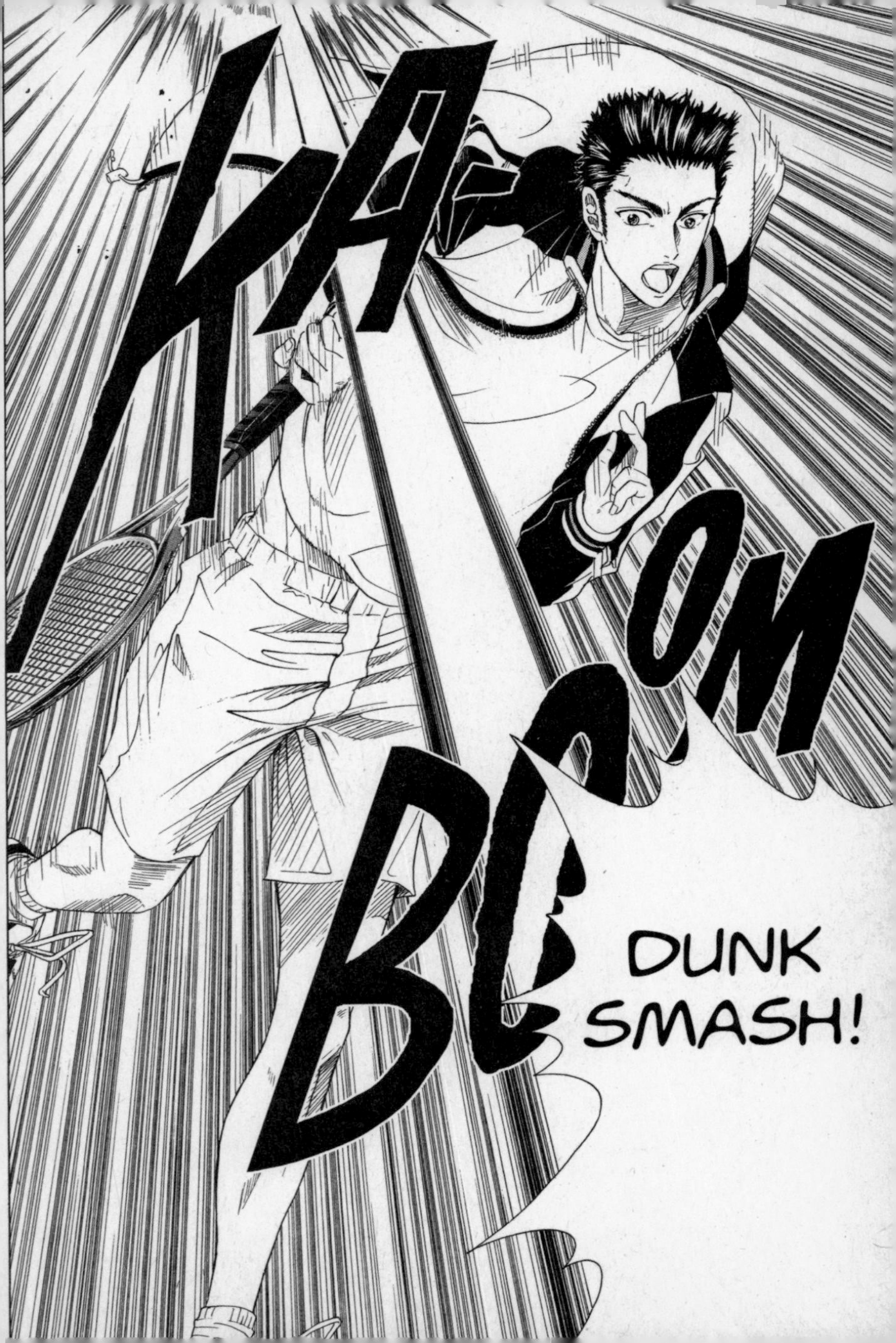
KA-
BOOM
DUNK
SMASH!

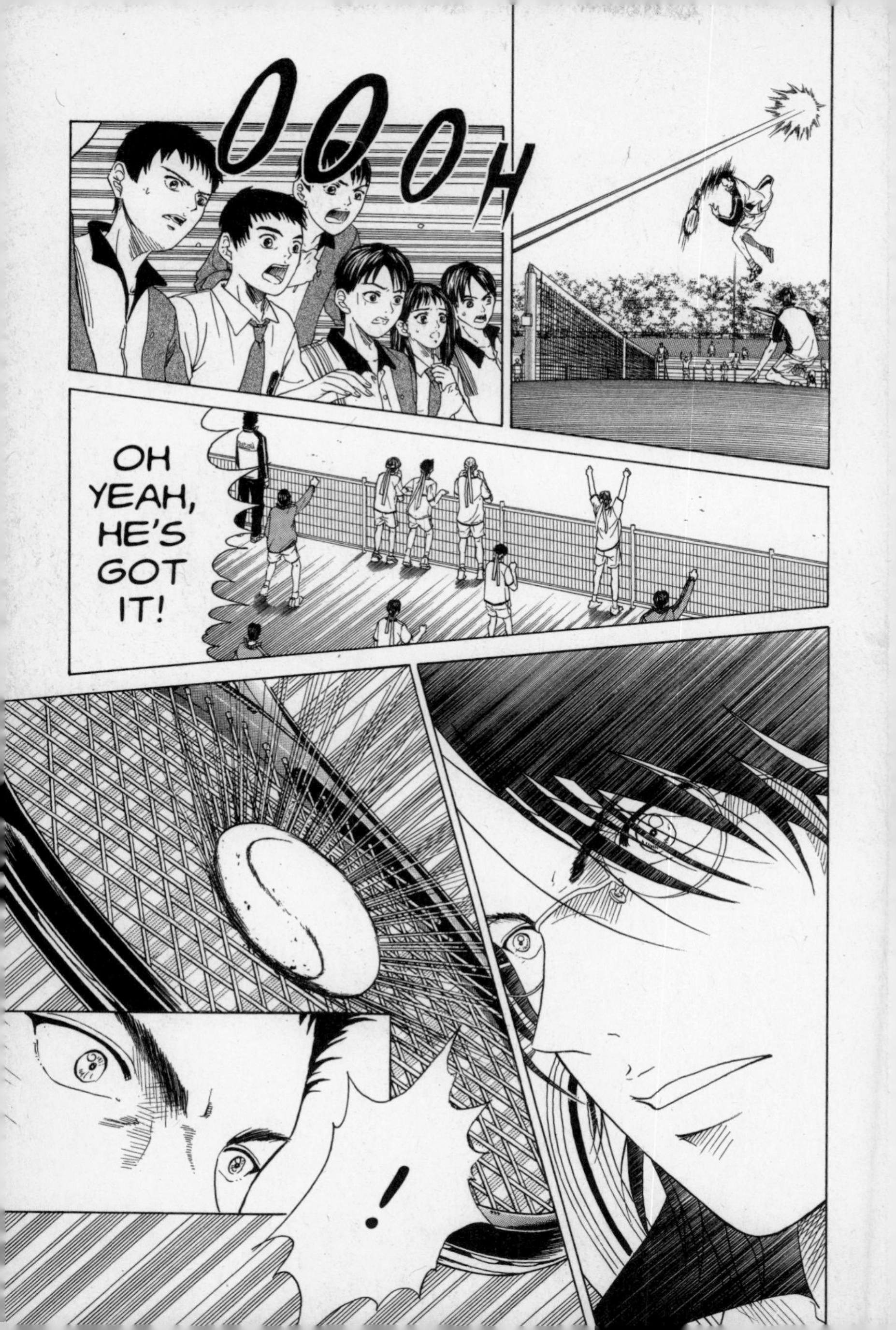
OOOOH
OH YEAH, HE'S GOT IT!
!

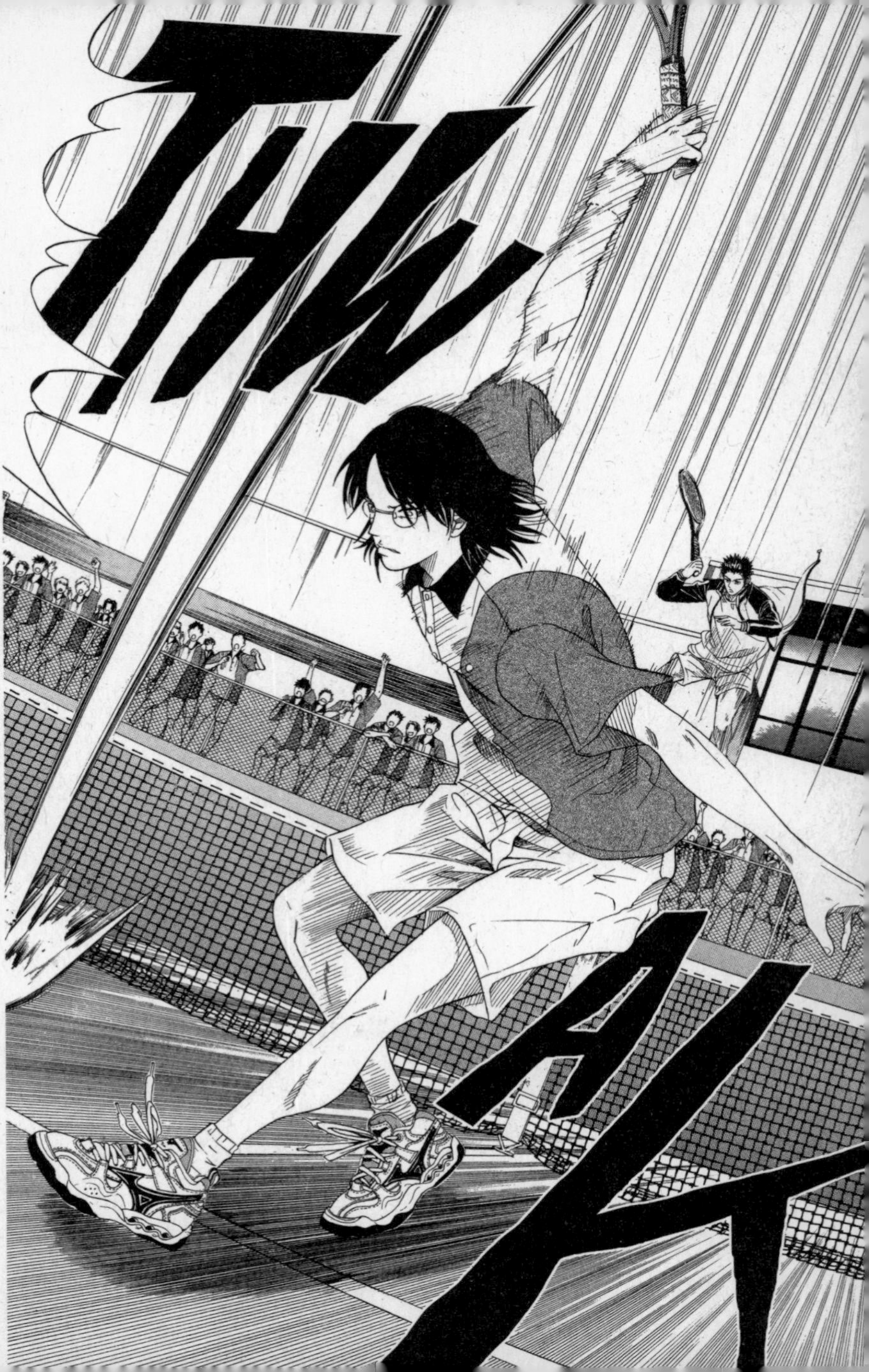

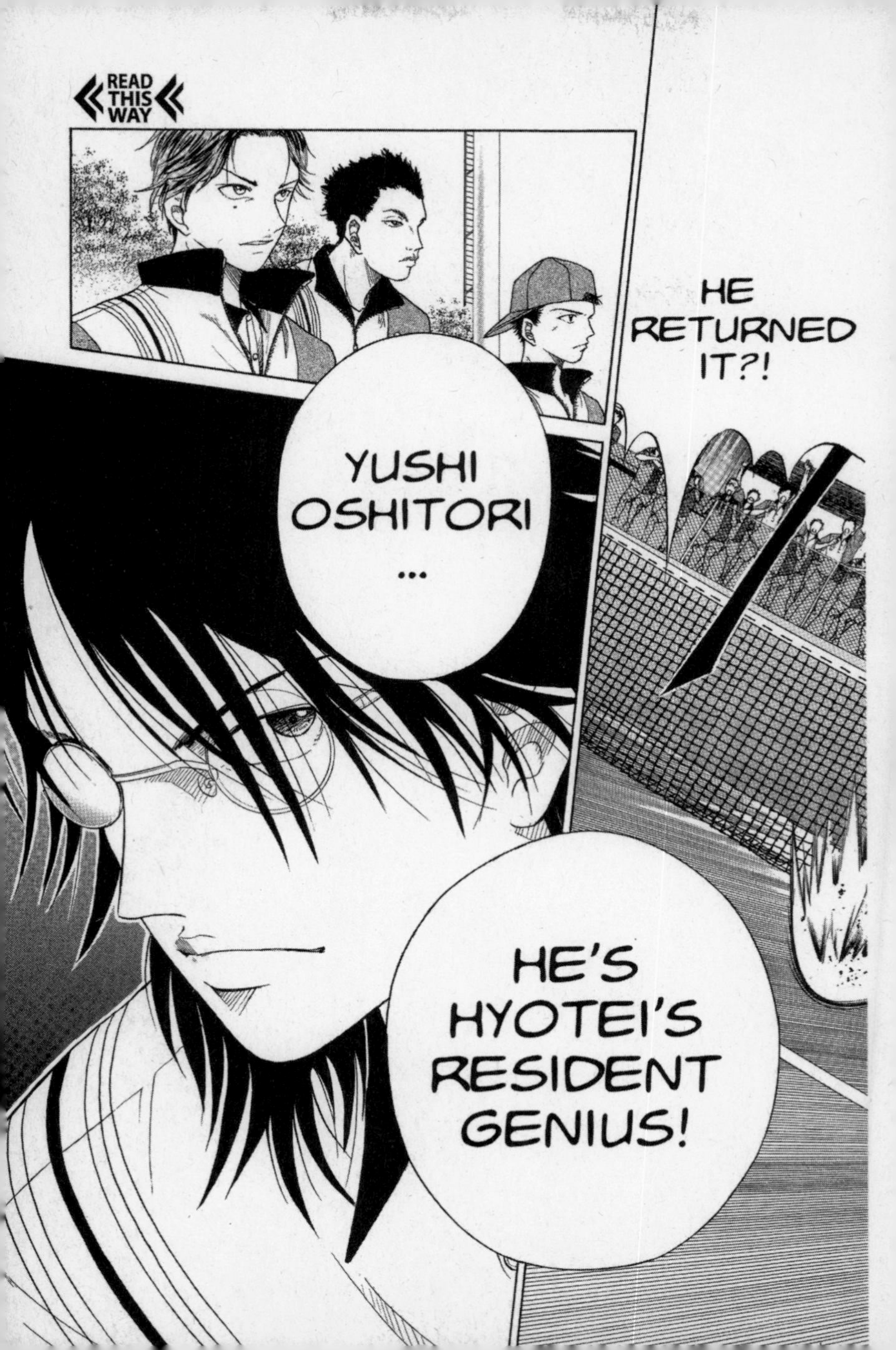
READ THIS WAY
HE RETURNED IT?!
YUSHI OSHITORI ...
HE'S HYOTEI'S RESIDENT GENIUS!

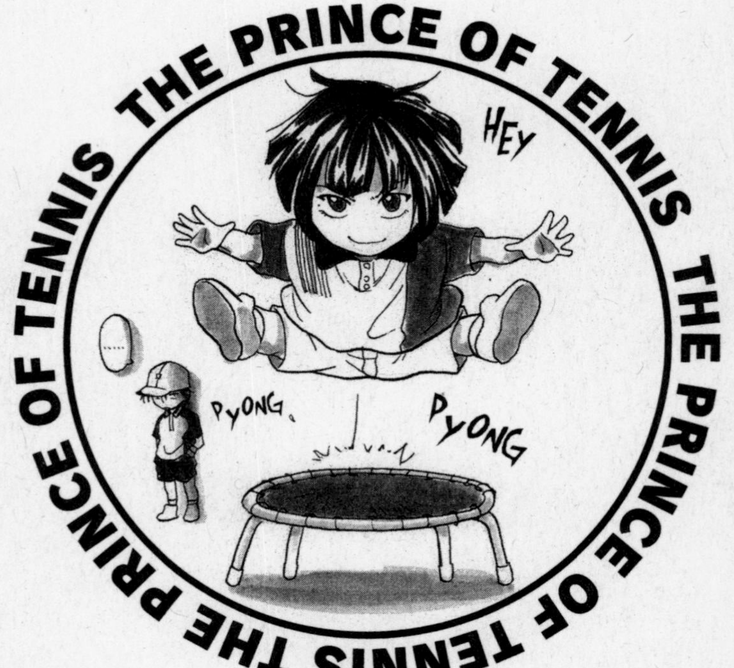
THE PRINCE OF TENNIS THE PRINCE OF TENNIS THE PRINCE OF TENNIS
HEY
......
PYONG
PYONG

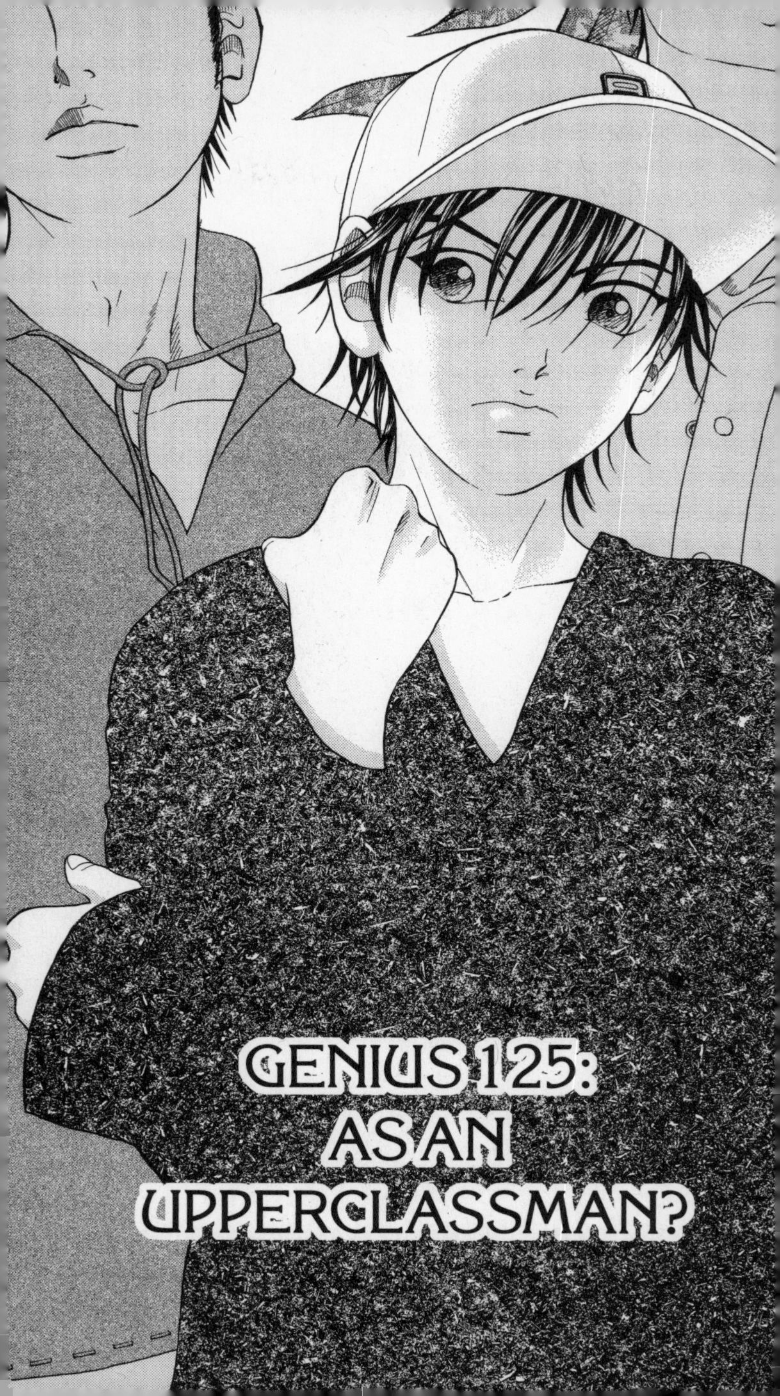
GENIUS 125:
AS AN
UPPERCLASSMAN?

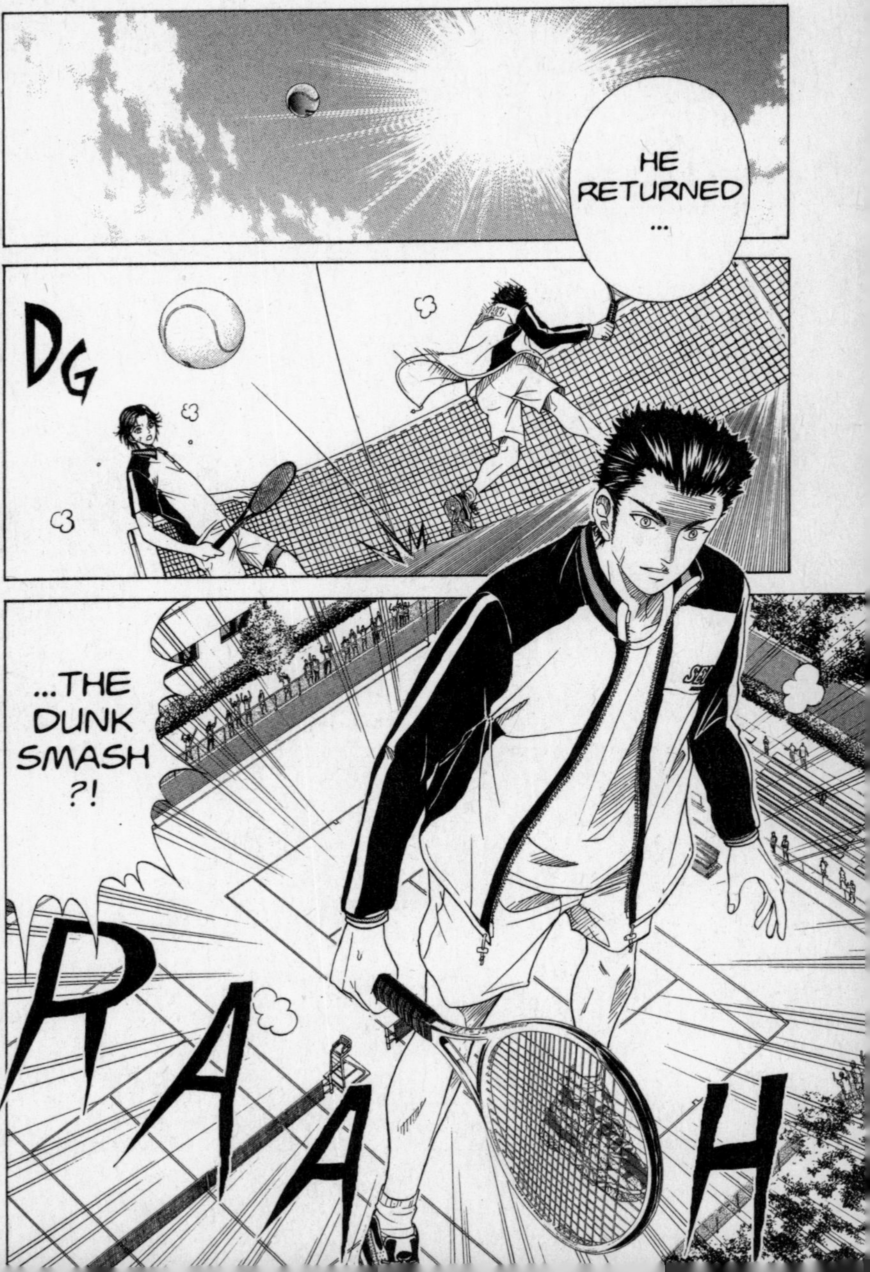
HE RETURNED ...
DG
...THE DUNK SMASH ?!
RAAAH

READ THIS WAY

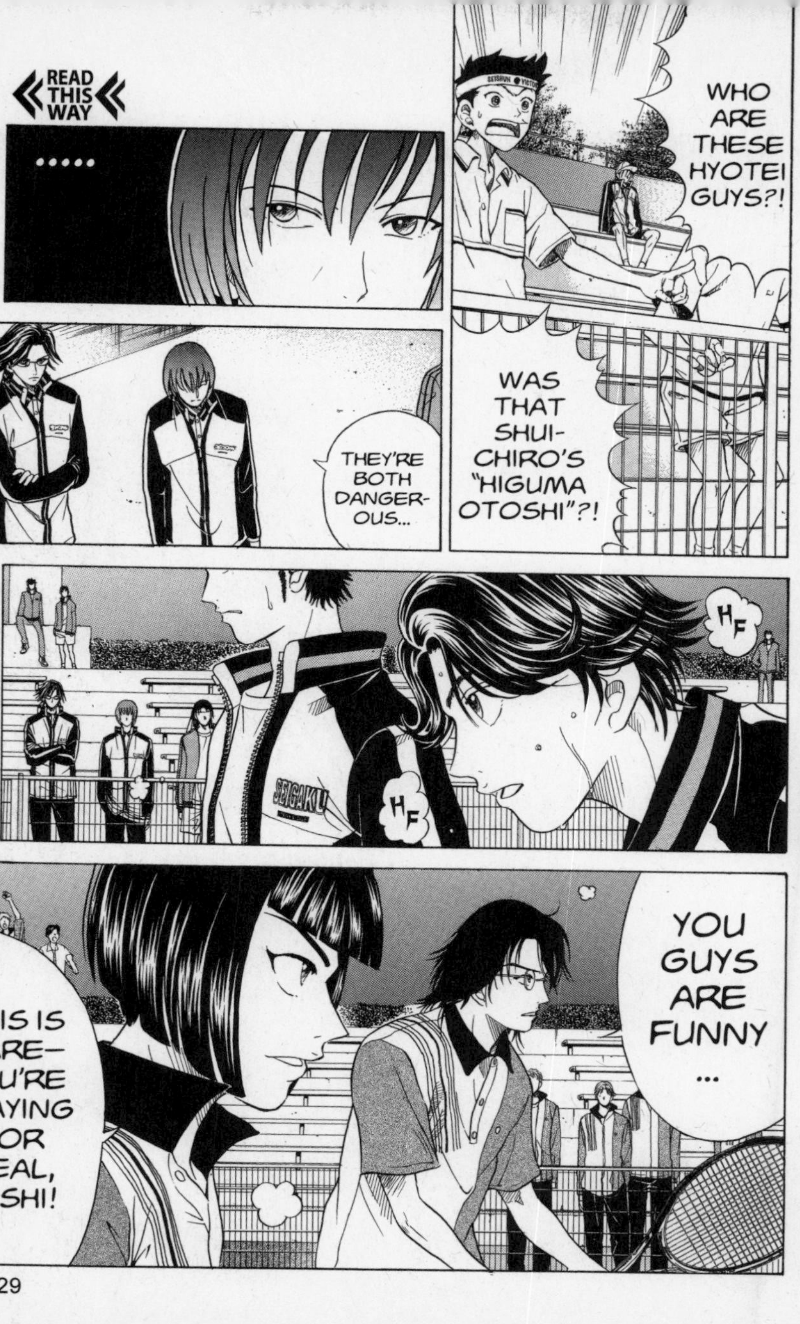

WHO ARE THESE HYOTEI GUYS?!
.....
WAS THAT SHUICHIRO'S "HIGUMA OTOSHI"?!
THEY'RE BOTH DANGEROUS...
HF
HF
YOU GUYS ARE FUNNY...
THIS IS RARE—YOU'RE PLAYING FOR REAL, YUSHI!

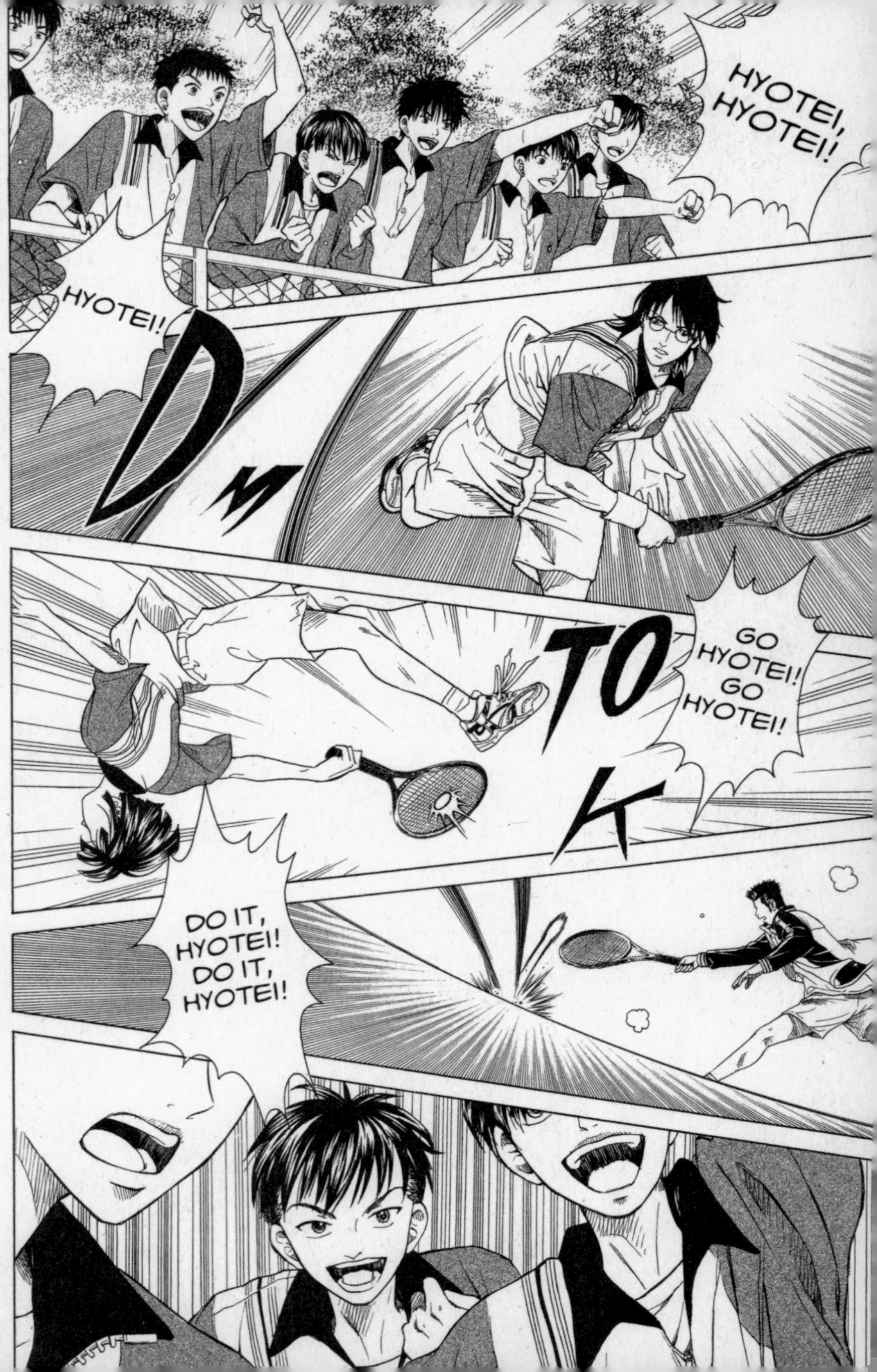
HYOTEI, HYOTEI!
HYOTEI!
DM
GO HYOTEI! GO HYOTEI!
TOK
DO IT, HYOTEI! DO IT, HYOTEI!

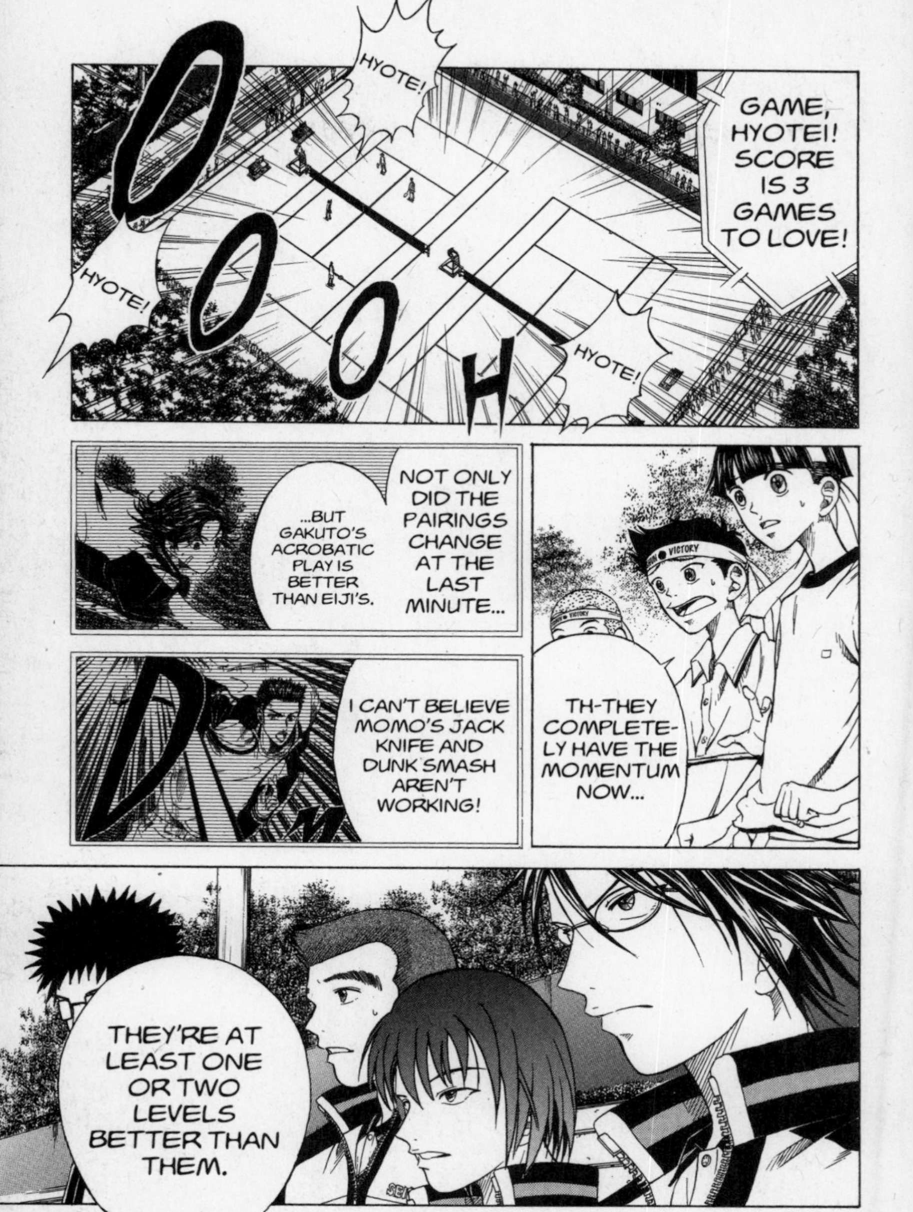
GAME, HYOTEI! SCORE IS 3 GAMES TO LOVE!
HYOTE!
HYOTE!
OOOOH
HYOTE!
TH-THEY COMPLETE-LY HAVE THE MOMENTUM NOW...
NOT ONLY DID THE PAIRINGS CHANGE AT THE LAST MINUTE...
...BUT GAKUTO'S ACROBATIC PLAY IS BETTER THAN EIJI'S.
I CAN'T BELIEVE MOMO'S JACK KNIFE AND DUNK SMASH AREN'T WORKING!
THEY'RE AT LEAST ONE OR TWO LEVELS BETTER THAN THEM.

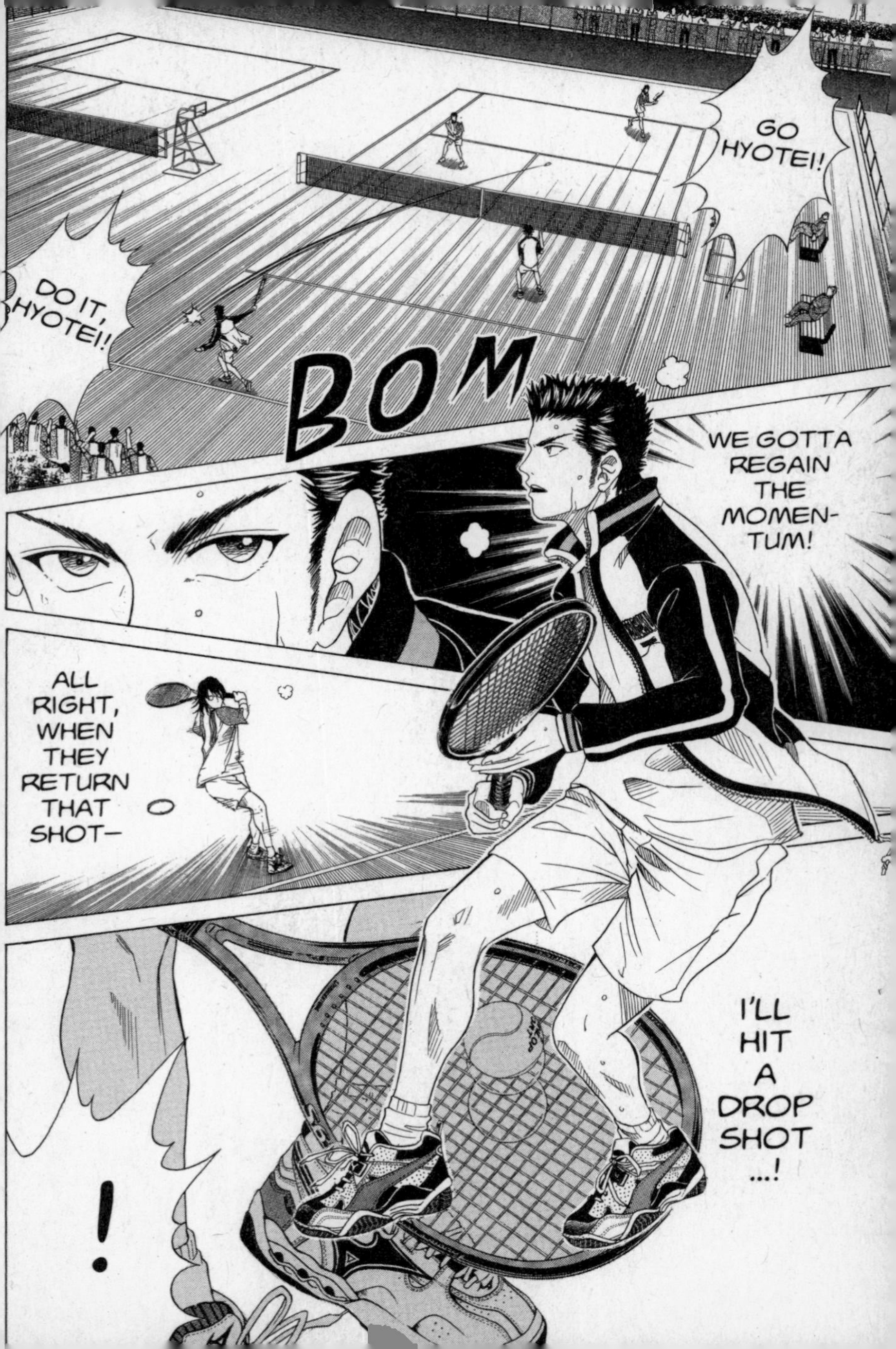
GO HYOTEI!
DO IT, HYOTEI!!
BOM
WE GOTTA REGAIN THE MOMENTUM!
ALL RIGHT, WHEN THEY RETURN THAT SHOT—
I'LL HIT A DROP SHOT ...!
!

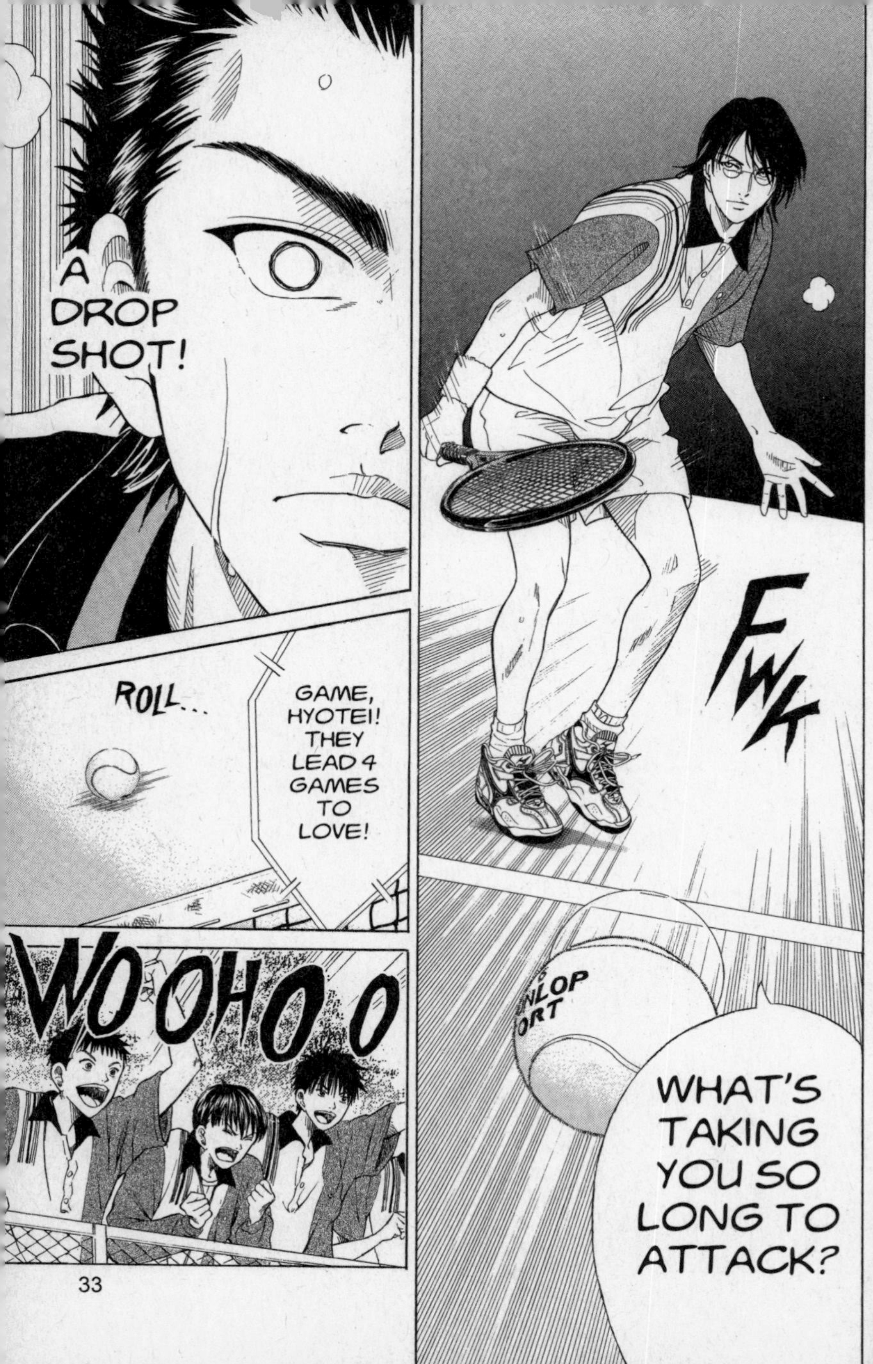
FWK
WHAT'S TAKING YOU SO LONG TO ATTACK?
A DROP SHOT!
ROLL...
GAME, HYOTEI! THEY LEAD 4 GAMES TO LOVE!
WOOHOOO

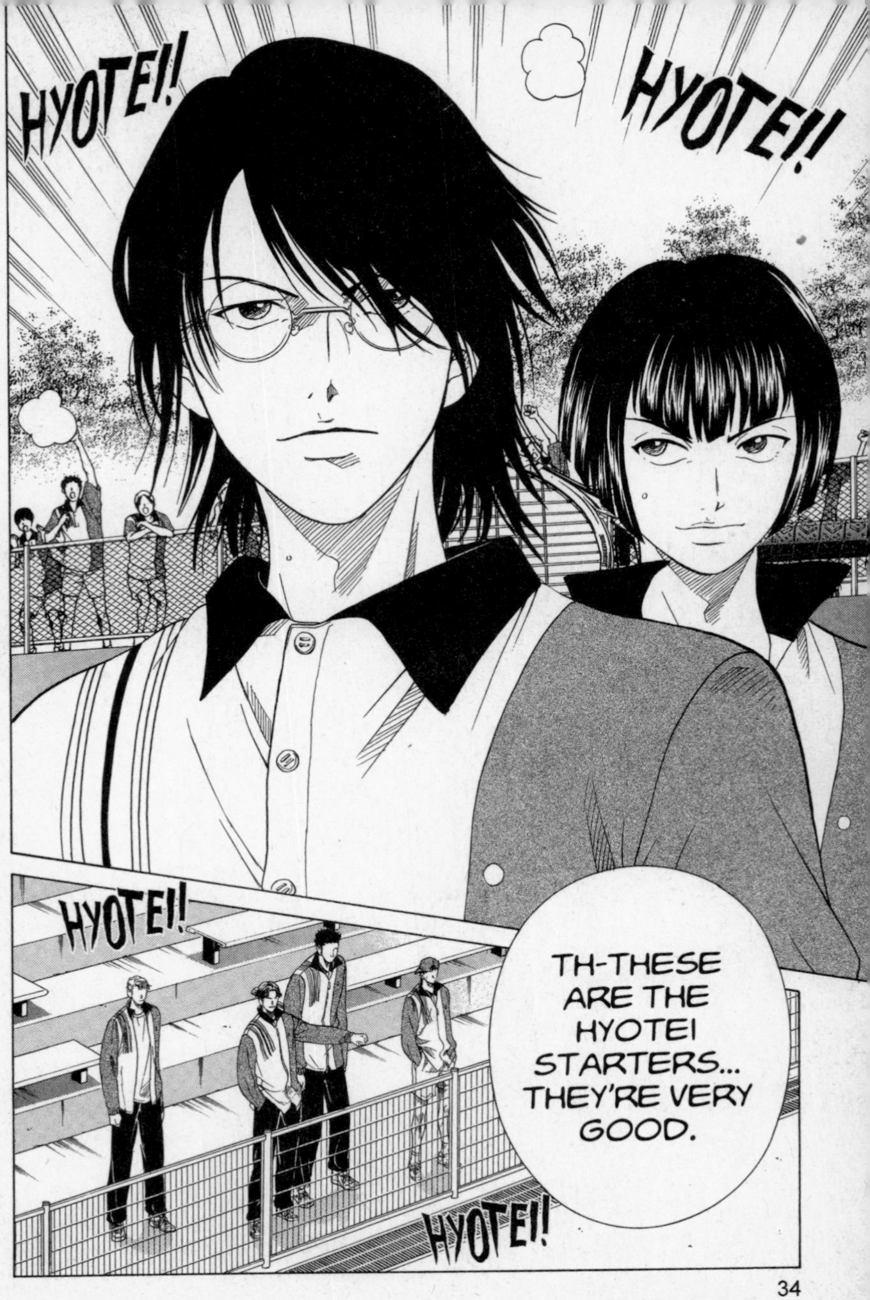
HYOTEI!!
HYOTEI!
TH-THESE ARE THE HYOTEI STARTERS... THEY'RE VERY GOOD.
HYOTEI!
HYOTEI!

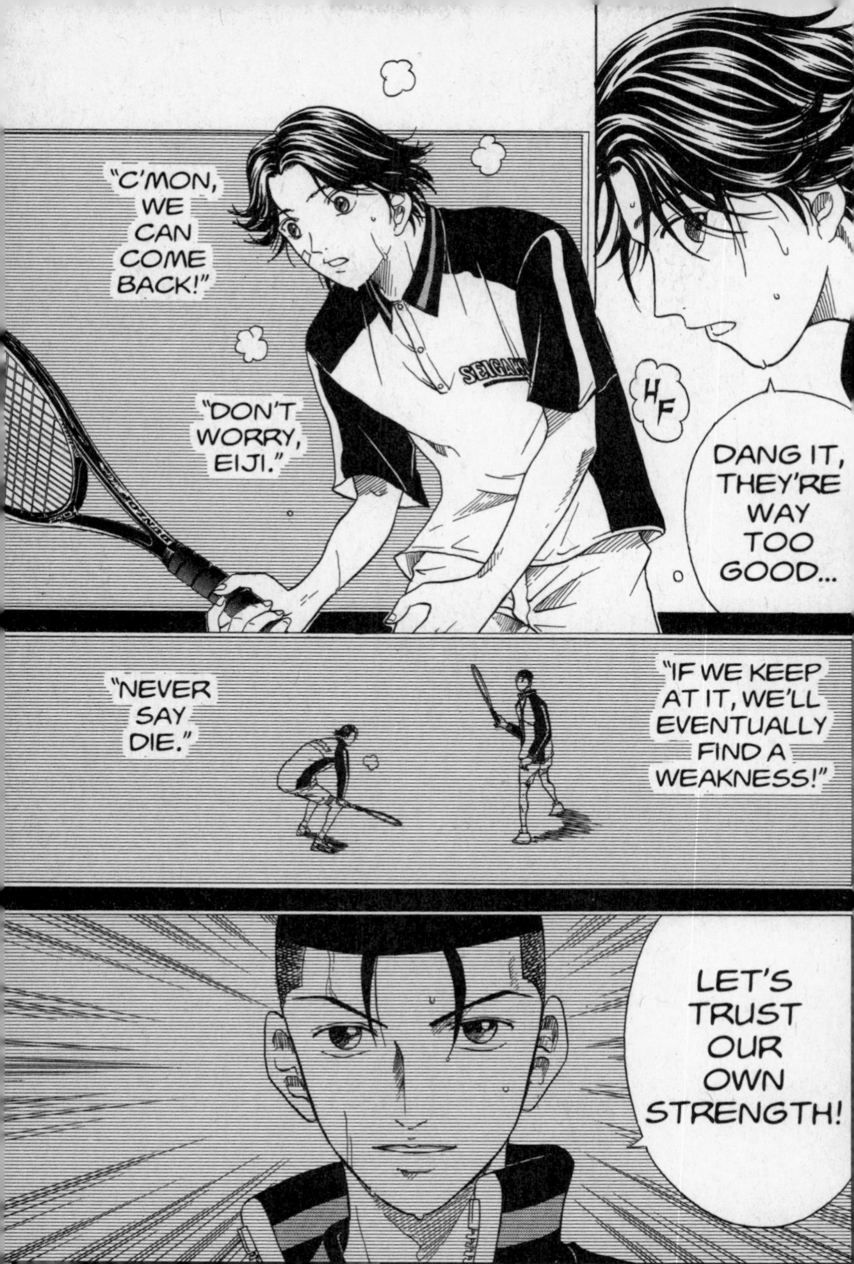
HF
DANG IT, THEY'RE WAY TOO GOOD...
"C'MON, WE CAN COME BACK!"
"DON'T WORRY, EIJI."
SEIGAKU
"IF WE KEEP AT IT, WE'LL EVENTUALLY FIND A WEAKNESS!"
"NEVER SAY DIE."
LET'S TRUST OUR OWN STRENGTH!

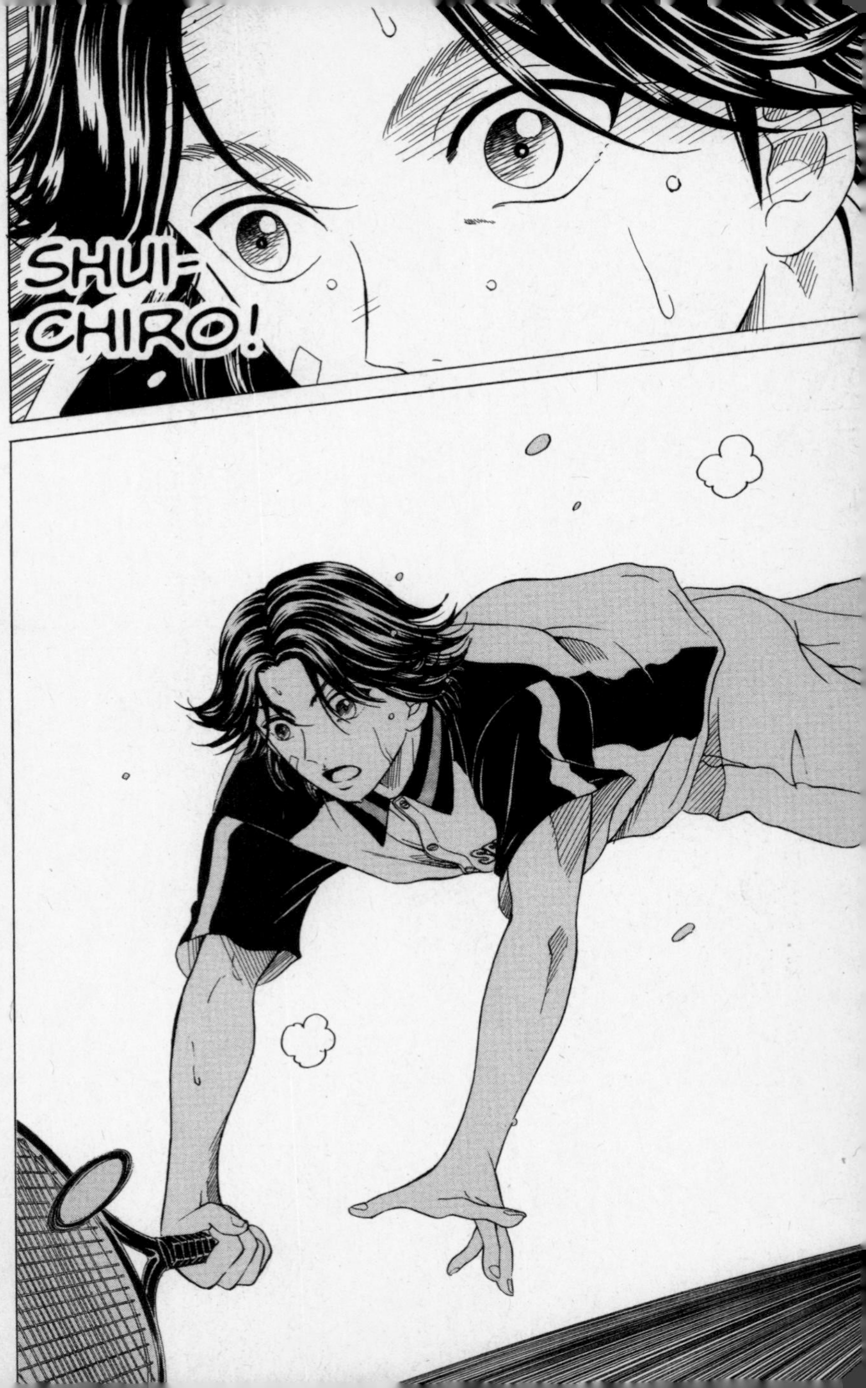
SHUI-
CHIRO!

READ THIS WAY

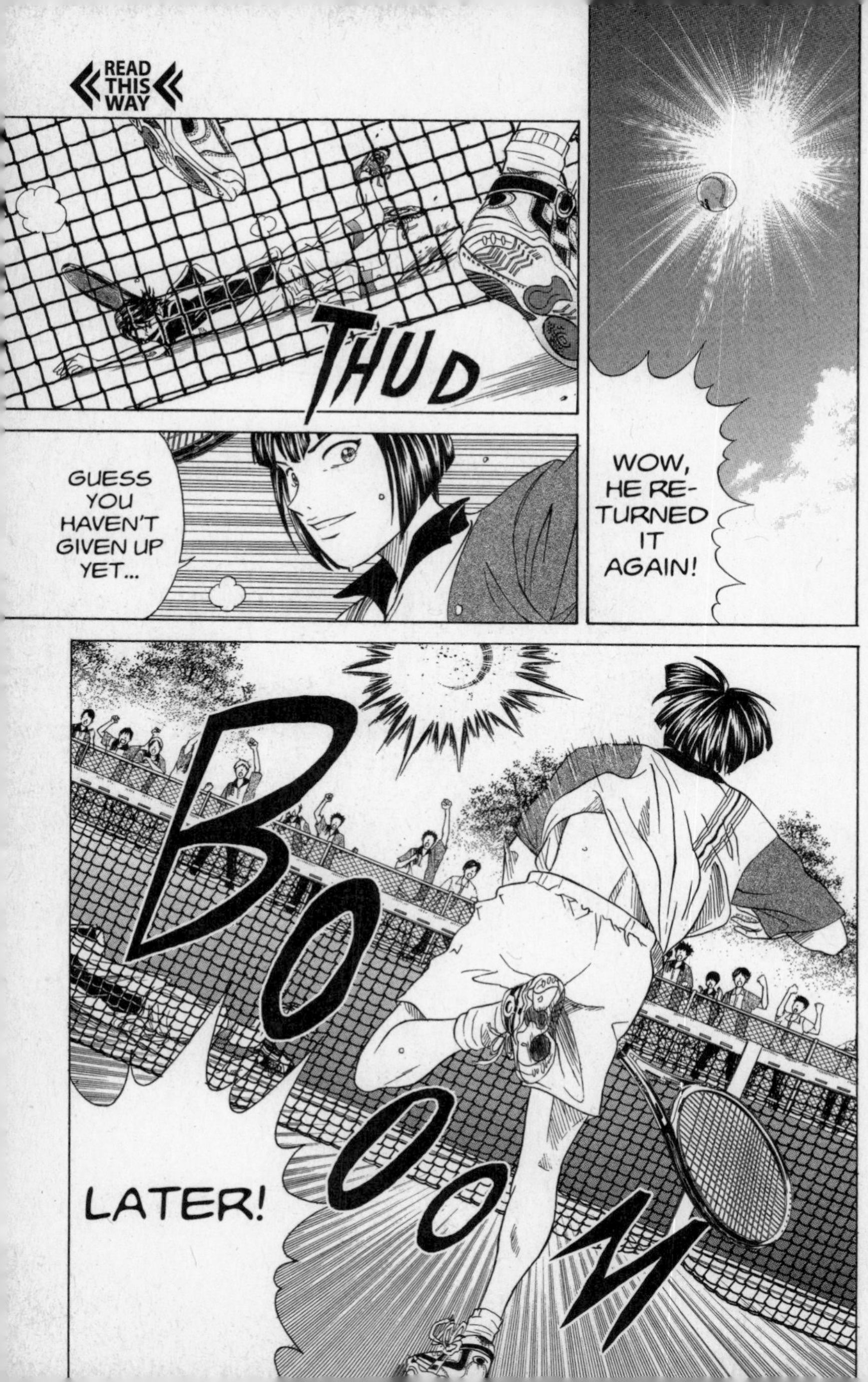
WOW, HE RE-TURNED IT AGAIN!
THUD
GUESS YOU HAVEN'T GIVEN UP YET...
BOOOOM
LATER!

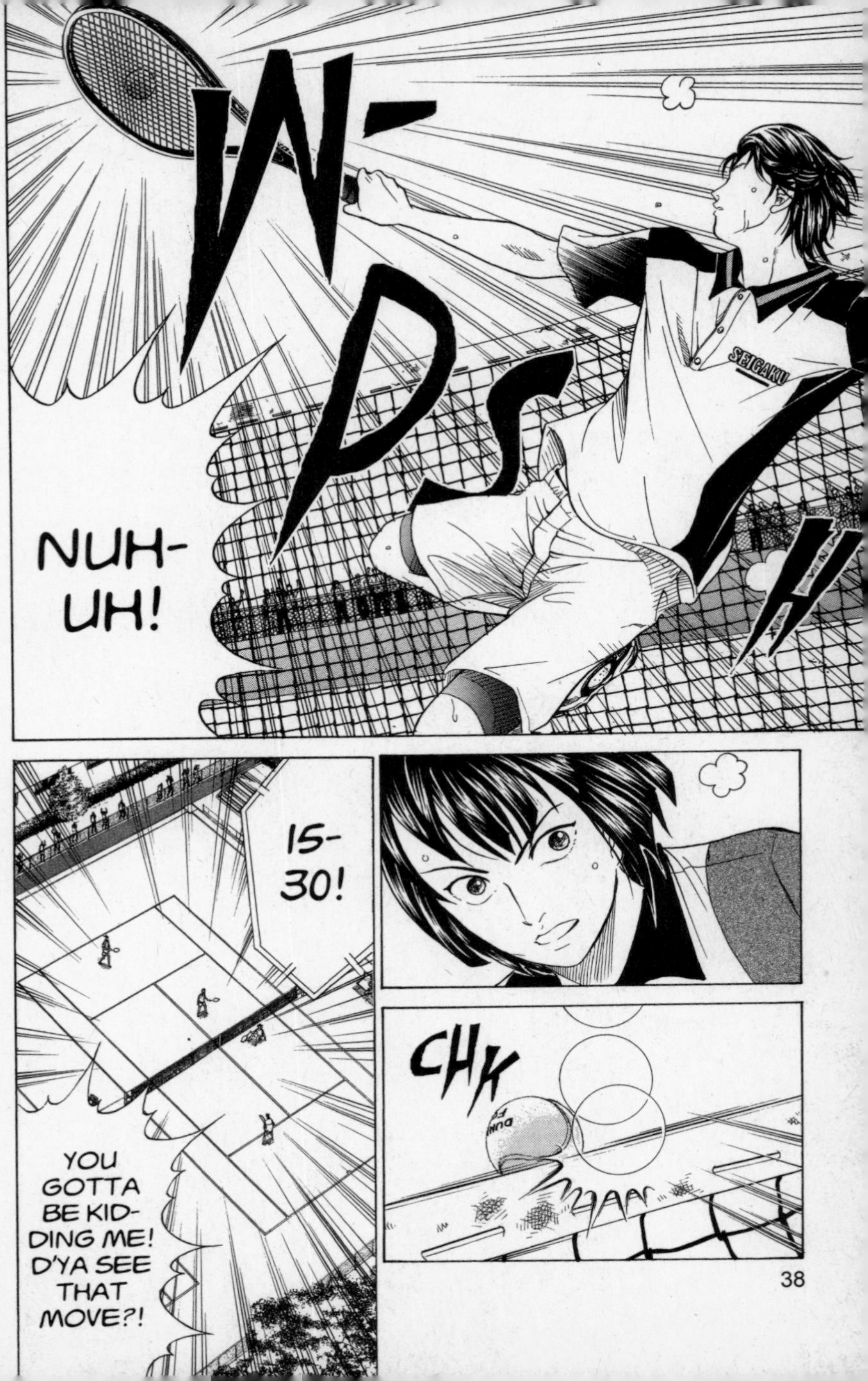
W-PSSH
NUH-UH!
CHK
15-30!
YOU GOTTA BE KID-DING ME! D'YA SEE THAT MOVE?!

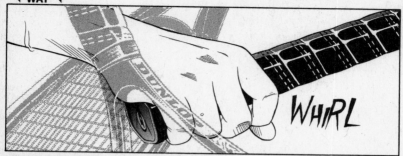

WHIRL

HE'S GOT A DIFFERENT LOOK IN HIS EYES!

WHIRL

WHIRL

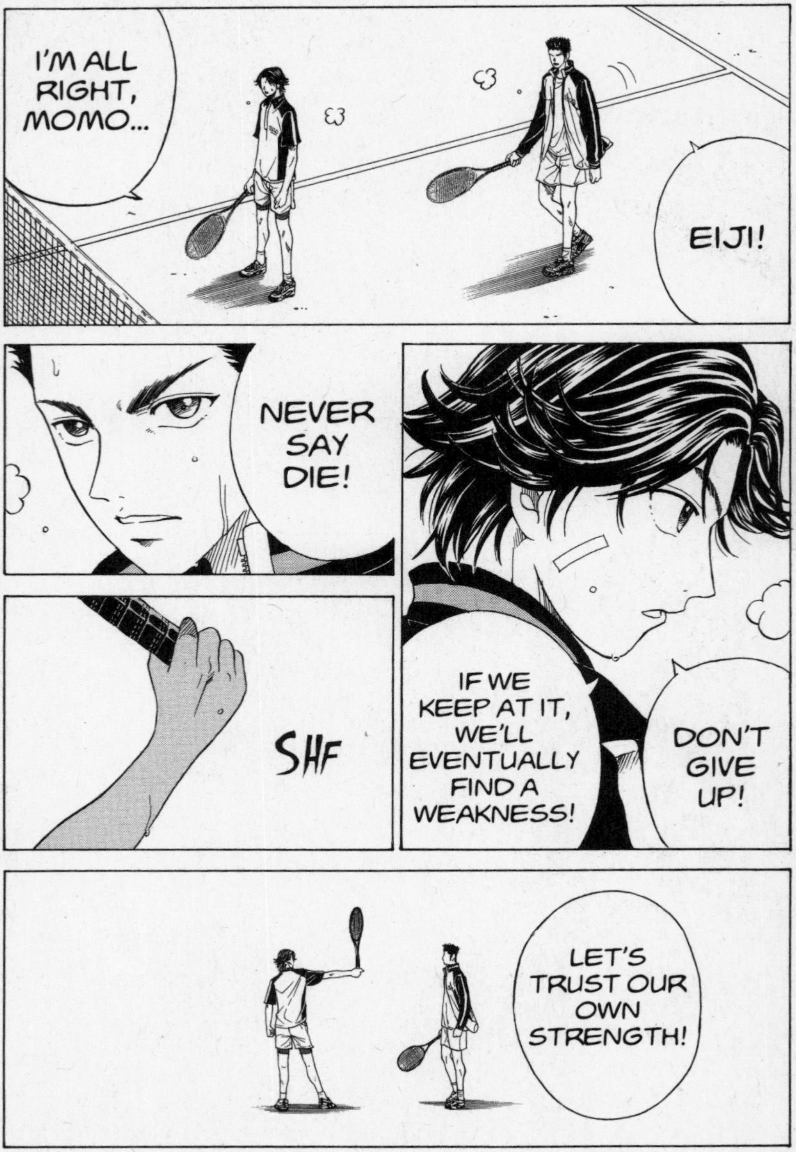
EIJI!
I'M ALL RIGHT, MOMO...
DON'T GIVE UP!
IF WE KEEP AT IT, WE'LL EVENTUALLY FIND A WEAKNESS!
NEVER SAY DIE!
SHF
LET'S TRUST OUR OWN STRENGTH!

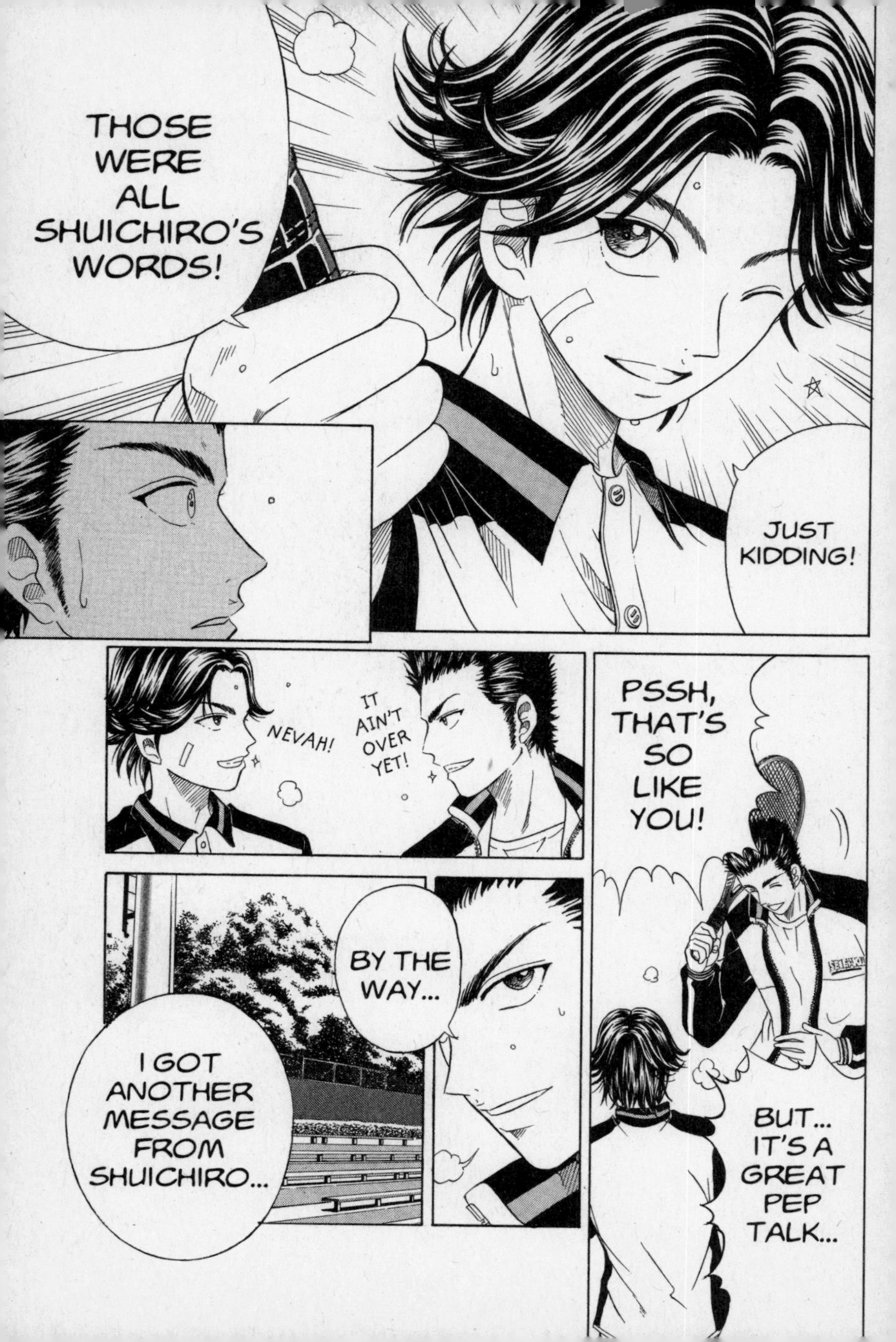
THOSE WERE ALL SHUICHIRO'S WORDS!
JUST KIDDING!
PSSH, THAT'S SO LIKE YOU!
BUT... IT'S A GREAT PEP TALK...
IT AIN'T OVER YET!
NEVAH!
BY THE WAY...
I GOT ANOTHER MESSAGE FROM SHUICHIRO...

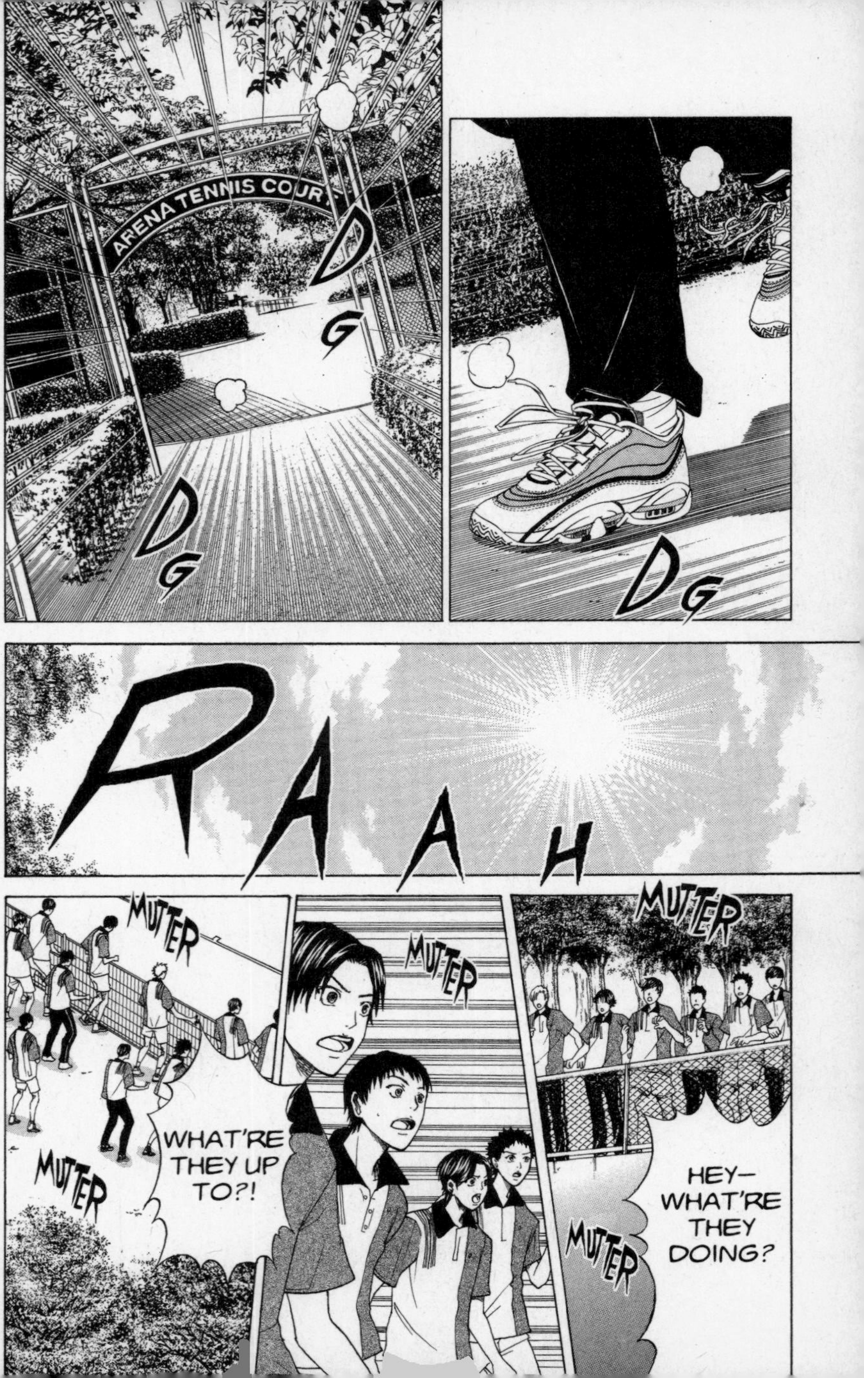
DG
ARENA TENNIS COUR
DG
DG
RAAH
MUTTER
HEY—
WHAT'RE
THEY
DOING?
MUTTER
MUTTER
MUTTER
WHAT'RE
THEY UP
TO?!
MUTTER

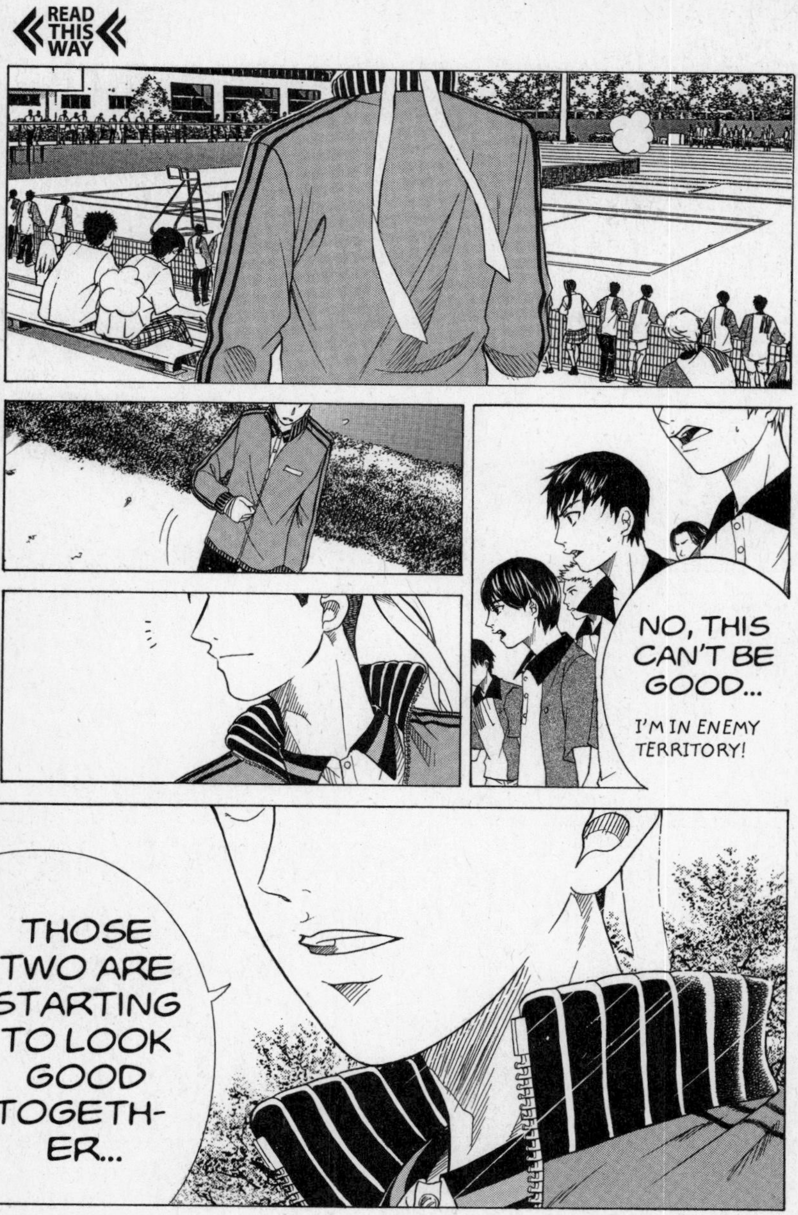
READ THIS WAY
NO, THIS CAN'T BE GOOD...
I'M IN ENEMY TERRITORY!
THOSE TWO ARE STARTING TO LOOK GOOD TOGETH-ER...

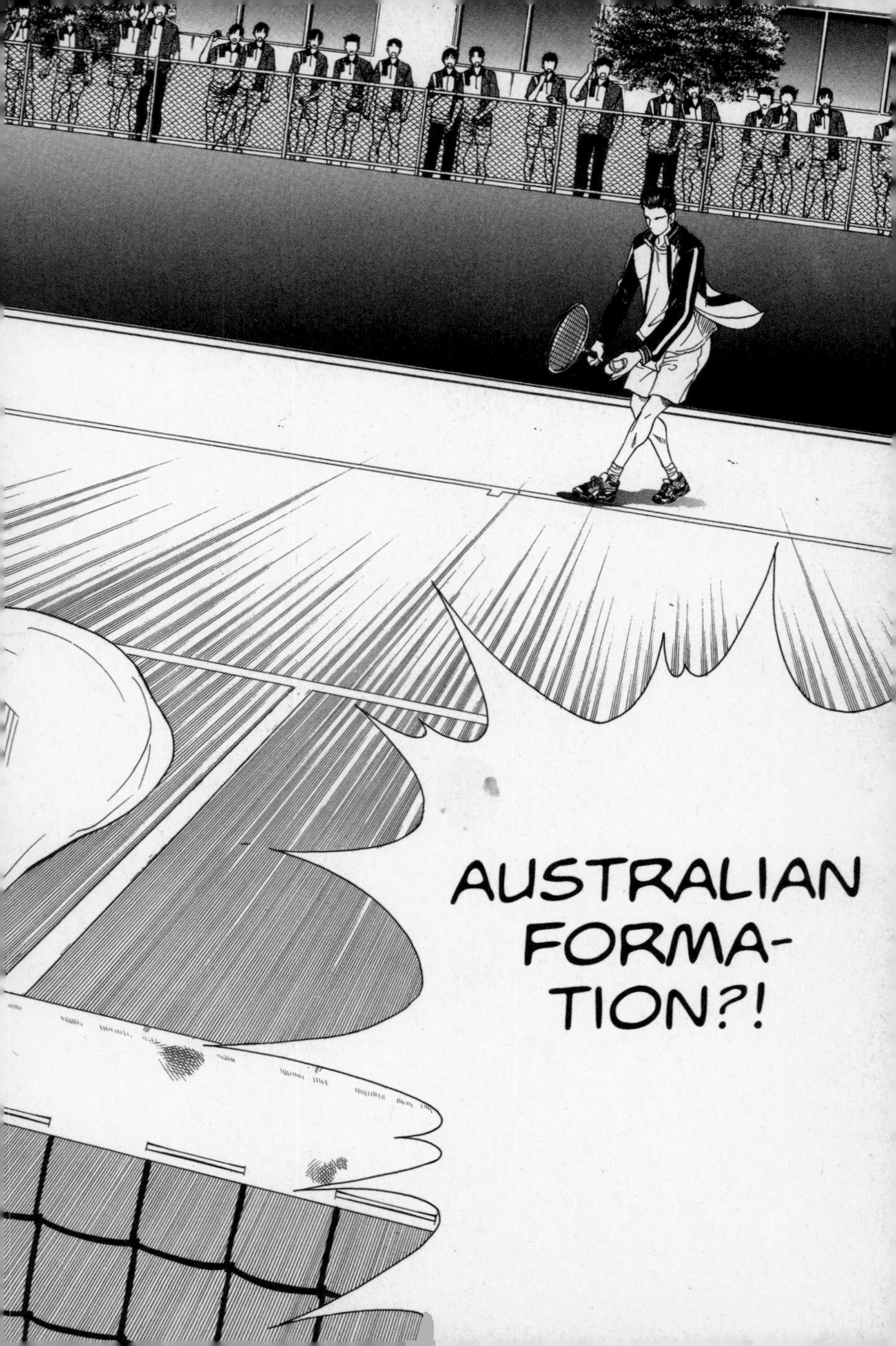
AUSTRALIAN FORMA-TION?!

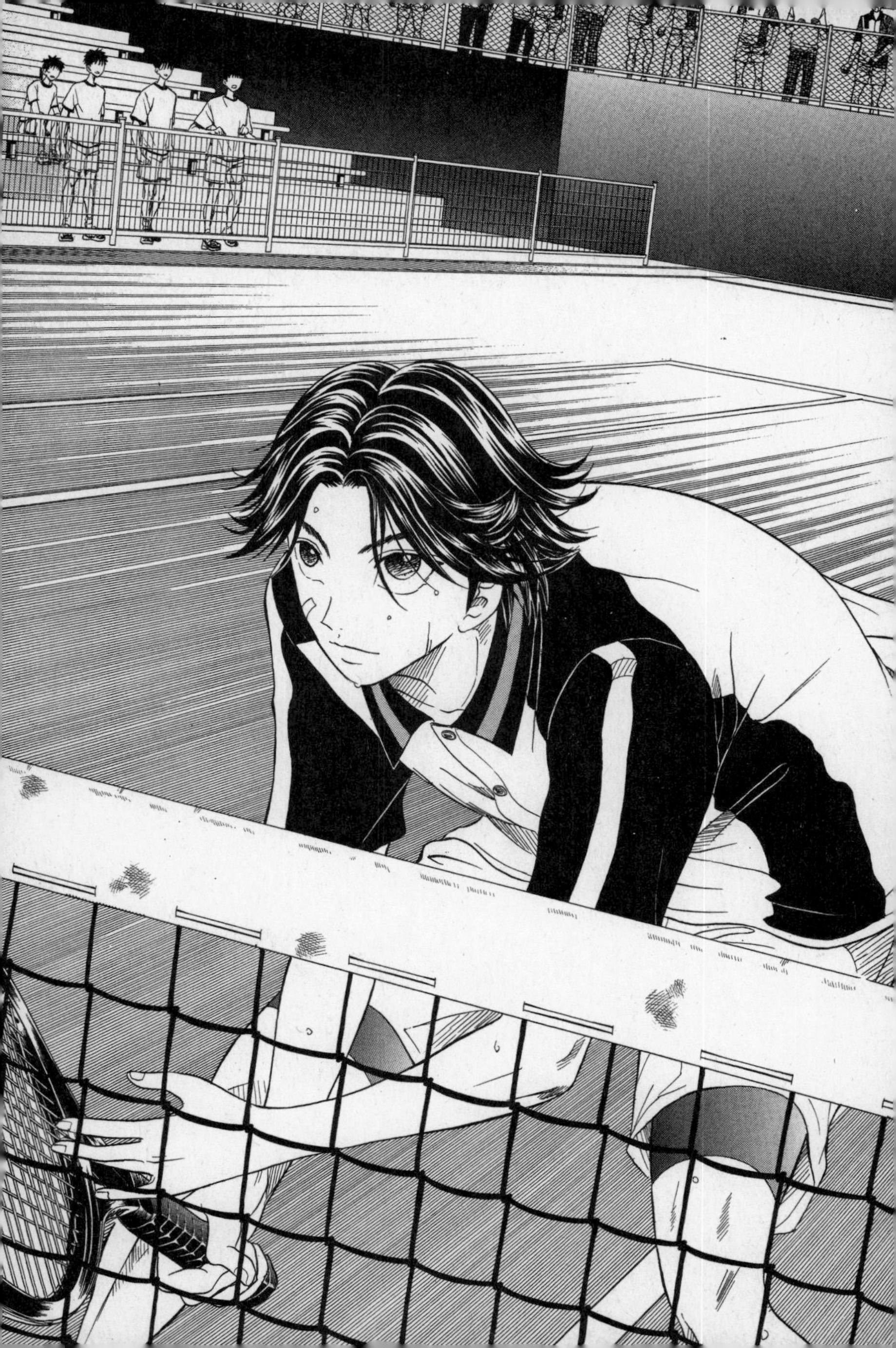

THE PRINCE OF TENNIS THE PRINCE OF TENNIS THE PRINCE OF TENNIS THE PRINCE OF TENNIS

SILHOUETTE QUIZ

GENIUS 126:

THREE-MAN DOUBLES

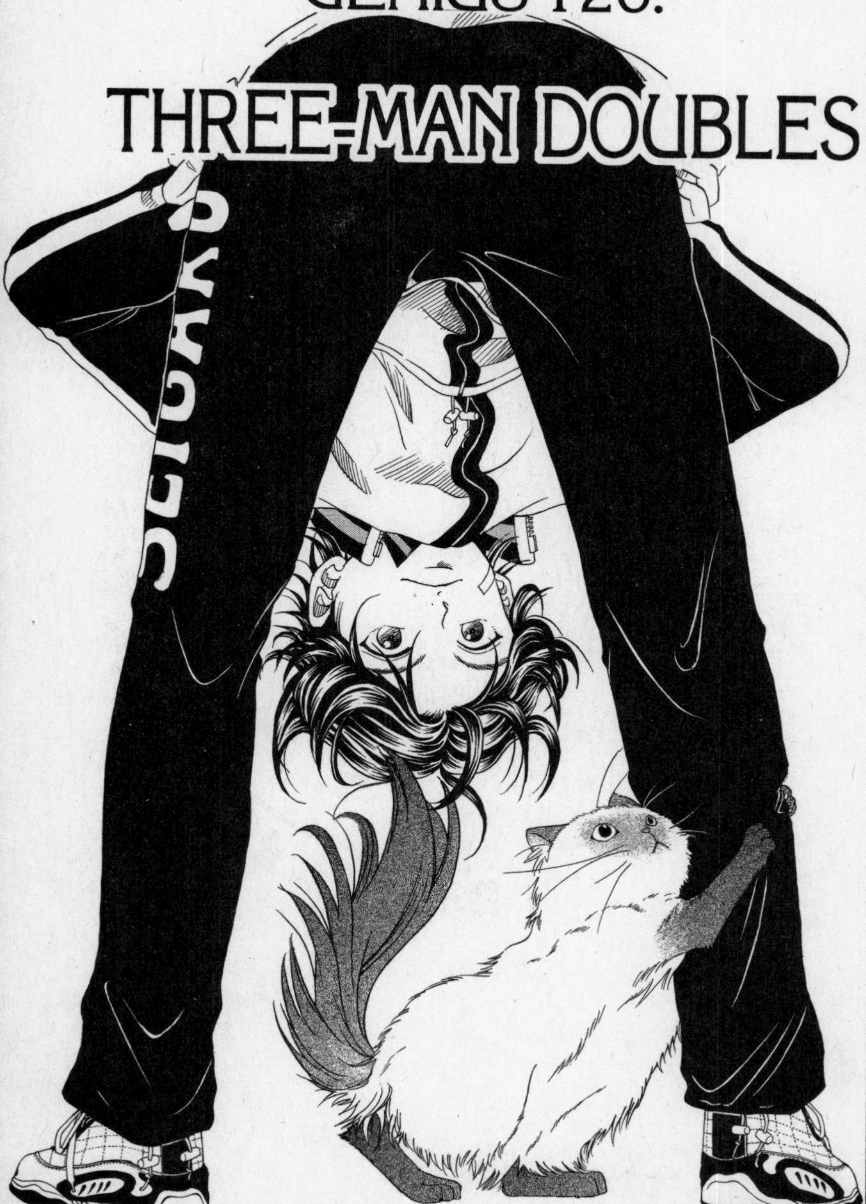

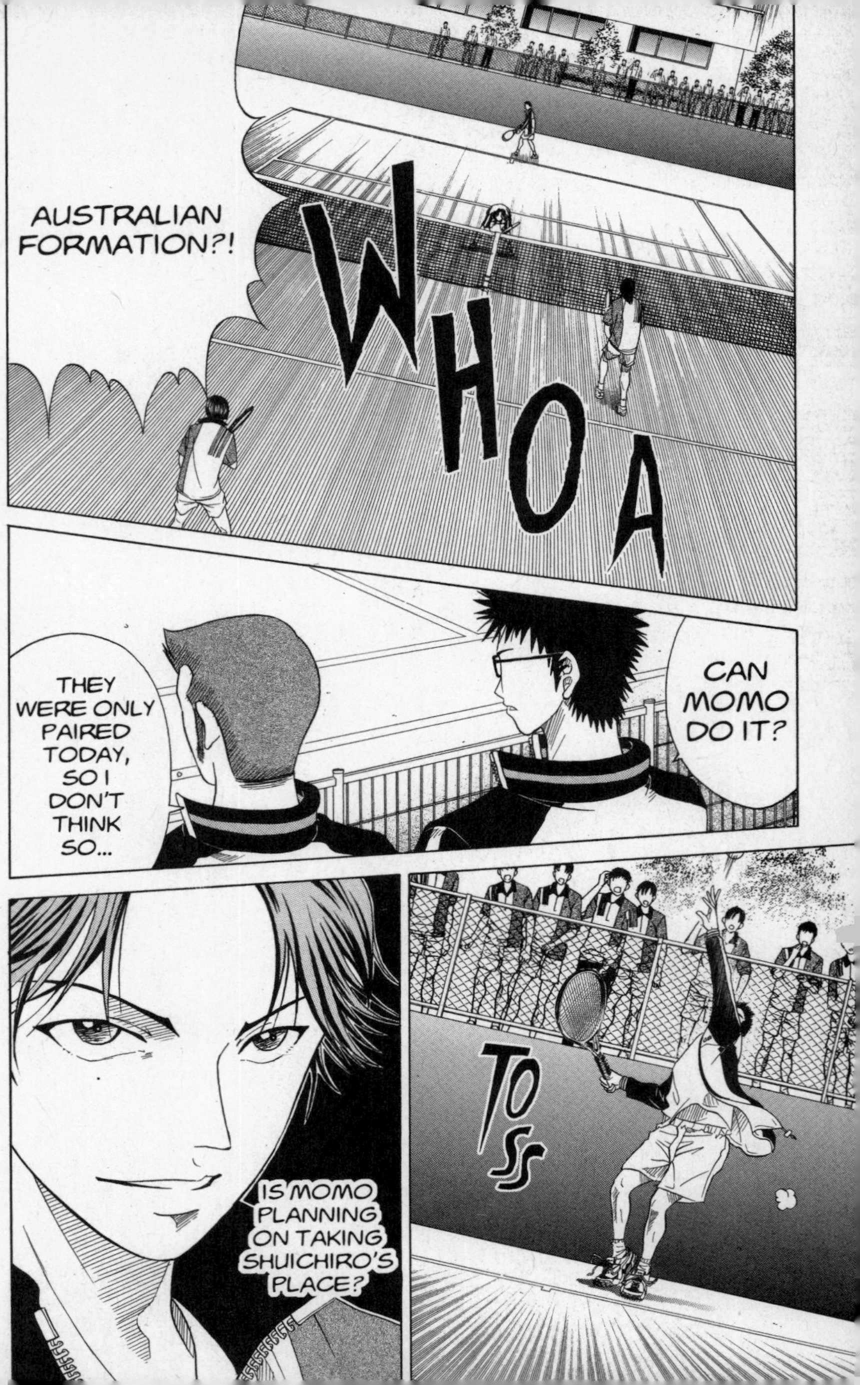
AUSTRALIAN FORMATION?!
WHOA
CAN MOMO DO IT?
THEY WERE ONLY PAIRED TODAY, SO I DON'T THINK SO...
TOSS
IS MOMO PLANNING ON TAKING SHUICHIRO'S PLACE?

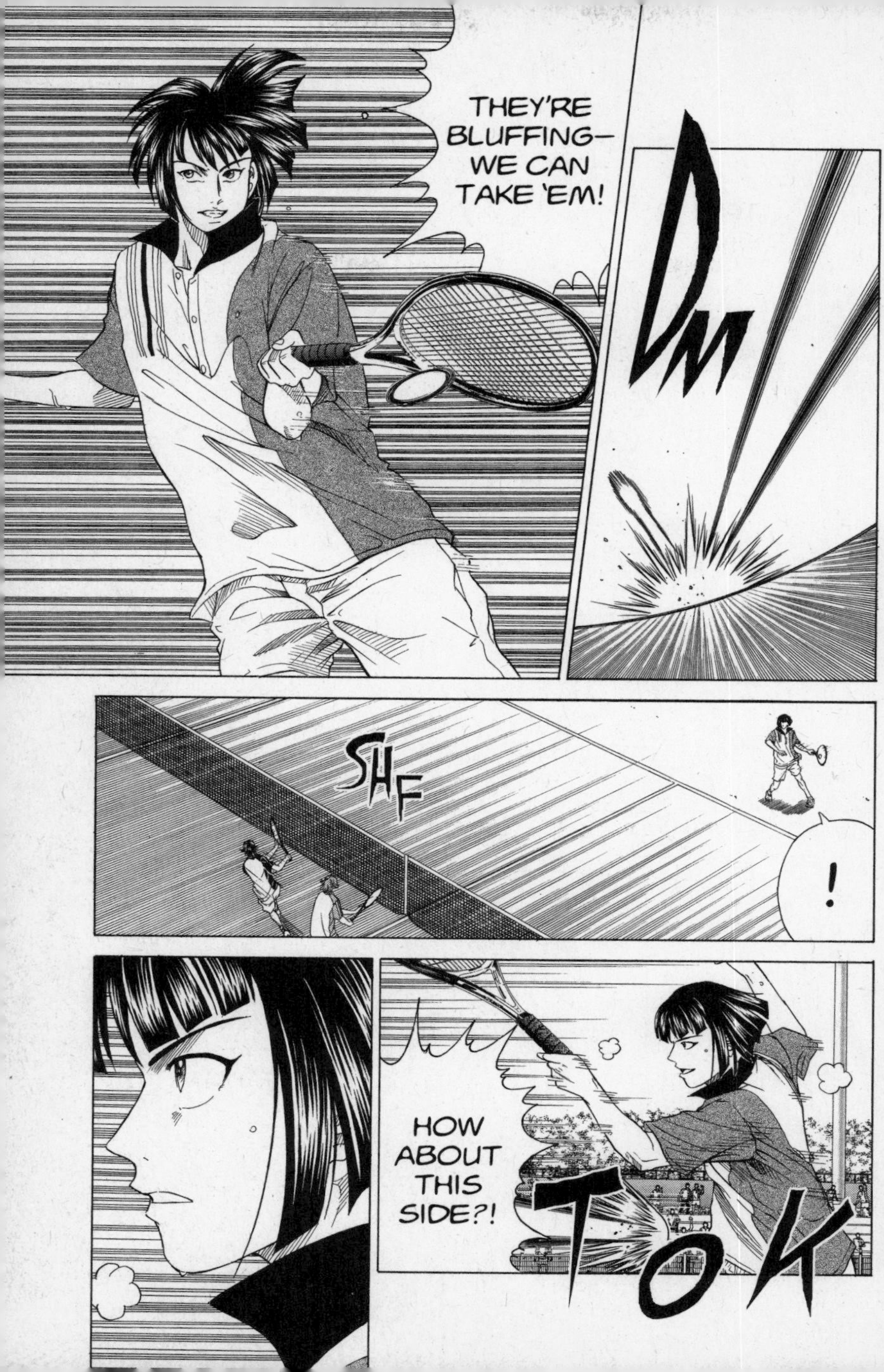
DM
THEY'RE BLUFFING—WE CAN TAKE 'EM!
!
SHF
HOW ABOUT THIS SIDE?!
TOK

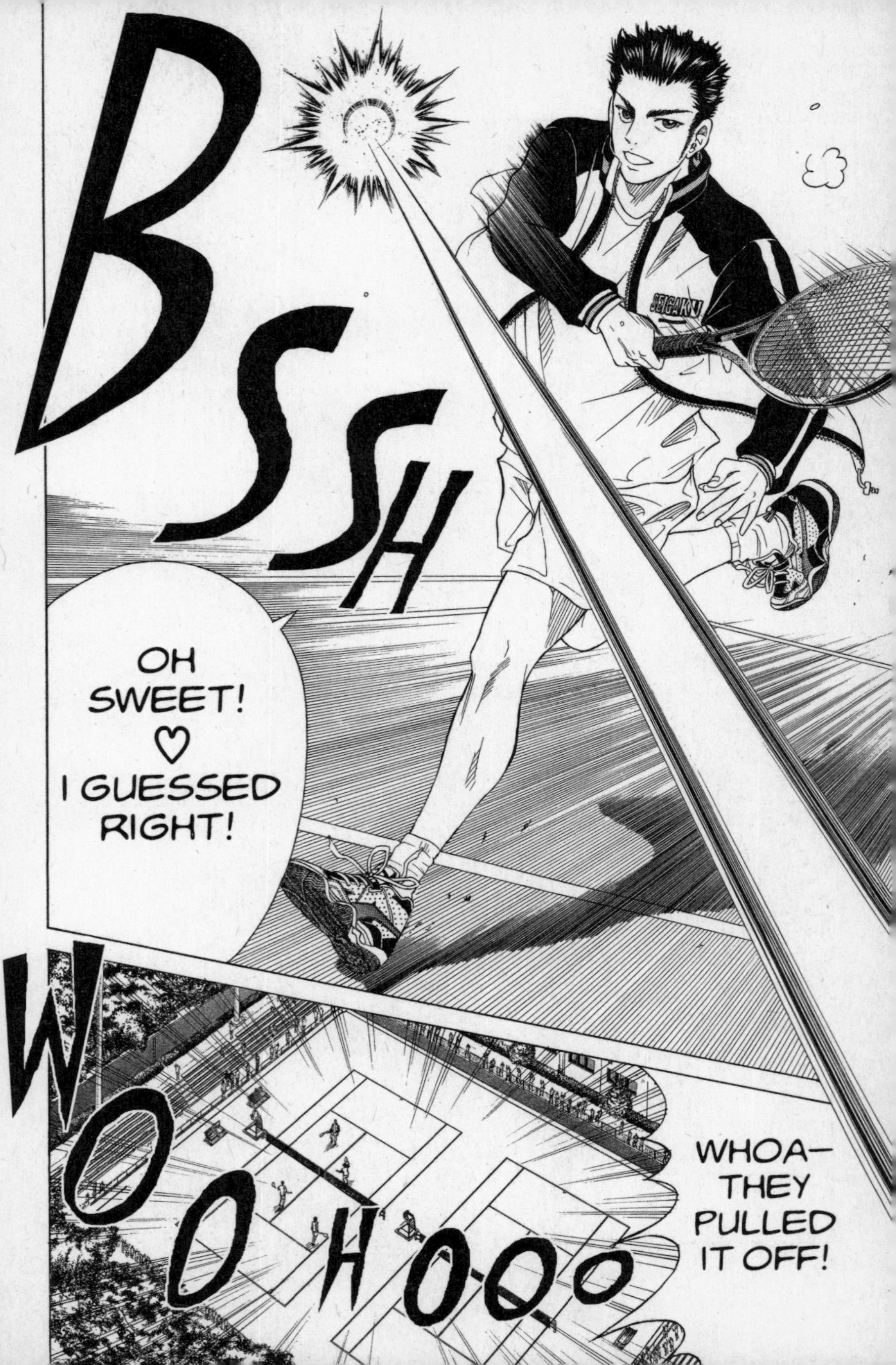
BSSH
OH SWEET! ♡ I GUESSED RIGHT!
WHOA— THEY PULLED IT OFF!
WOOHOOO

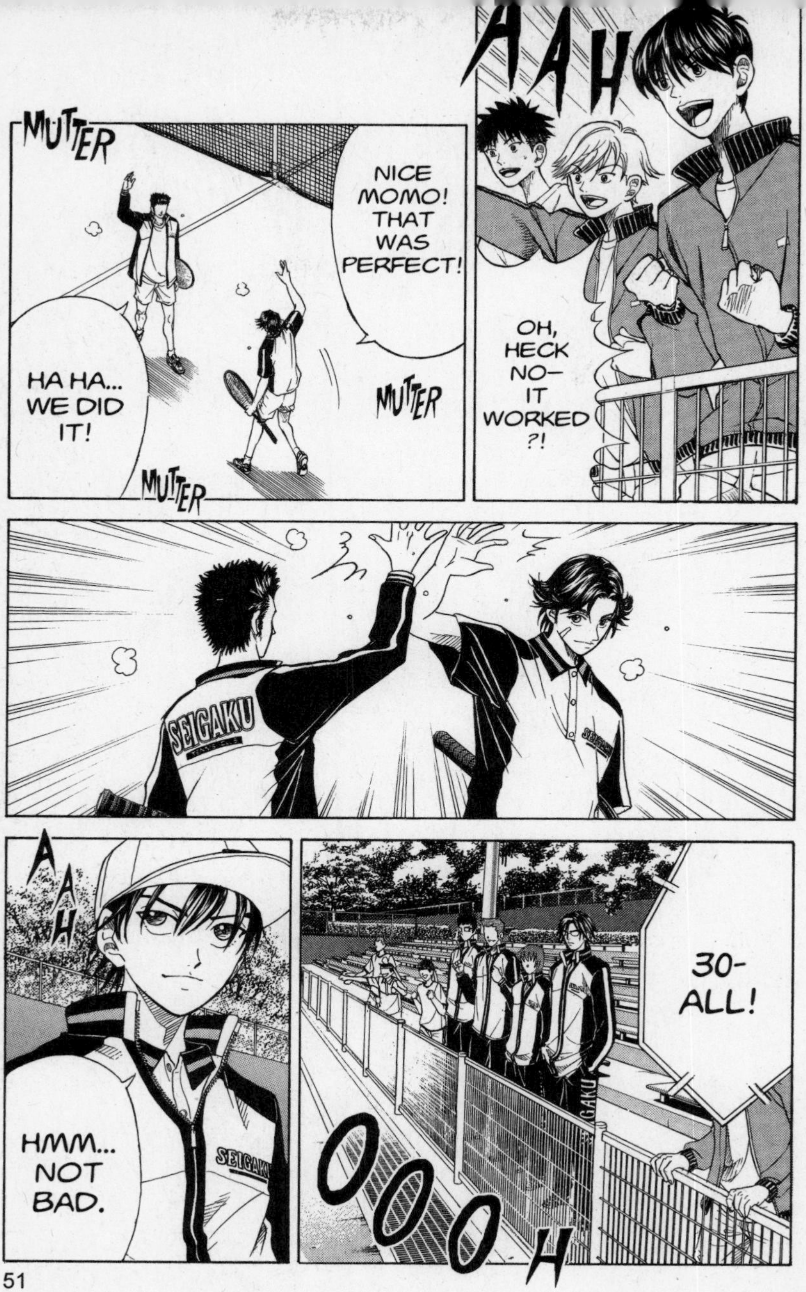
AAH
OH, HECK NO— IT WORKED ?!
MUTTER
NICE MOMO! THAT WAS PERFECT!
MUTTER
HA HA... WE DID IT!
MUTTER
30-ALL!
OOOOH
AAH
HMM... NOT BAD.

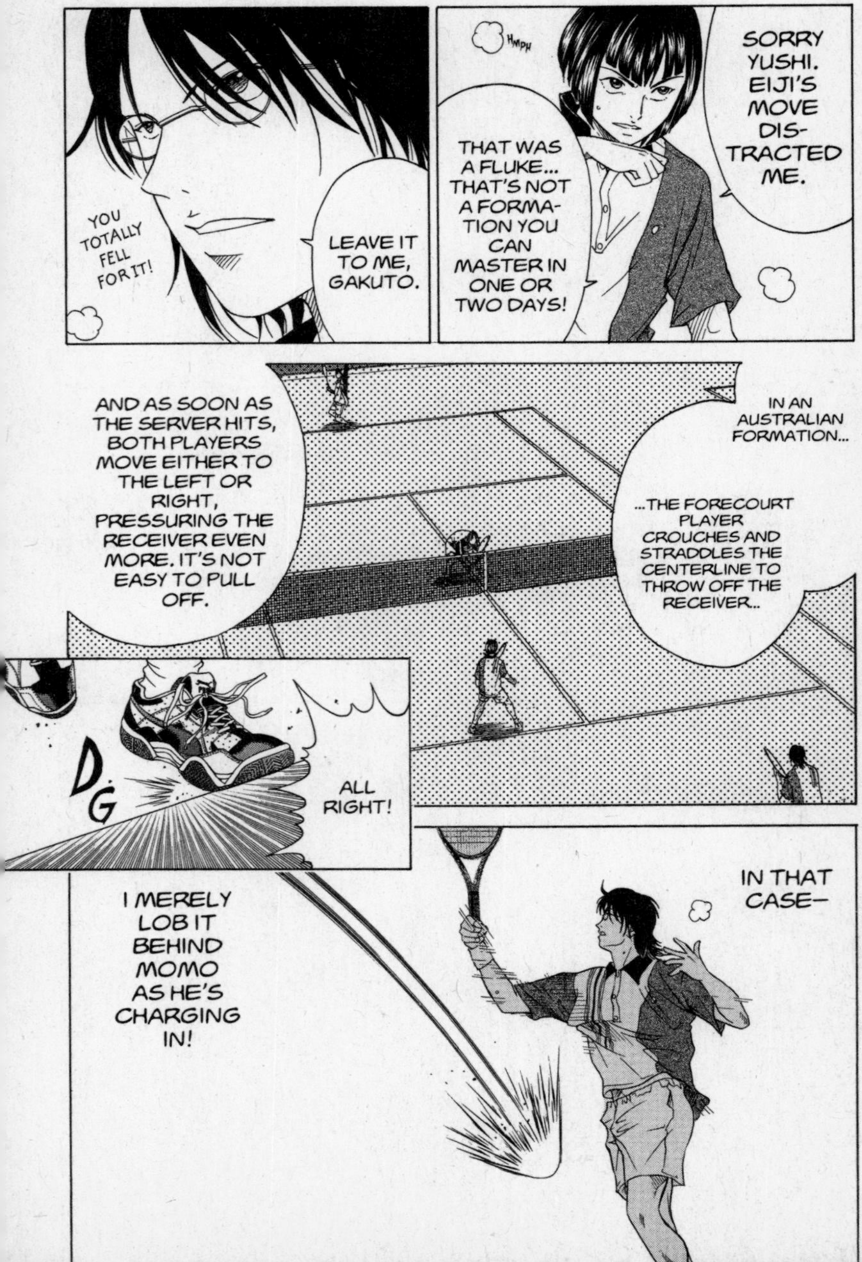
SORRY YUSHI. EIJI'S MOVE DIS-TRACTED ME.
HMPH
THAT WAS A FLUKE... THAT'S NOT A FORMA-TION YOU CAN MASTER IN ONE OR TWO DAYS!
LEAVE IT TO ME, GAKUTO.
YOU TOTALLY FELL FOR IT!
IN AN AUSTRALIAN FORMATION...
...THE FORECOURT PLAYER CROUCHES AND STRADDLES THE CENTERLINE TO THROW OFF THE RECEIVER..
AND AS SOON AS THE SERVER HITS, BOTH PLAYERS MOVE EITHER TO THE LEFT OR RIGHT, PRESSURING THE RECEIVER EVEN MORE. IT'S NOT EASY TO PULL OFF.
ALL RIGHT!
DG
IN THAT CASE—
I MERELY LOB IT BEHIND MOMO AS HE'S CHARGING IN!

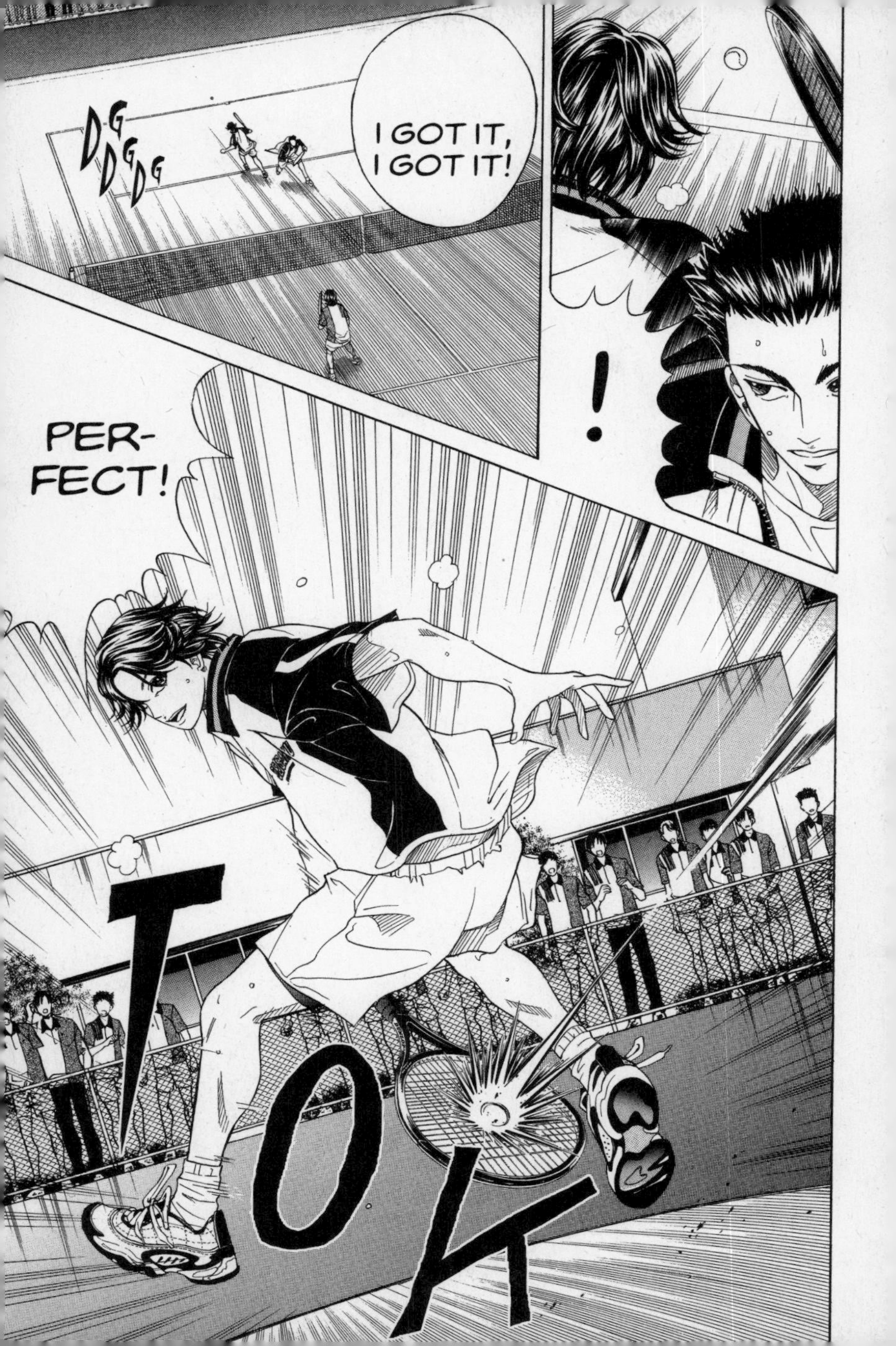
!
I GOT IT, I GOT IT!
DGDGDG
PER-FECT!
TOK

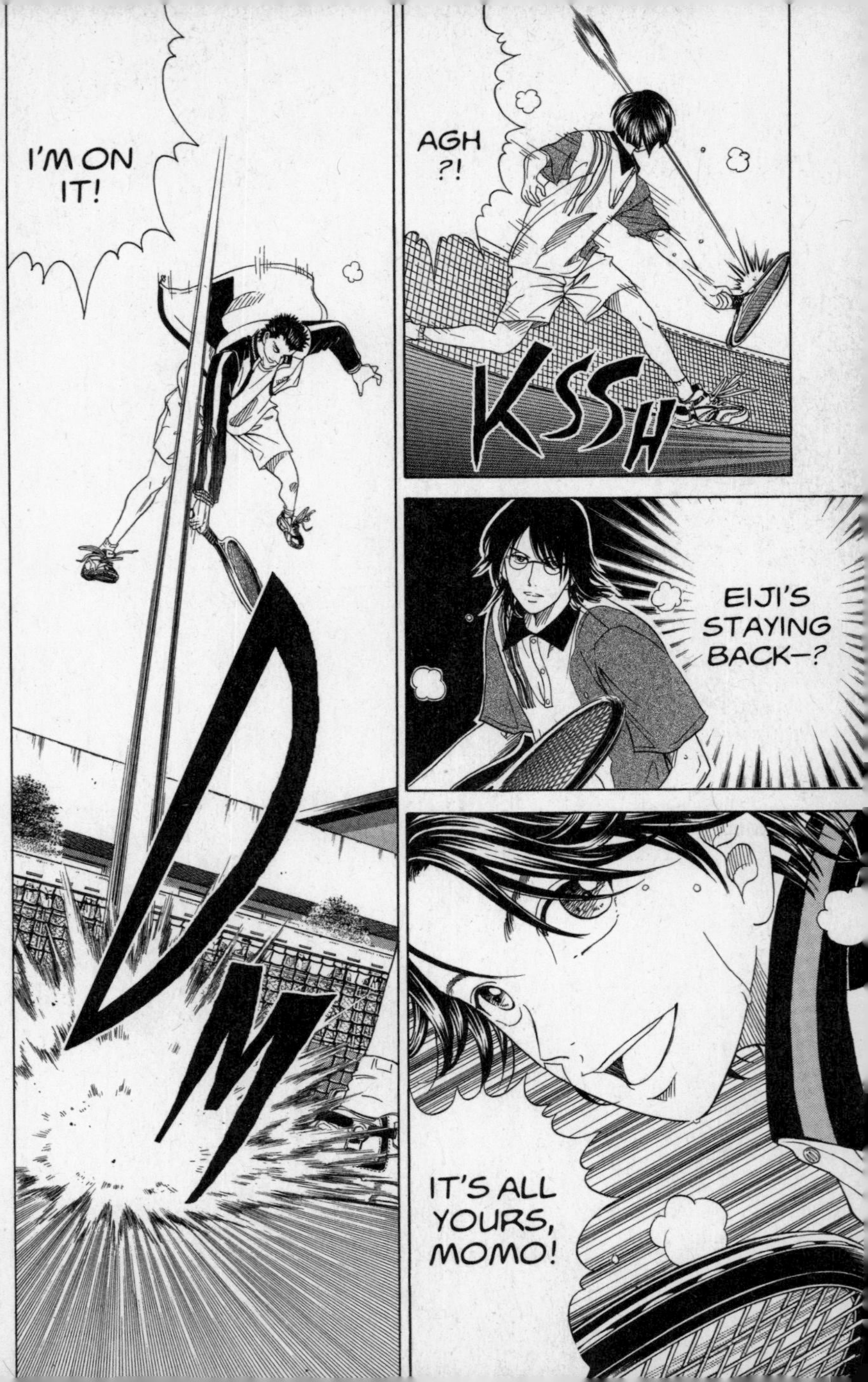
AGH ?!
KSSH
EIJI'S STAYING BACK—?
IT'S ALL YOURS, MOMO!
I'M ON IT!
DM

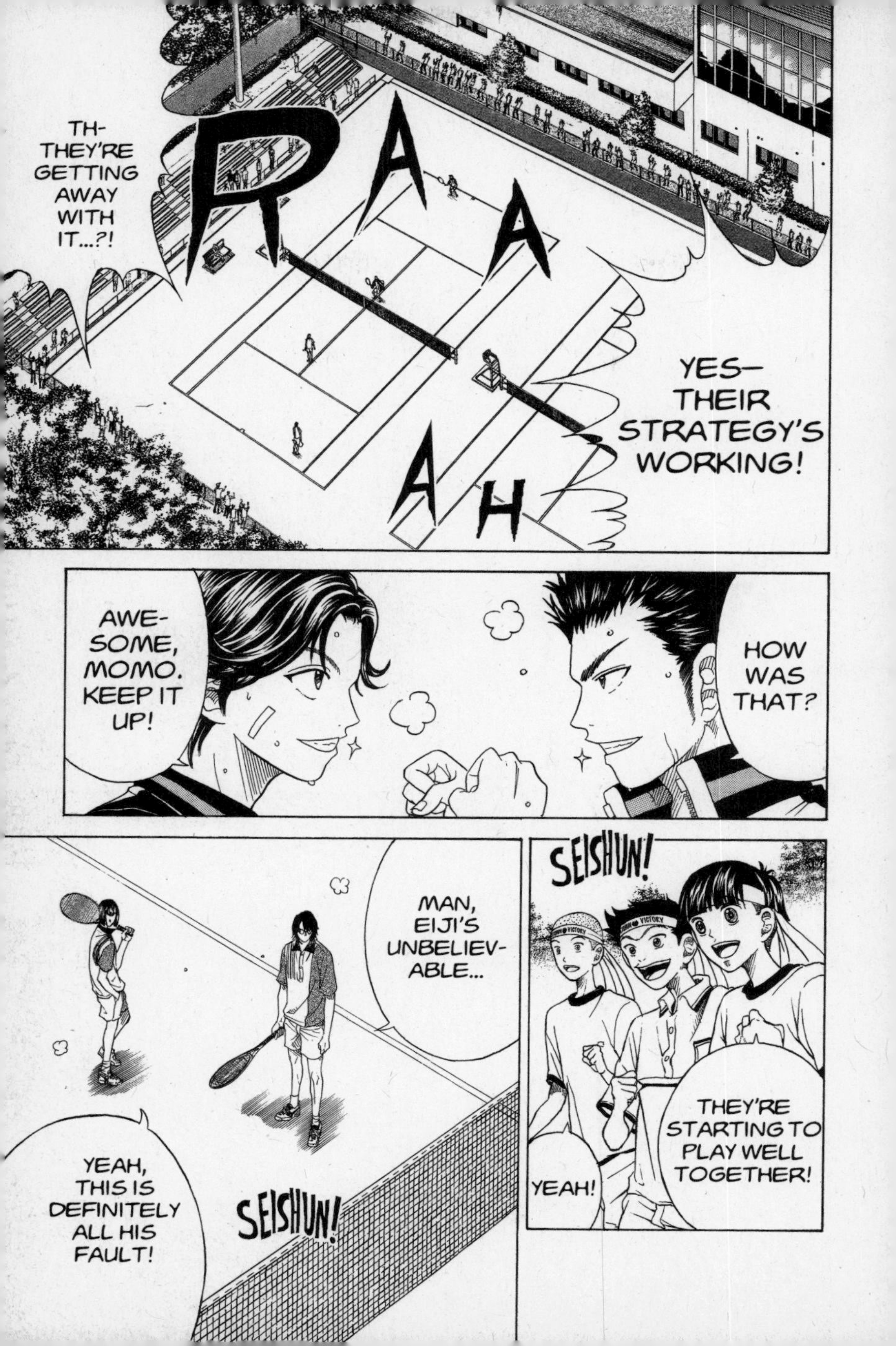
TH- THEY'RE GETTING AWAY WITH IT...?!
RAAAH
YES— THEIR STRATEGY'S WORKING!
HOW WAS THAT?
AWE- SOME, MOMO. KEEP IT UP!
SEISHUN!
THEY'RE STARTING TO PLAY WELL TOGETHER!
YEAH!
MAN, EIJI'S UNBELIEV- ABLE...
YEAH, THIS IS DEFINITELY ALL HIS FAULT!
SEISHUN!

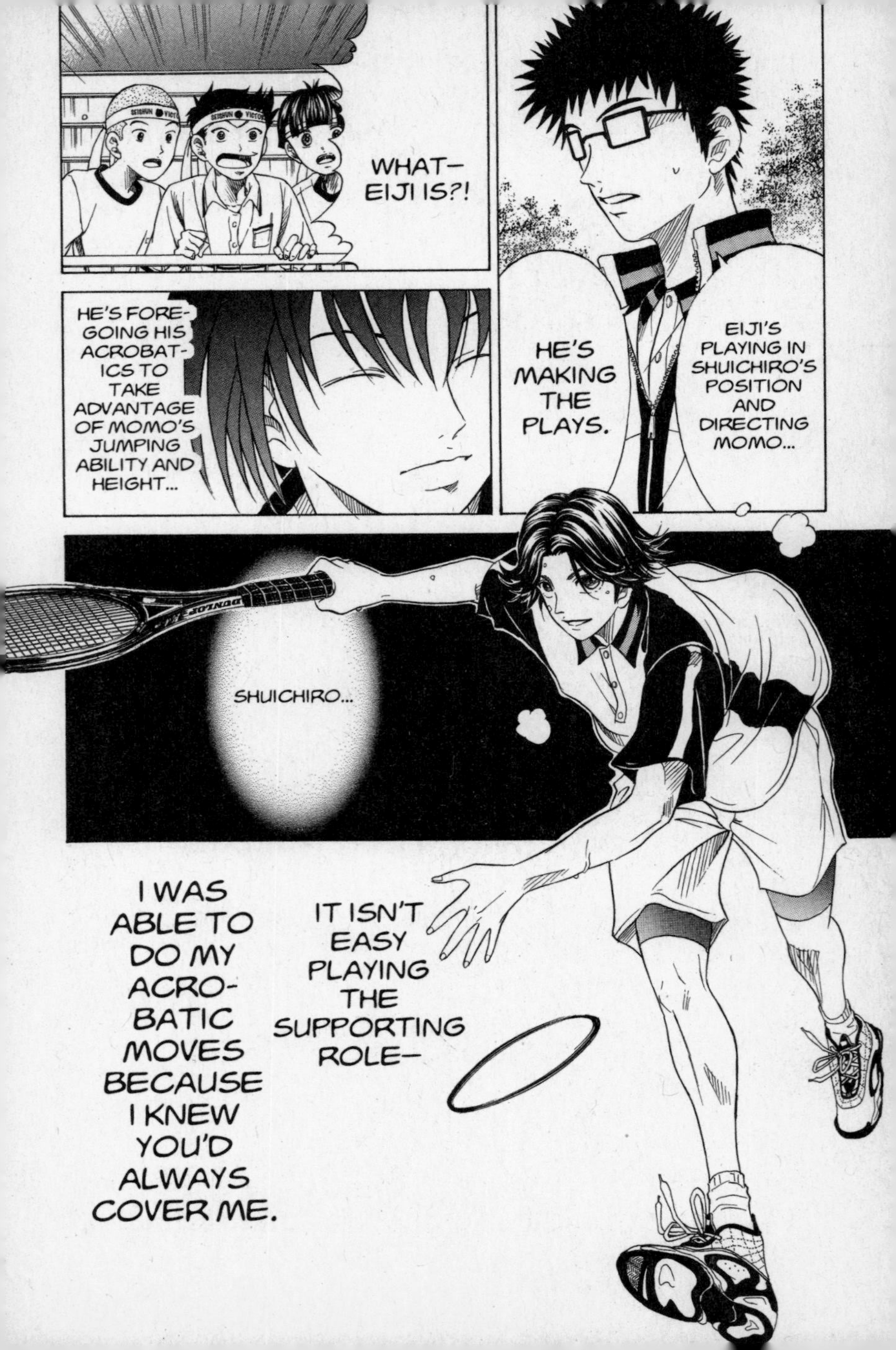
EIJI'S PLAYING IN SHUICHIRO'S POSITION AND DIRECTING MOMO...
HE'S MAKING THE PLAYS.
WHAT— EIJI IS?!
HE'S FORE-GOING HIS ACROBAT-ICS TO TAKE ADVANTAGE OF MOMO'S JUMPING ABILITY AND HEIGHT...
SHUICHIRO...
IT ISN'T EASY PLAYING THE SUPPORTING ROLE—
I WAS ABLE TO DO MY ACRO-BATIC MOVES BECAUSE I KNEW YOU'D ALWAYS COVER ME.

READ THIS WAY

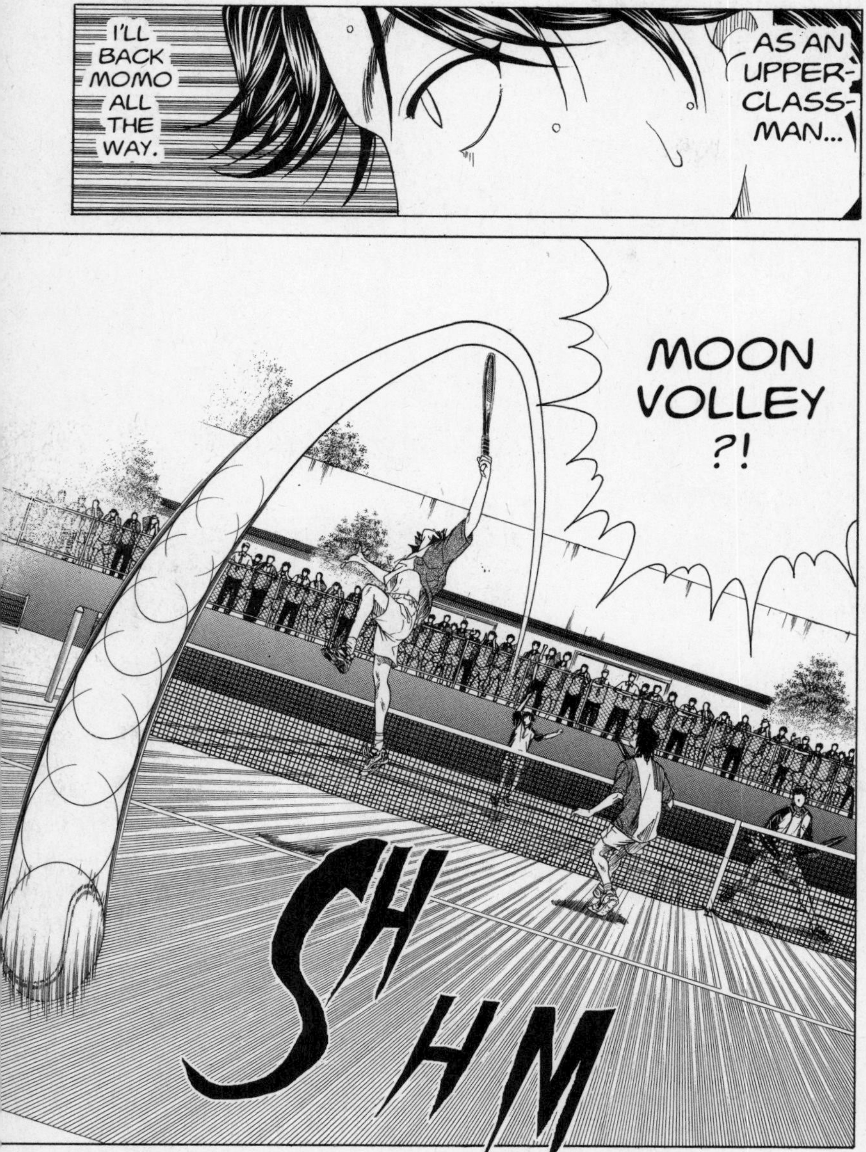
AS AN UPPER-CLASSMAN...
I'LL BACK MOMO ALL THE WAY.
MOON VOLLEY ?!
SHHM

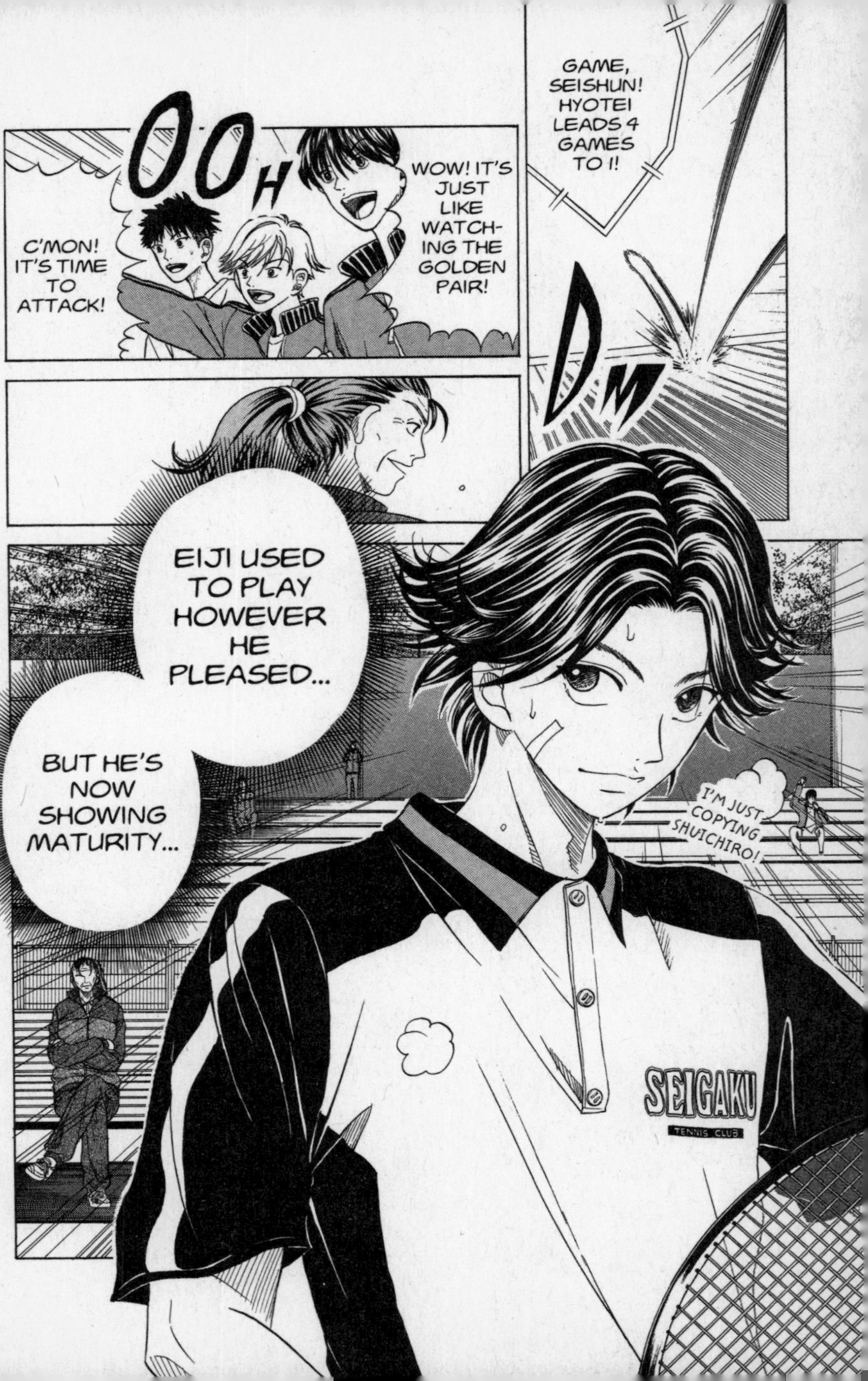
GAME, SEISHUN! HYOTEI LEADS 4 GAMES TO 1!
DM
OOH
WOW! IT'S JUST LIKE WATCHING THE GOLDEN PAIR!
C'MON! IT'S TIME TO ATTACK!
I'M JUST COPYING SHUICHIRO!
EIJI USED TO PLAY HOWEVER HE PLEASED...
BUT HE'S NOW SHOWING MATURITY...
SEIGAKU
TENNIS CLUB

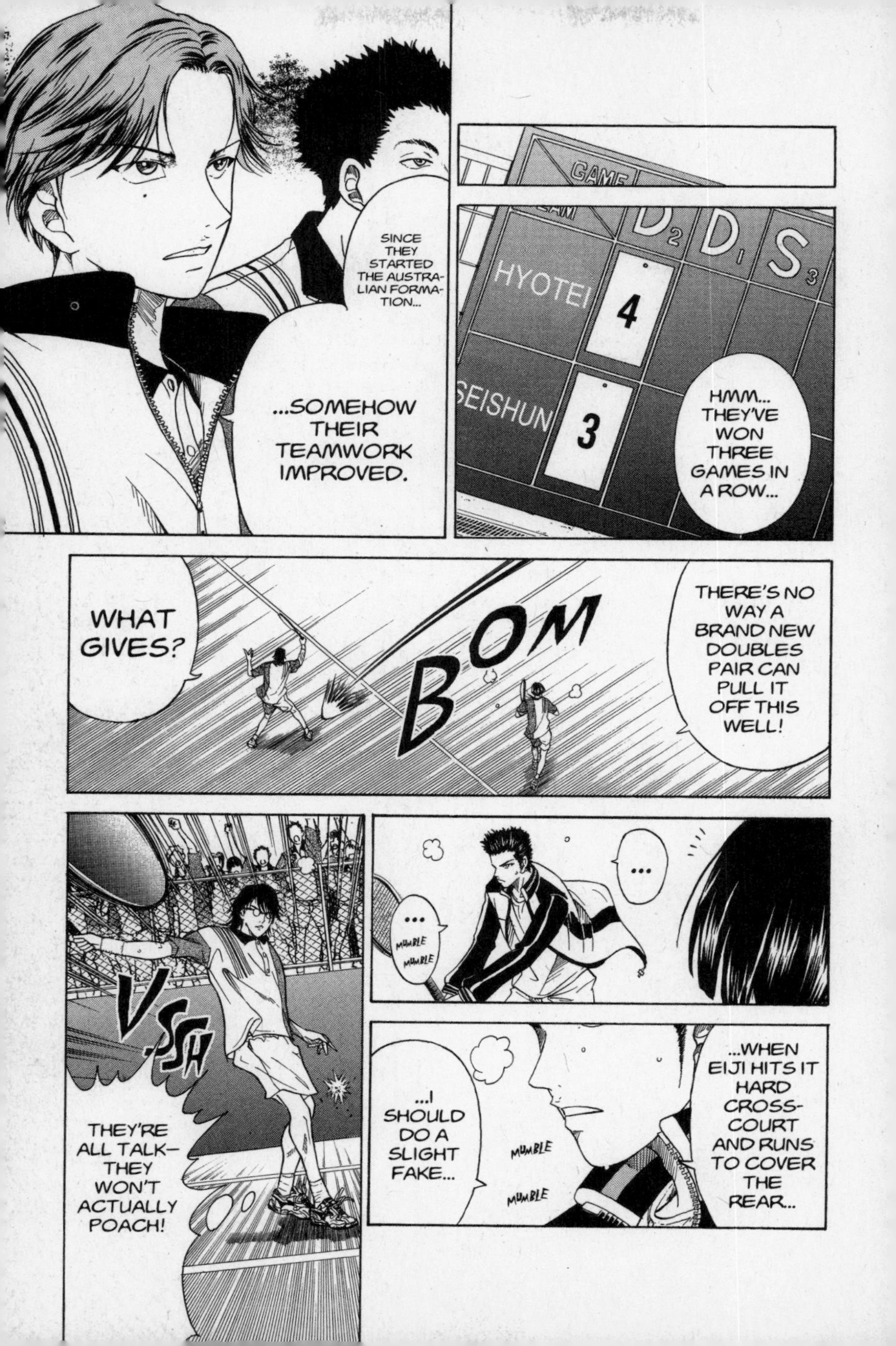
GAME
D2 D1 S3
HYOTEI 4
SEISHUN 3
HMM... THEY'VE WON THREE GAMES IN A ROW...
SINCE THEY STARTED THE AUSTRALIAN FORMATION...
...SOMEHOW THEIR TEAMWORK IMPROVED.
THERE'S NO WAY A BRAND NEW DOUBLES PAIR CAN PULL IT OFF THIS WELL!
BOM
WHAT GIVES?
...
...
MUMBLE MUMBLE
...WHEN EIJI HITS IT HARD CROSS-COURT AND RUNS TO COVER THE REAR...
MUMBLE
MUMBLE
...I SHOULD DO A SLIGHT FAKE...
VSSH
THEY'RE ALL TALK—THEY WON'T ACTUALLY POACH!

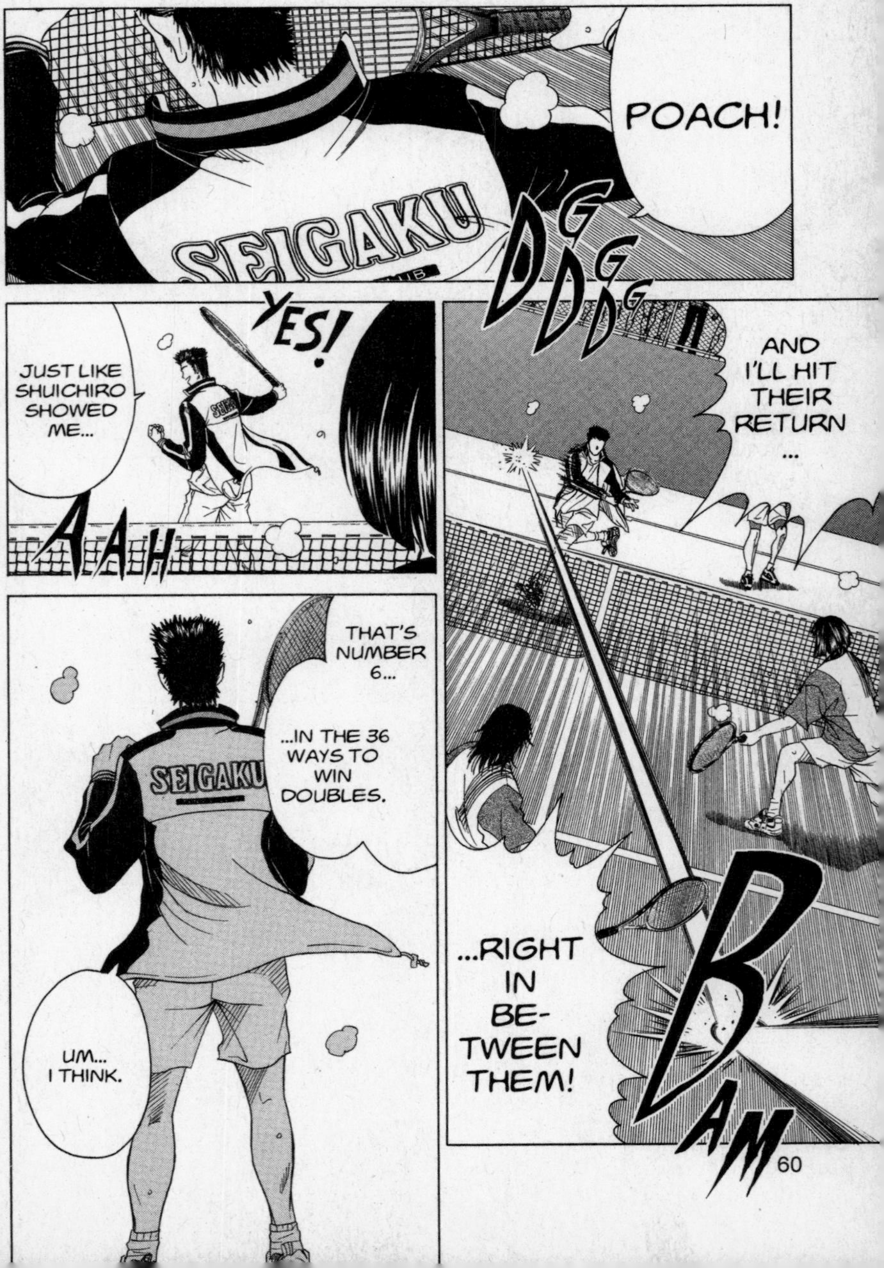
POACH!
AND I'LL HIT THEIR RETURN ...
...RIGHT IN BE-TWEEN THEM!
BAM
YES!
JUST LIKE SHUICHIRO SHOWED ME...
AAH
THAT'S NUMBER 6...
...IN THE 36 WAYS TO WIN DOUBLES.
UM... I THINK.

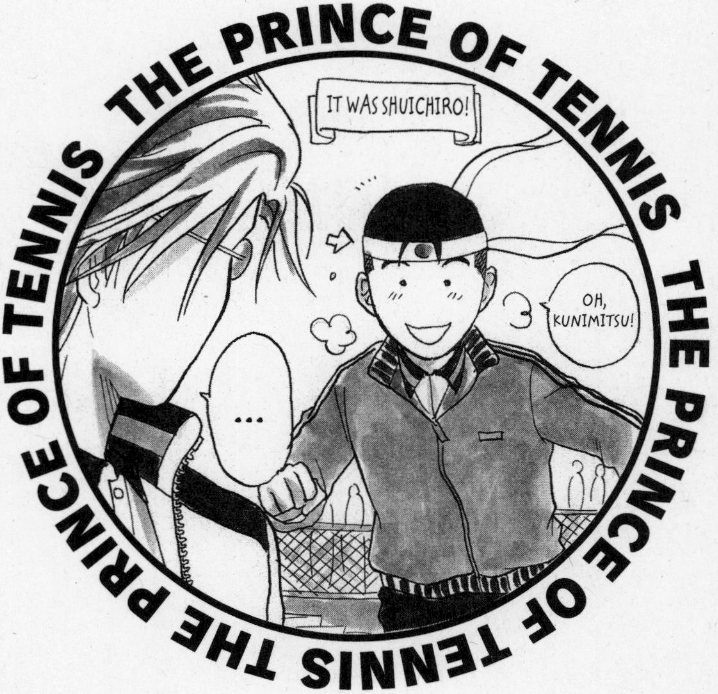
THE PRINCE OF TENNIS THE PRINCE OF TENNIS THE PRINCE OF TENNIS
IT WAS SHUICHIRO!
OH, KUNIMITSU!
...

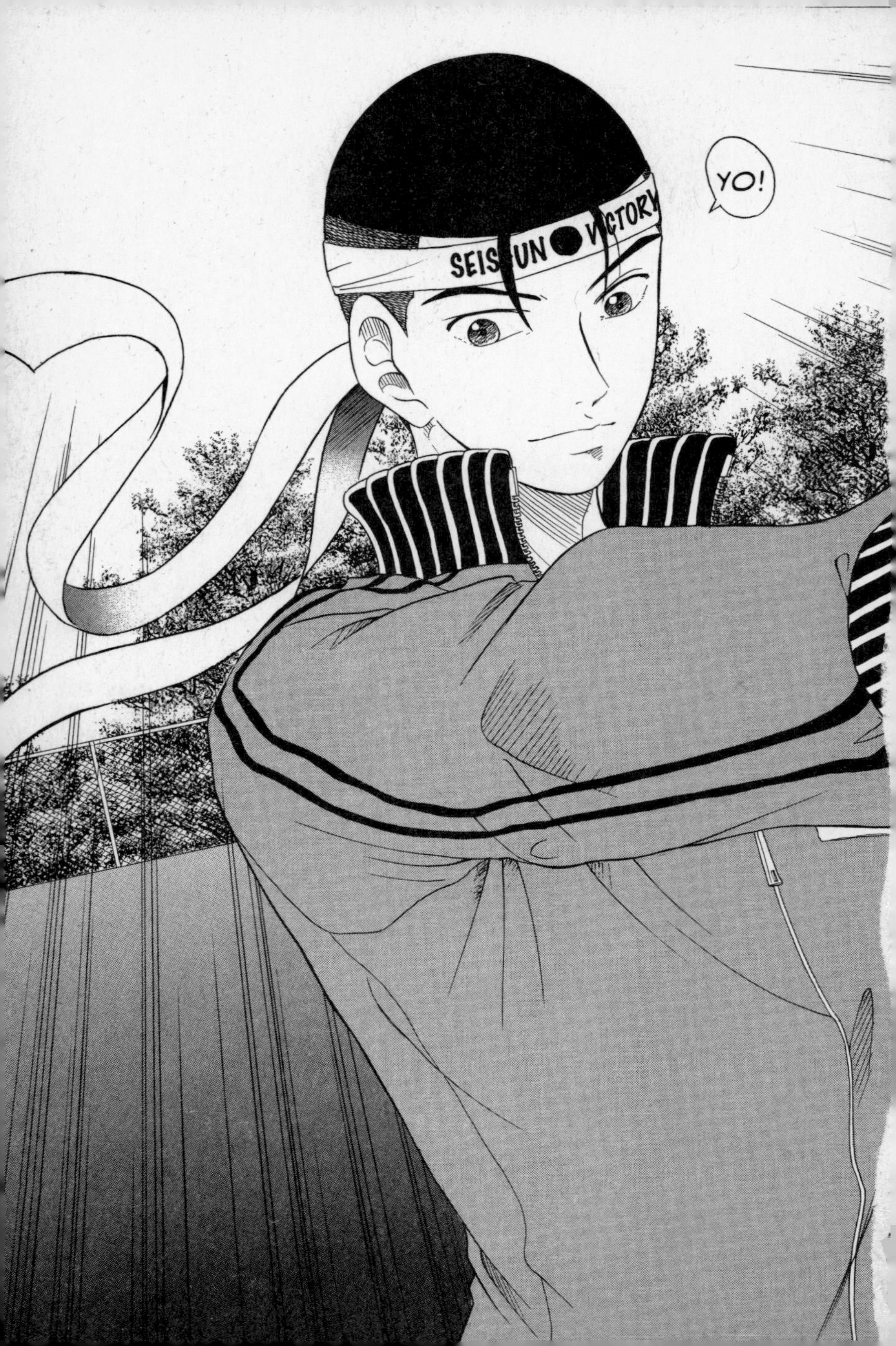
YO!

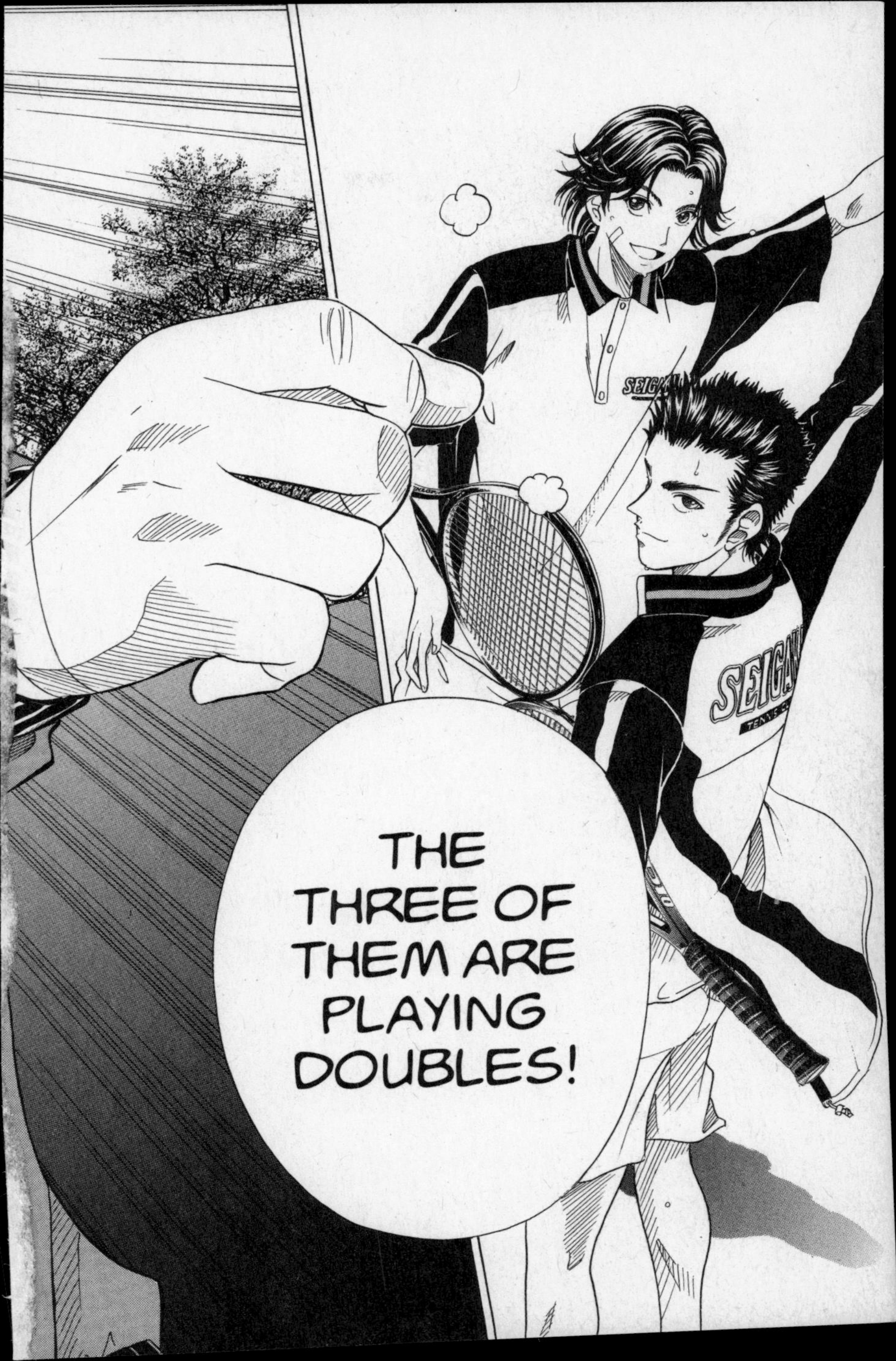
THE THREE OF THEM ARE PLAYING DOUBLES!

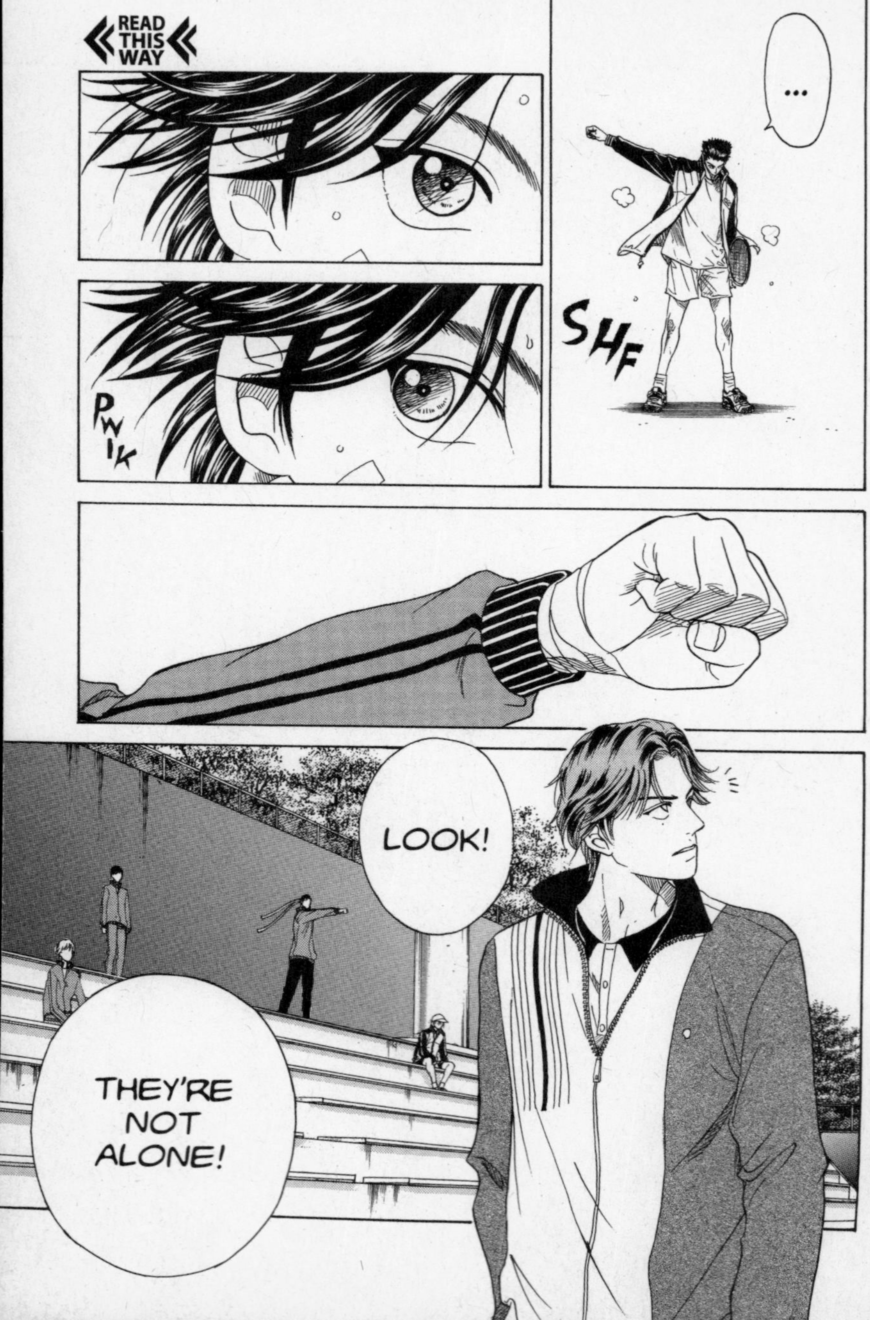
READ THIS WAY
...
SHF
PWIK
LOOK!
THEY'RE NOT ALONE!

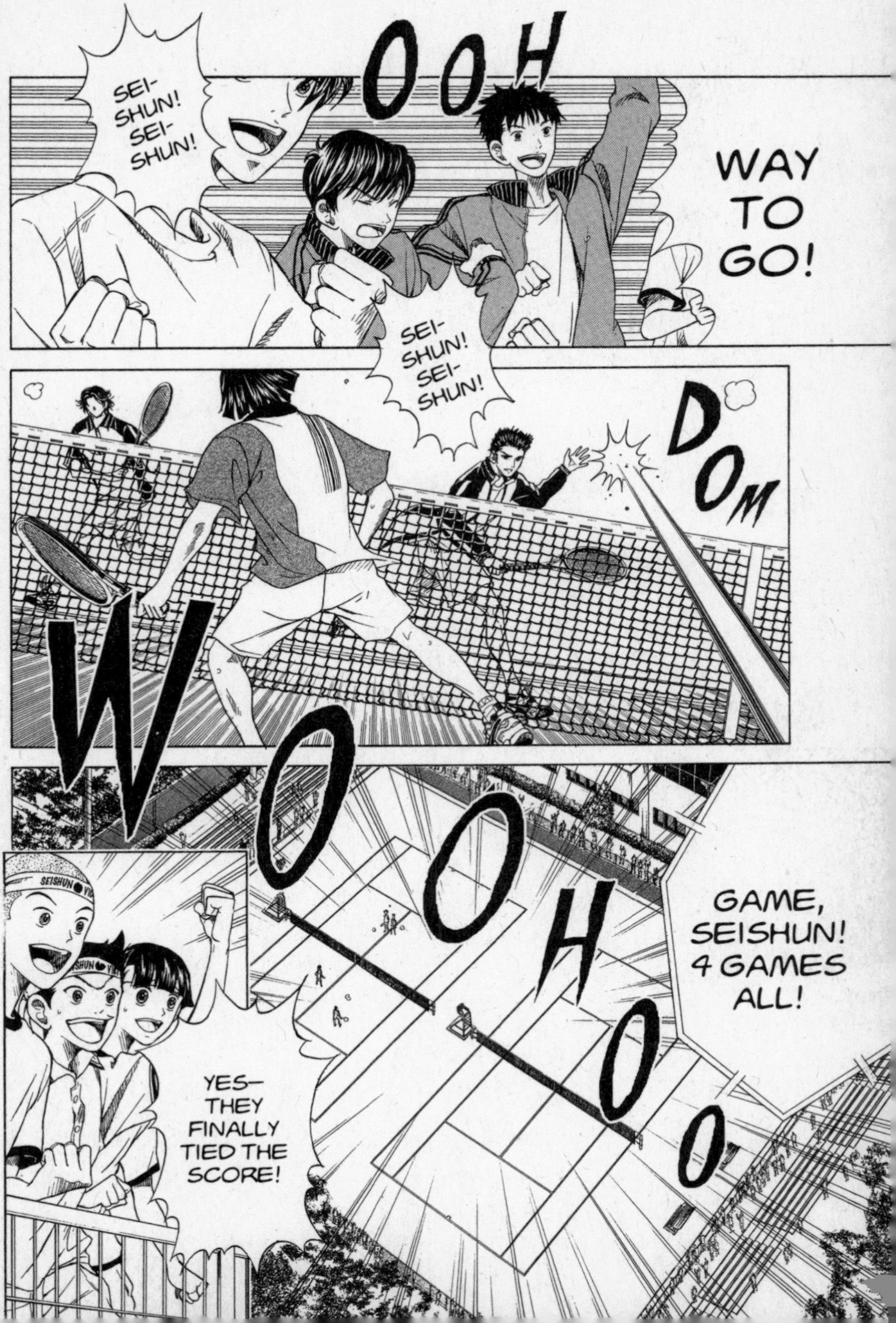

WAY TO GO!
OOOH
SEI-SHUN! SEI-SHUN!
SEI-SHUN! SEI-SHUN!
DOM
DOM
GAME, SEISHUN! 4 GAMES ALL!
WOOOHOOOO
YES—THEY FINALLY TIED THE SCORE!

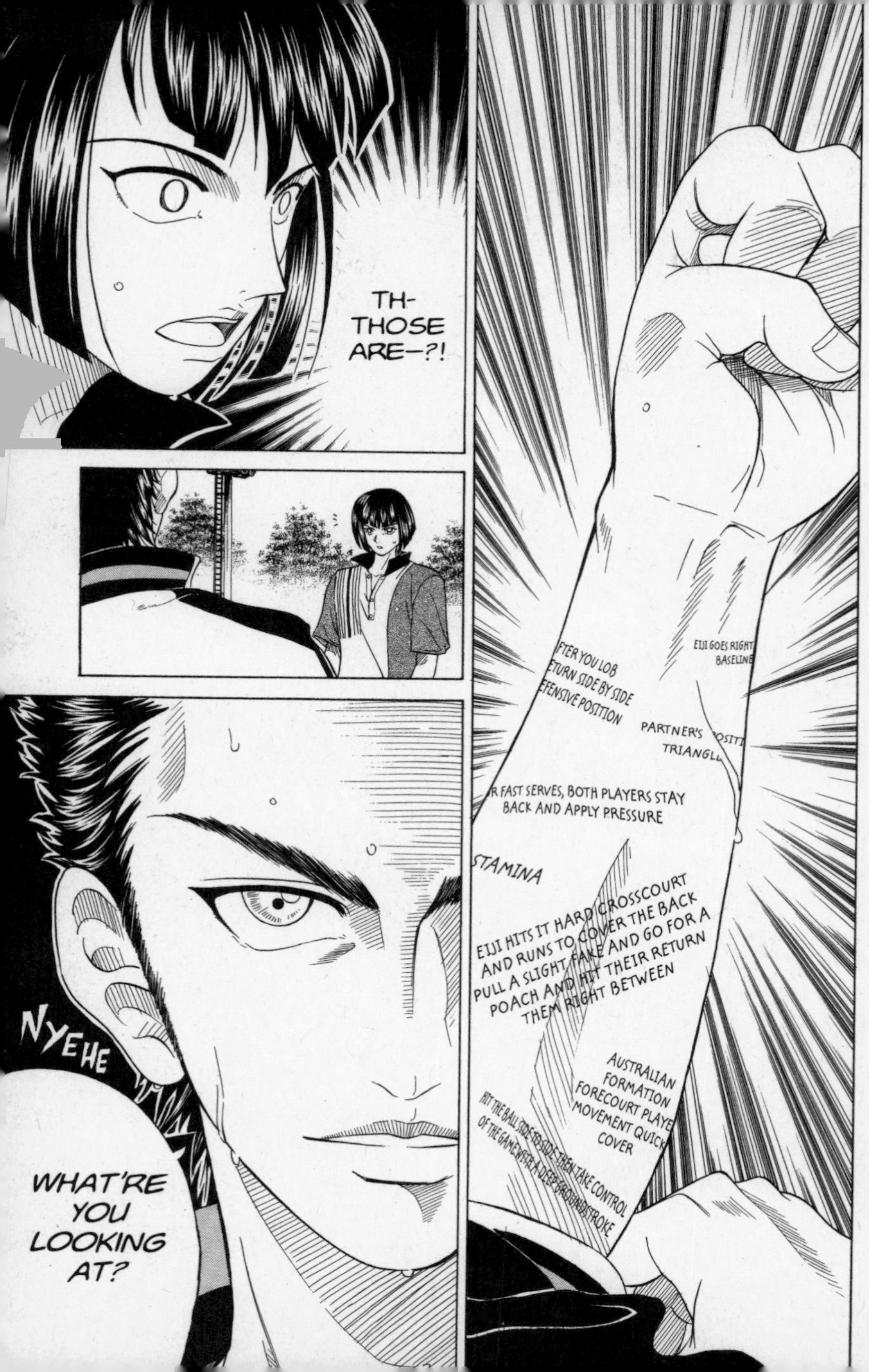
EIJI GOES RIGHT BASELINE
FTER YOU LOB
ETURN SIDE BY SIDE
EFENSIVE POSITION
PARTNER'S POSITI
TRIANGL
R FAST SERVES, BOTH PLAYERS STAY BACK AND APPLY PRESSURE
STAMINA
EIJI HITS IT HARD CROSSCOURT AND RUNS TO COVER THE BACK PULL A SLIGHT FAKE AND GO FOR A POACH AND HIT THEIR RETURN RIGHT BETWEEN THEM
AUSTRALIAN FORMATION
FORECOURT PLAYE
MOVEMENT QUICK
COVER
HIT THE BALL SIDE TO SIDE THEN TAKE CONTROL OF THE GAME WITH A DEEP GROUNDSTROKE
TH- THOSE ARE--?!
NYEHE
WHAT'RE YOU LOOKING AT?

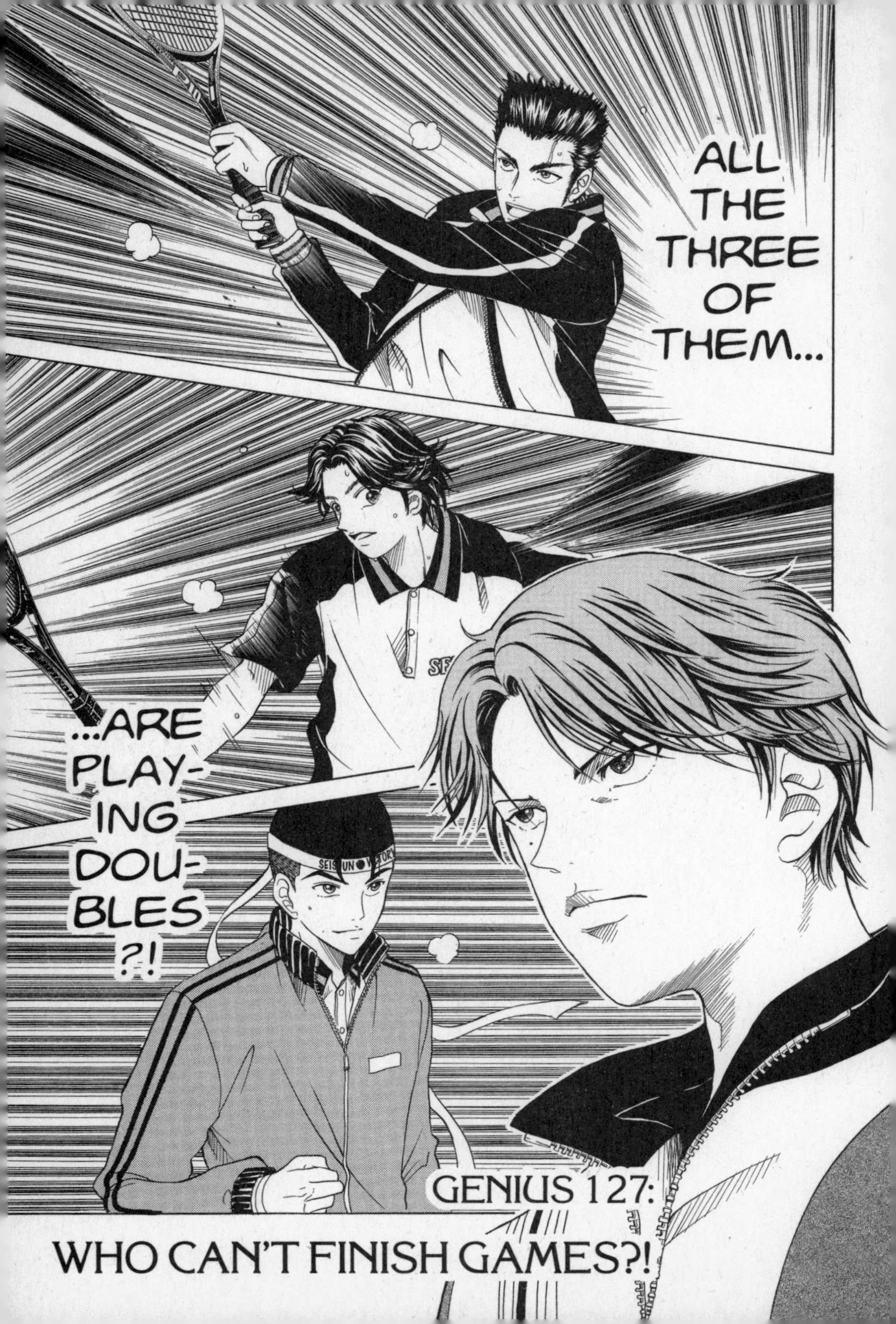
ALL THE THREE OF THEM...
...ARE PLAY-ING DOU-BLES?!
SEISUN VICTORY
GENIUS 127:
WHO CAN'T FINISH GAMES?!

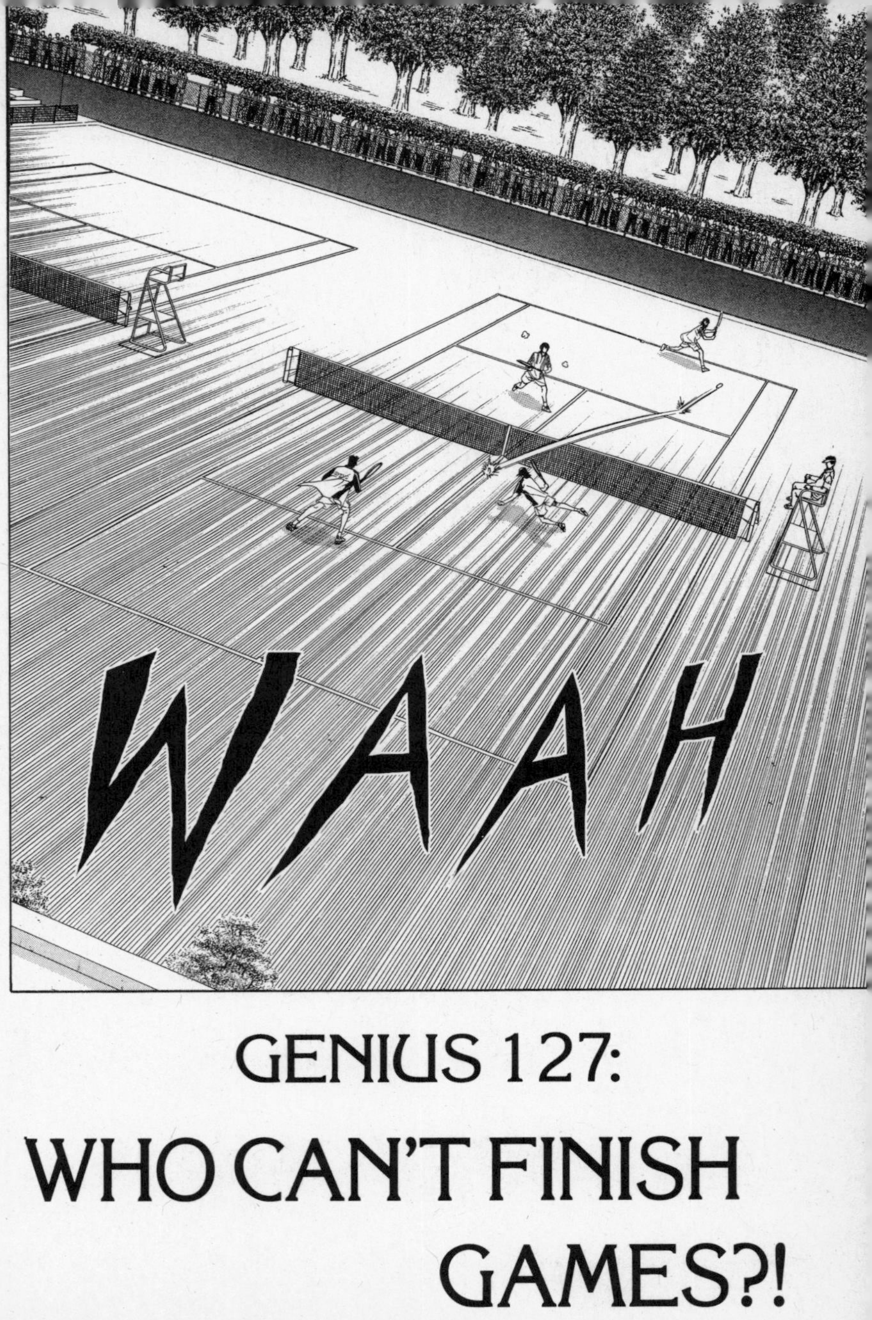
WAAH

GENIUS 127:

WHO CAN'T FINISH GAMES?!

READ THIS WAY

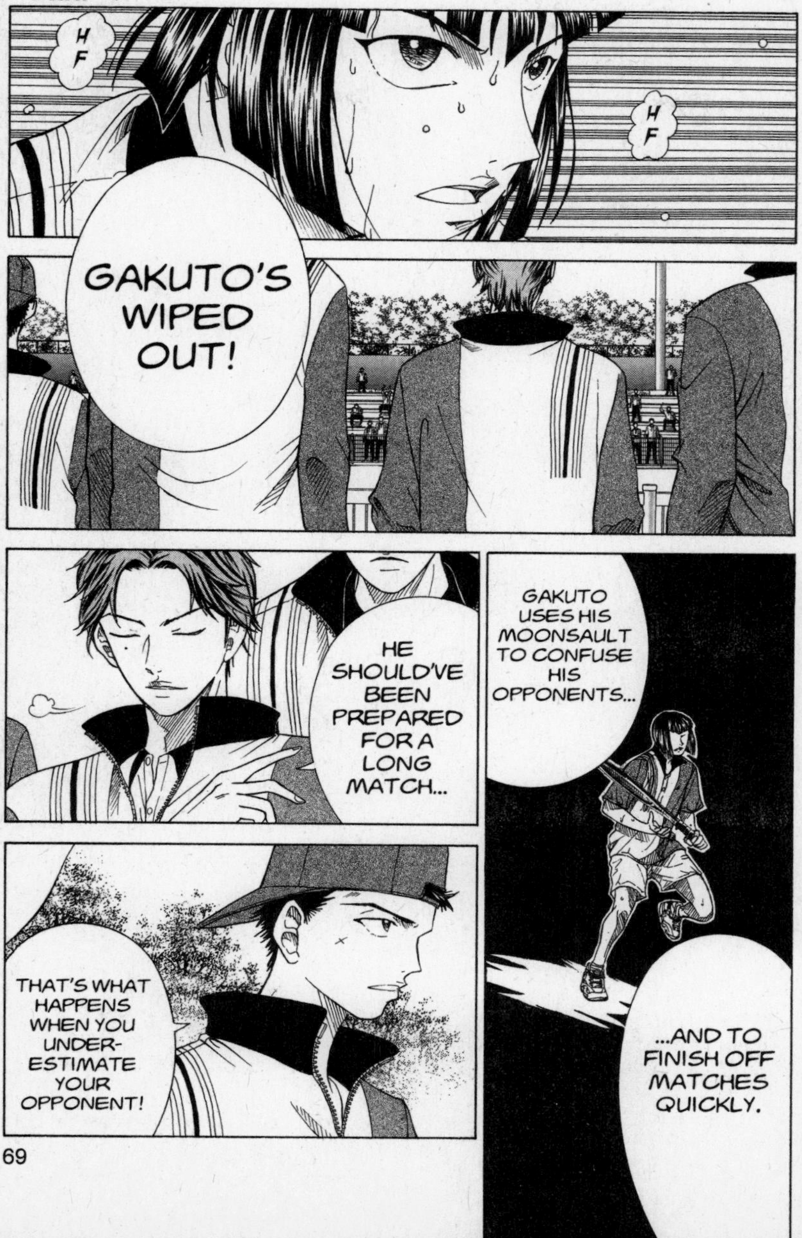
HF
HF
GAKUTO'S WIPED OUT!
GAKUTO USES HIS MOONSAULT TO CONFUSE HIS OPPONENTS...
...AND TO FINISH OFF MATCHES QUICKLY.
HE SHOULD'VE BEEN PREPARED FOR A LONG MATCH...
THAT'S WHAT HAPPENS WHEN YOU UNDER-ESTIMATE YOUR OPPONENT!

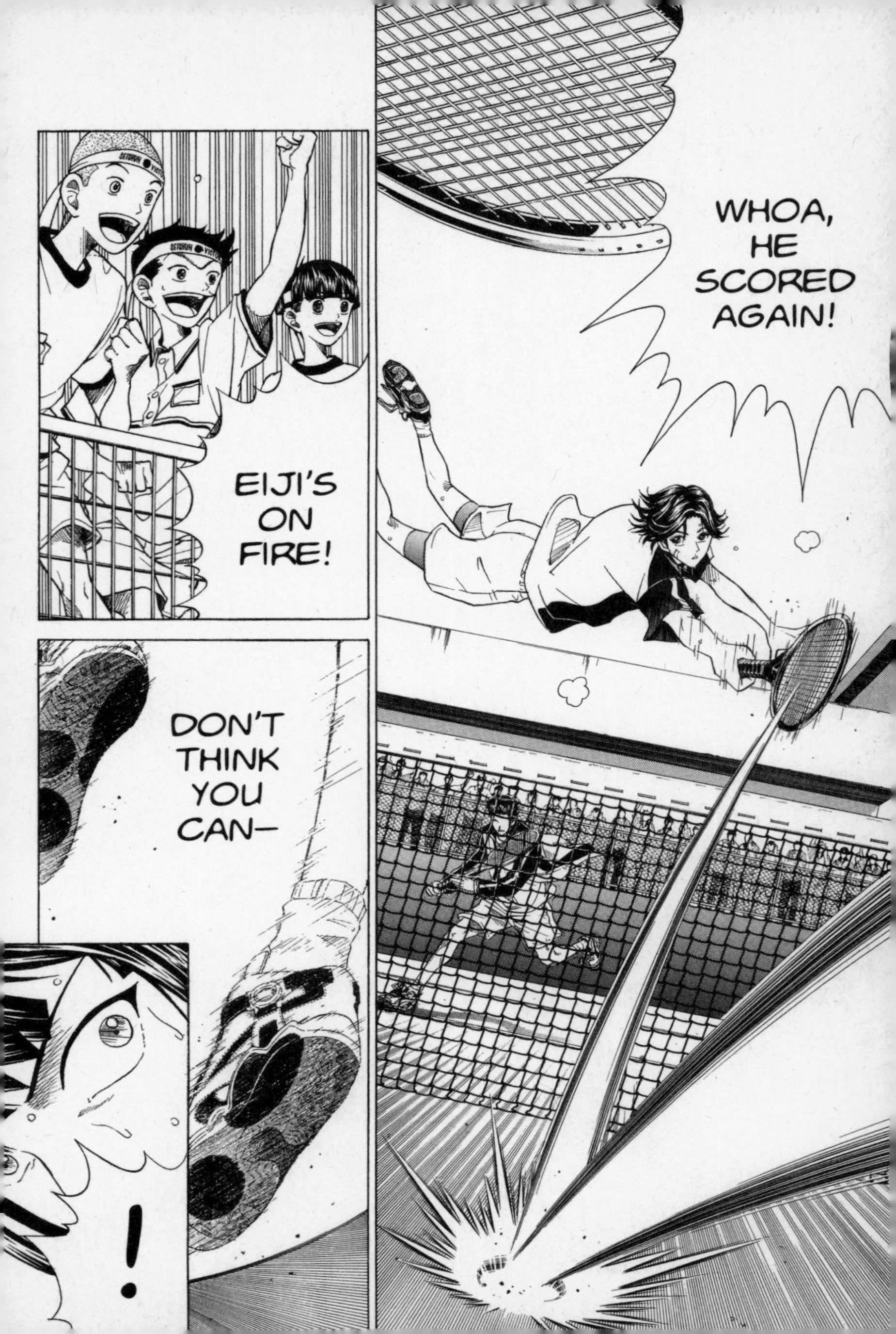
WHOA, HE SCORED AGAIN!
EIJI'S ON FIRE!
DON'T THINK YOU CAN—
!

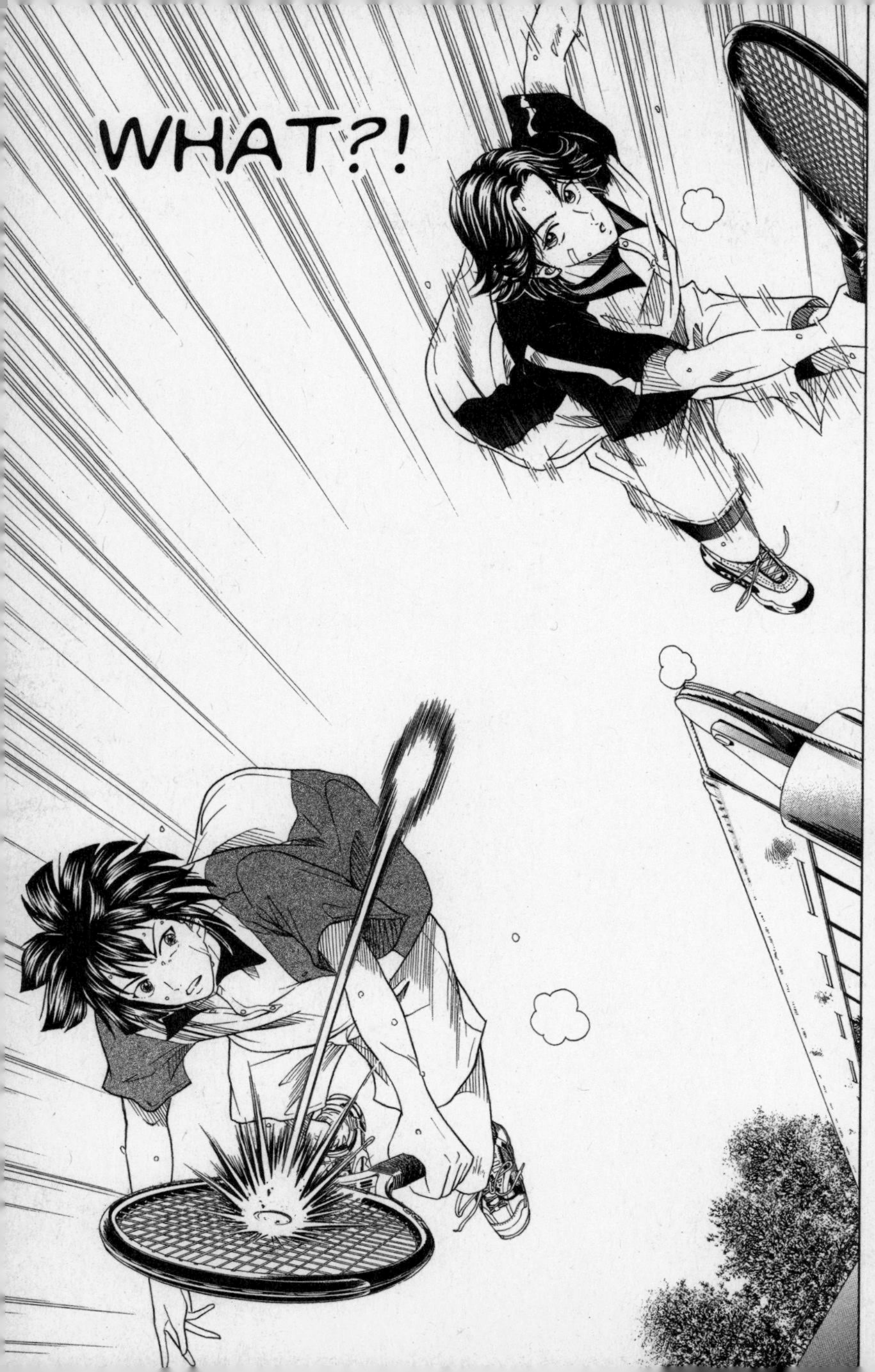
WHAT?!

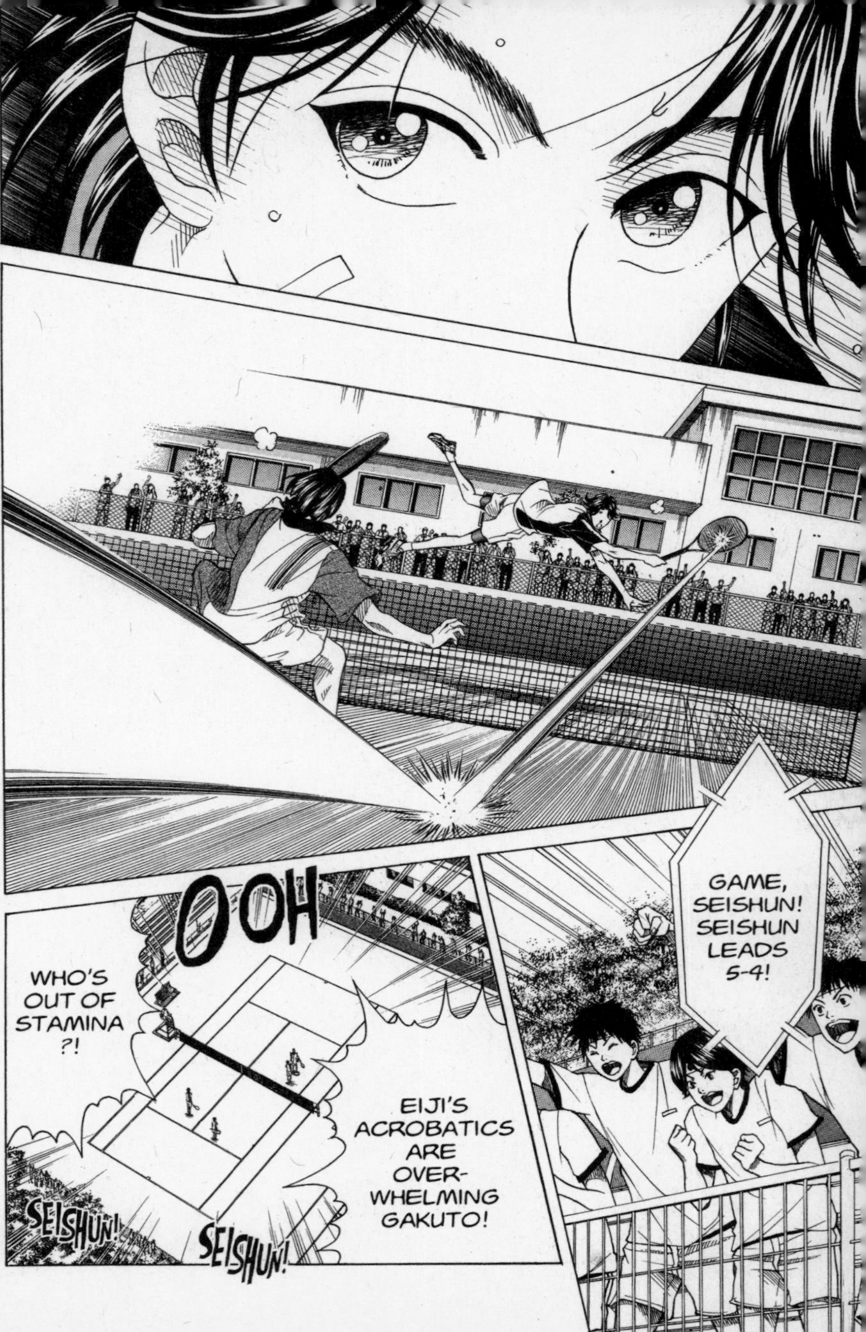
GAME, SEISHUN! SEISHUN LEADS 5-4!
OOH
WHO'S OUT OF STAMINA?!
EIJI'S ACROBATICS ARE OVER-WHELMING GAKUTO!
SEISHUN!
SEISHUN!

READ THIS WAY

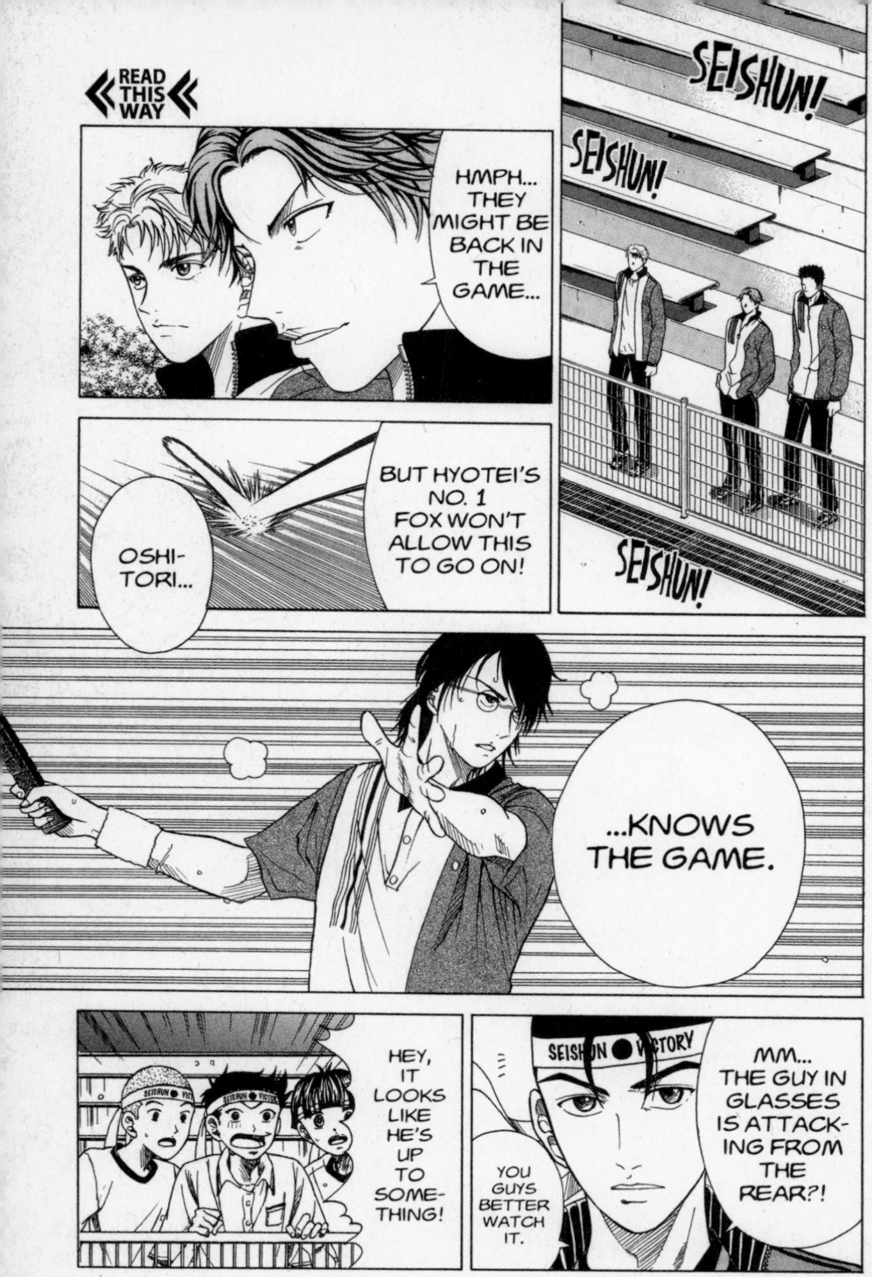
SEISHUN!
SEISHUN!
SEISHUN!
HMPH... THEY MIGHT BE BACK IN THE GAME...
BUT HYOTEI'S NO. 1 FOX WON'T ALLOW THIS TO GO ON!
OSHI-TORI...
...KNOWS THE GAME.
MM... THE GUY IN GLASSES IS ATTACK-ING FROM THE REAR?!
YOU GUYS BETTER WATCH IT.
HEY, IT LOOKS LIKE HE'S UP TO SOME-THING!

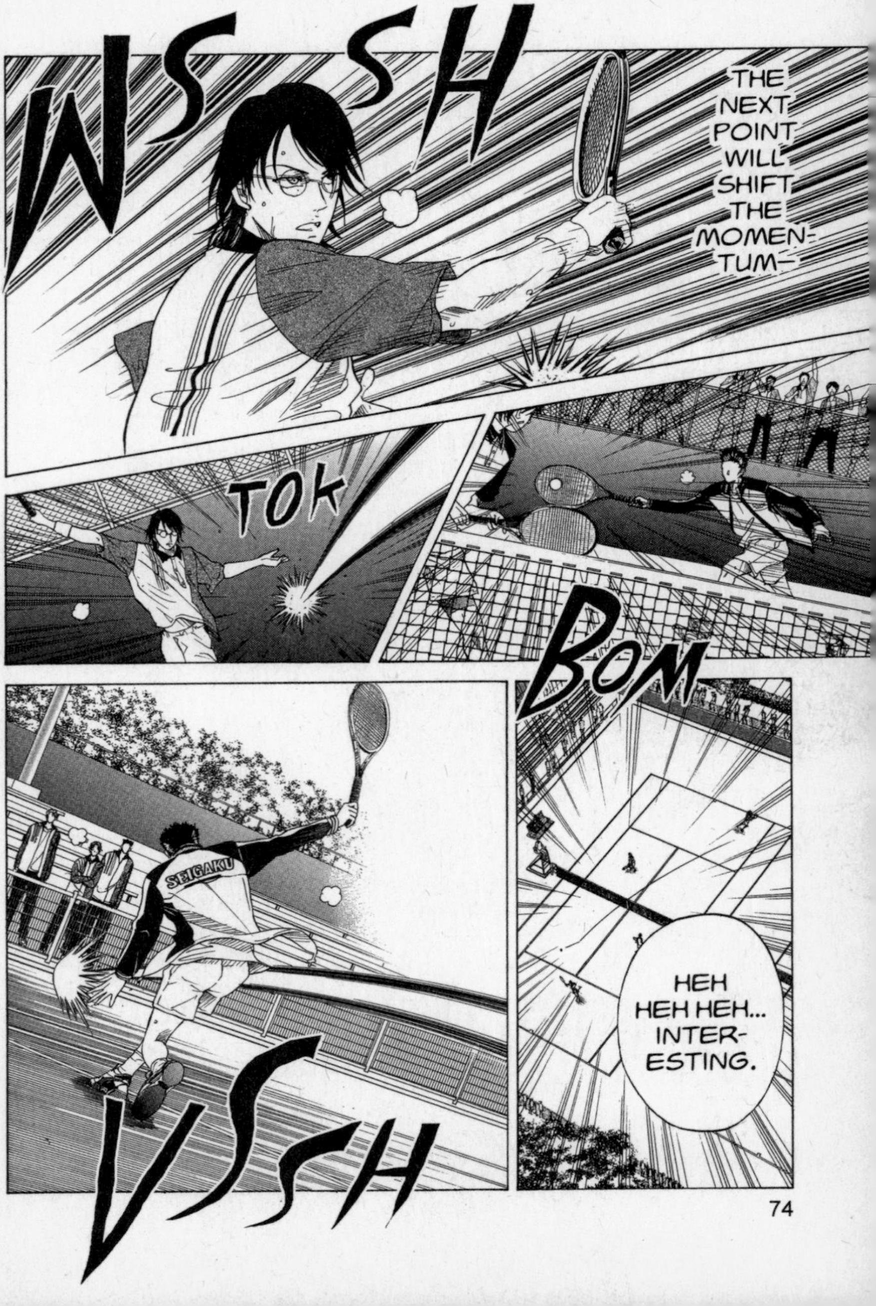
WSSH
THE NEXT POINT WILL SHIFT THE MOMEN-TUM—
BOM
TOK
HEH HEH HEH... INTER-ESTING.
VISSH

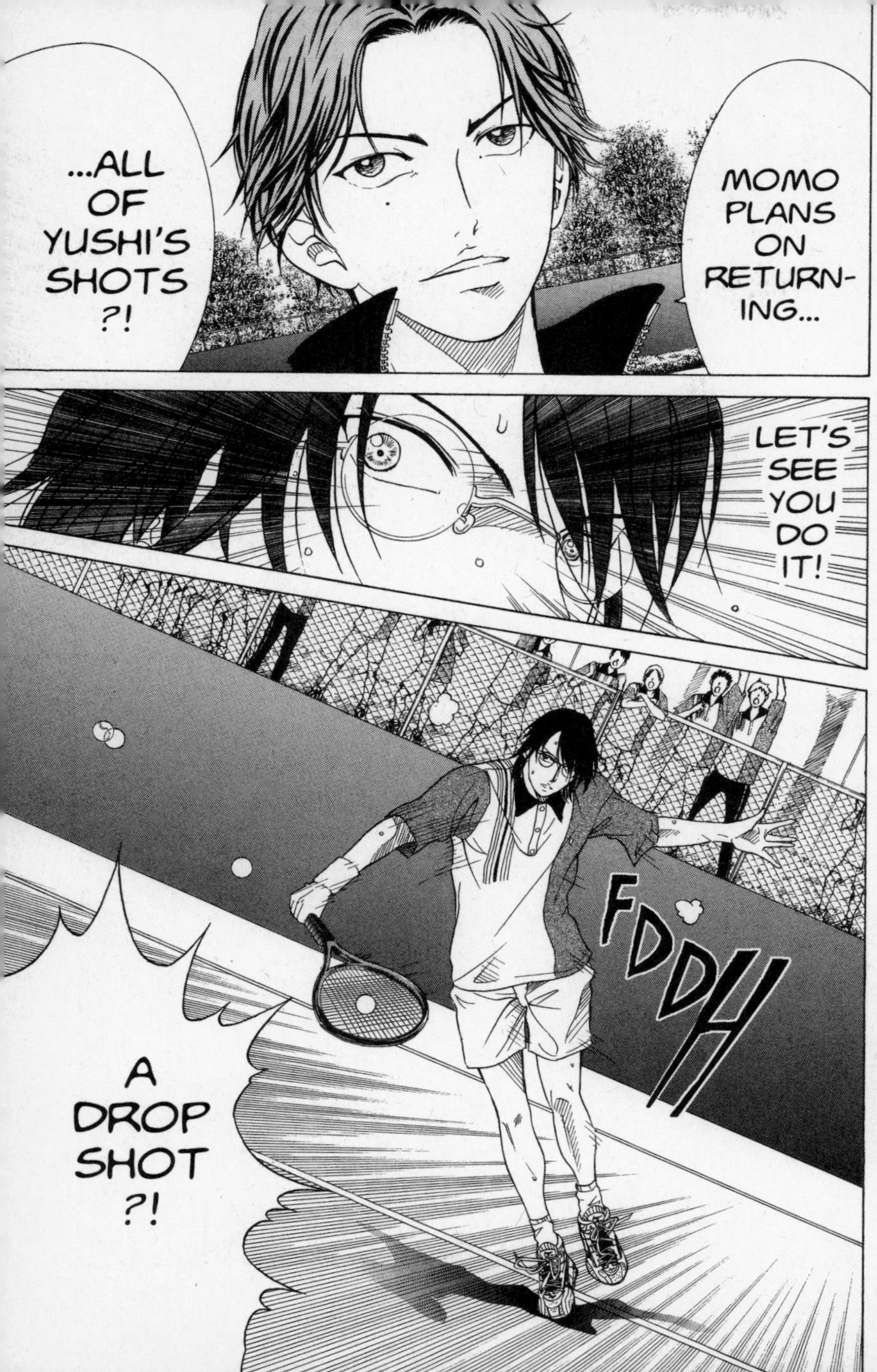
MOMO PLANS ON RETURN-ING...
...ALL OF YUSHI'S SHOTS ?!
LET'S SEE YOU DO IT!
FDDH
A DROP SHOT ?!

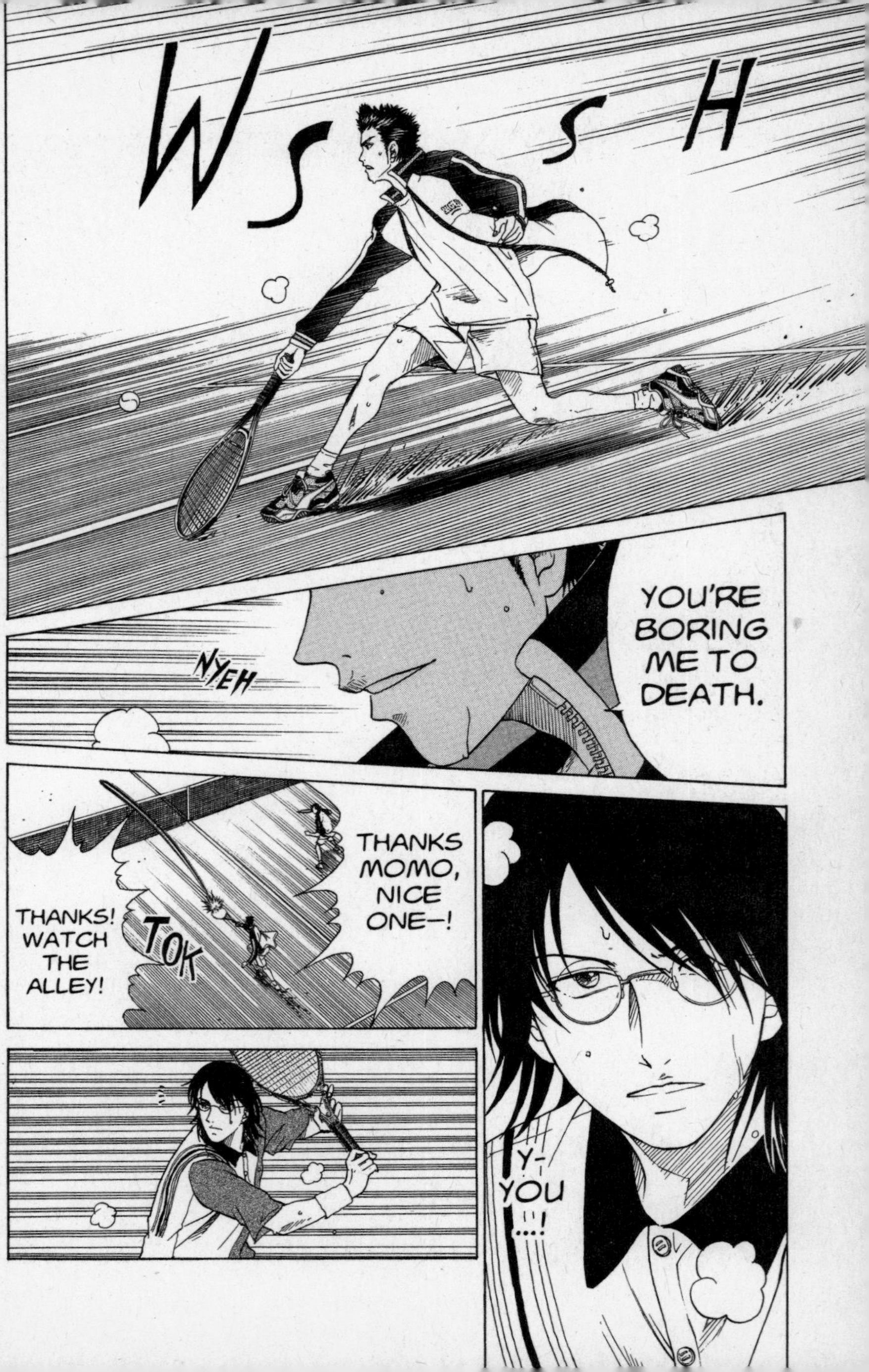
WSSH
YOU'RE BORING ME TO DEATH.
NYEH
Y- YOU !!!...!
THANKS MOMO, NICE ONE--!
TOK
THANKS! WATCH THE ALLEY!

READ THIS WAY

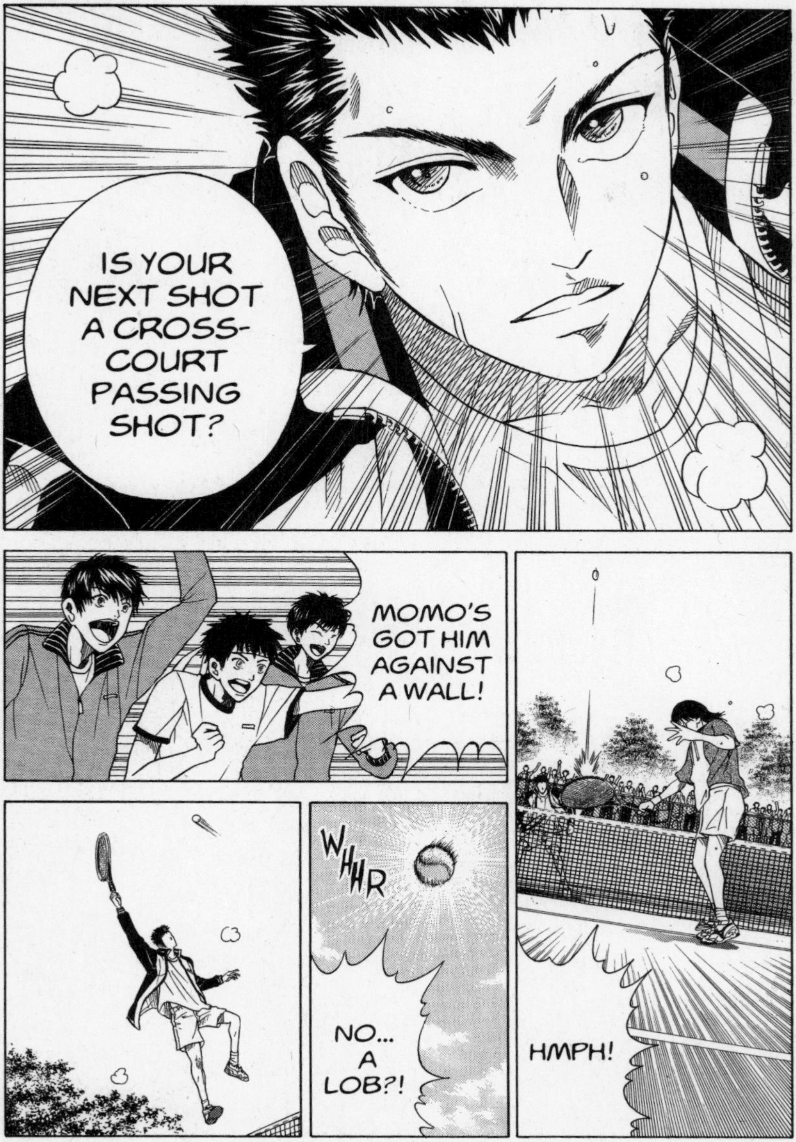

IS YOUR NEXT SHOT A CROSS-COURT PASSING SHOT?
HMPH!
MOMO'S GOT HIM AGAINST A WALL!
WHHR
NO... A LOB?!

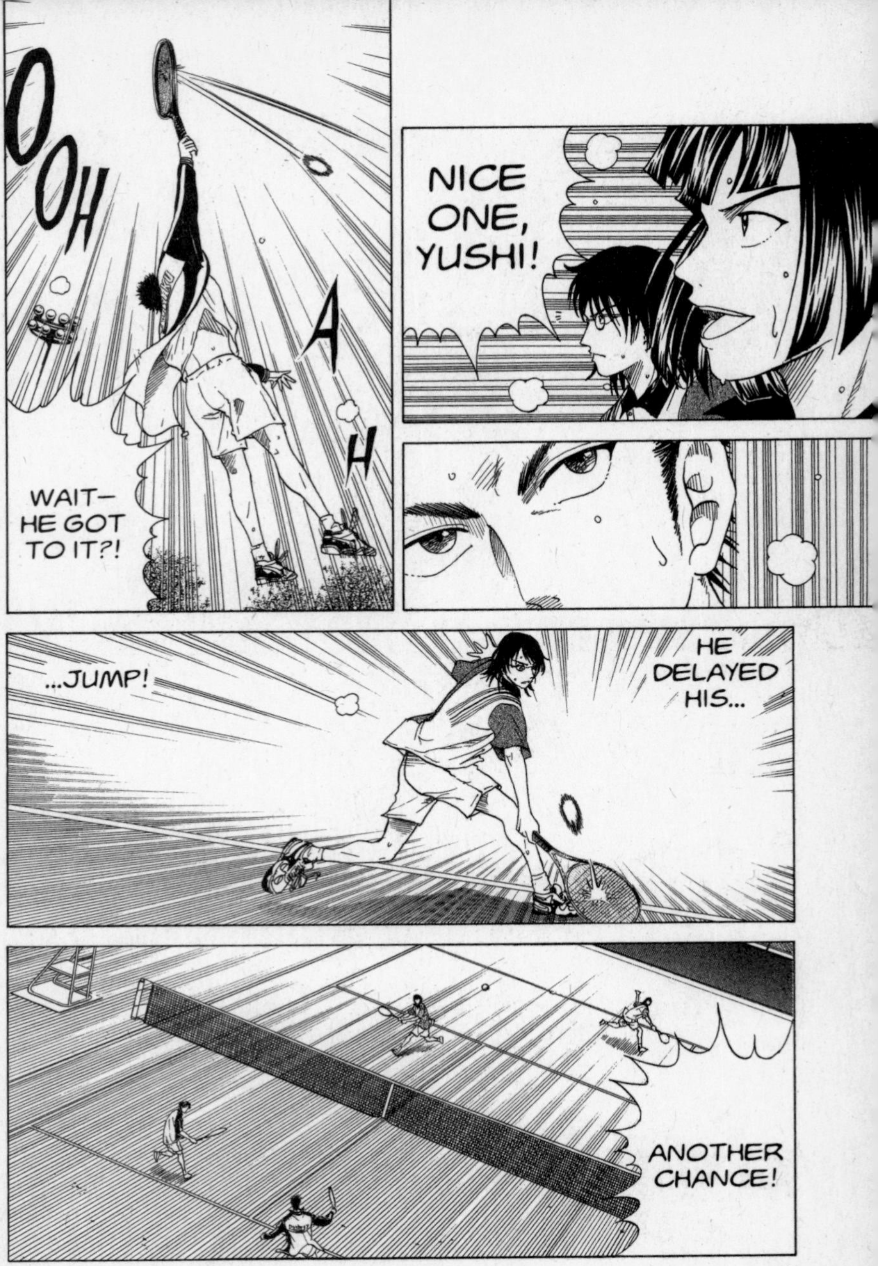
NICE ONE, YUSHI!
OOH
AH
WAIT— HE GOT TO IT?!
HE DELAYED HIS...
...JUMP!
ANOTHER CHANCE!

READ THIS WAY

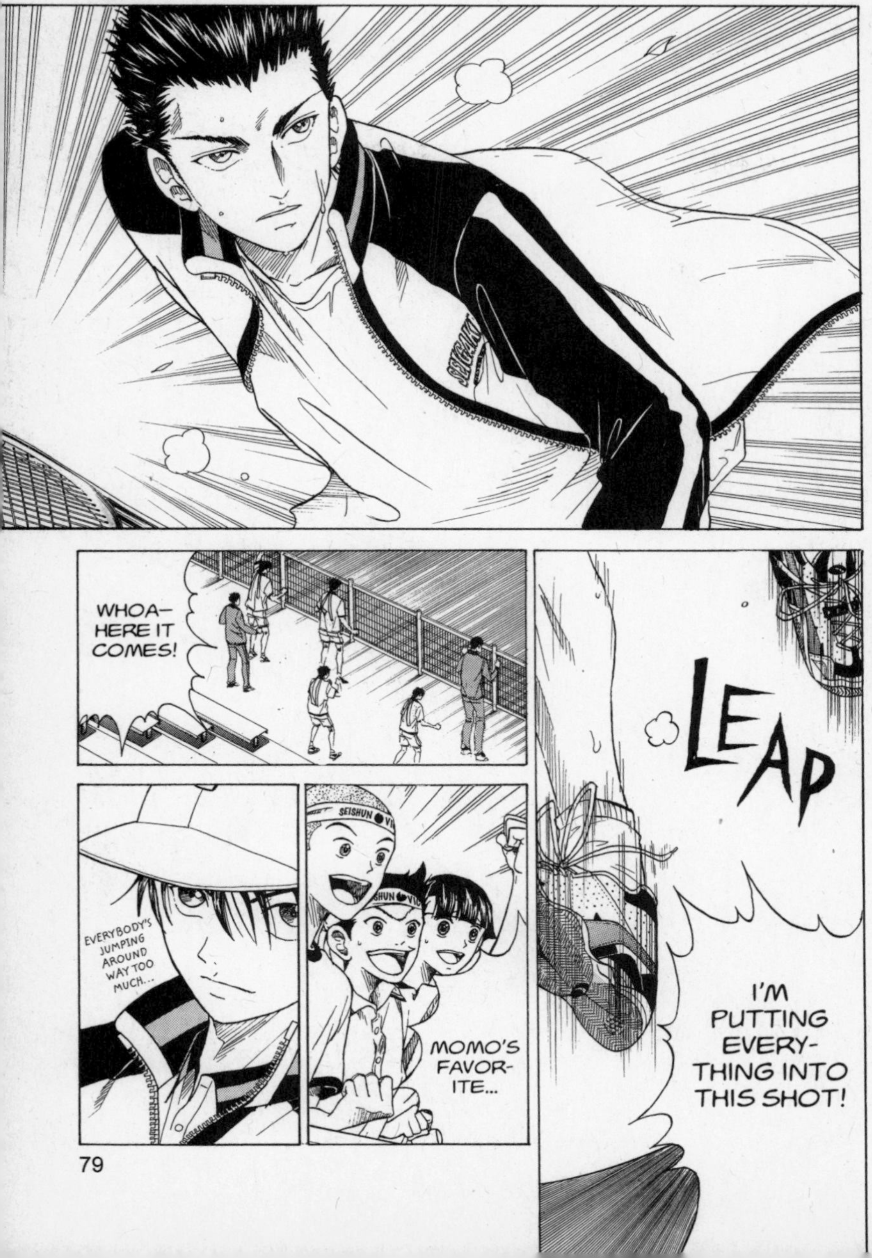
LEAP
I'M PUTTING EVERY-THING INTO THIS SHOT!
WHOA— HERE IT COMES!
MOMO'S FAVOR-ITE...
EVERYBODY'S JUMPING AROUND WAY TOO MUCH...

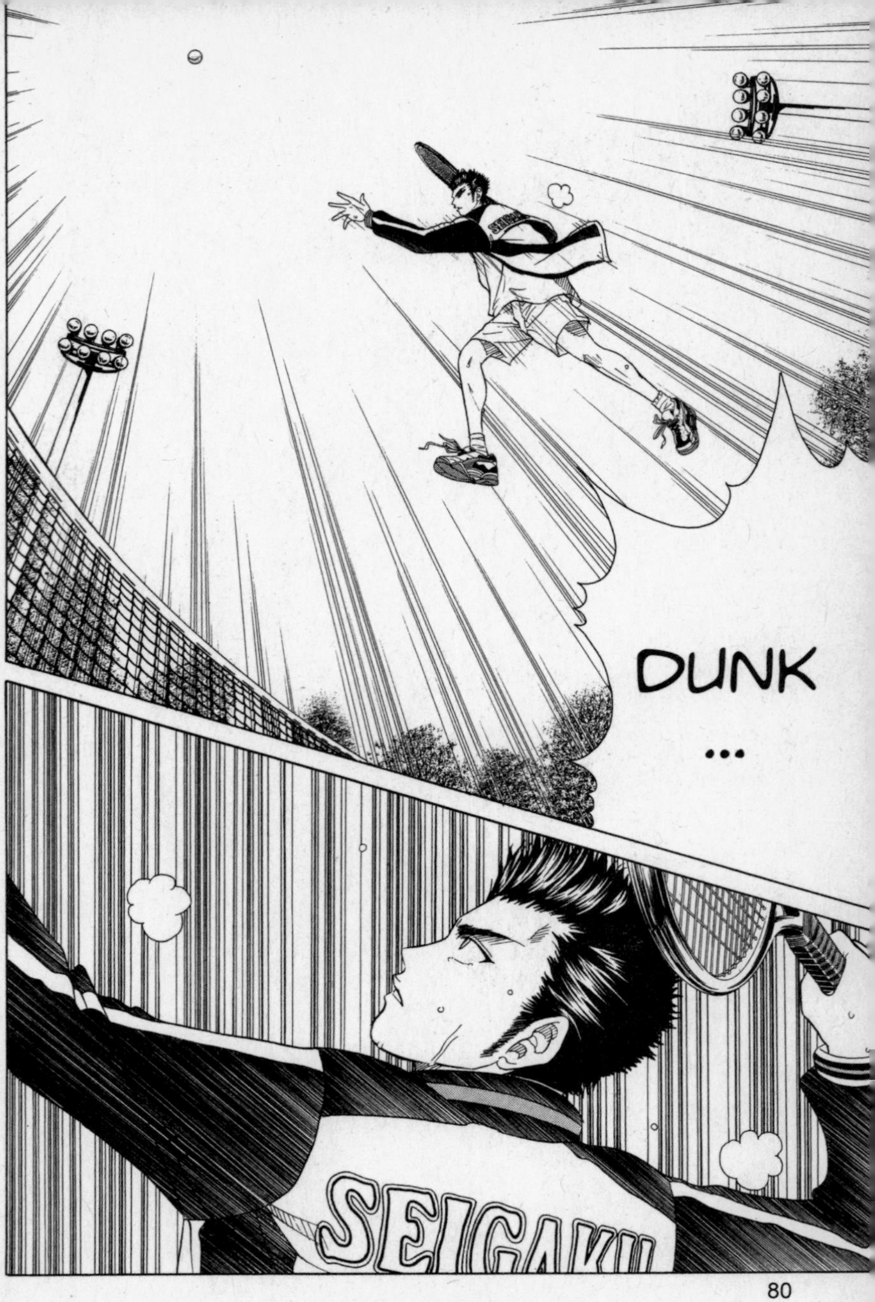
DUNK
...
SEIGAKU

READ THIS WAY

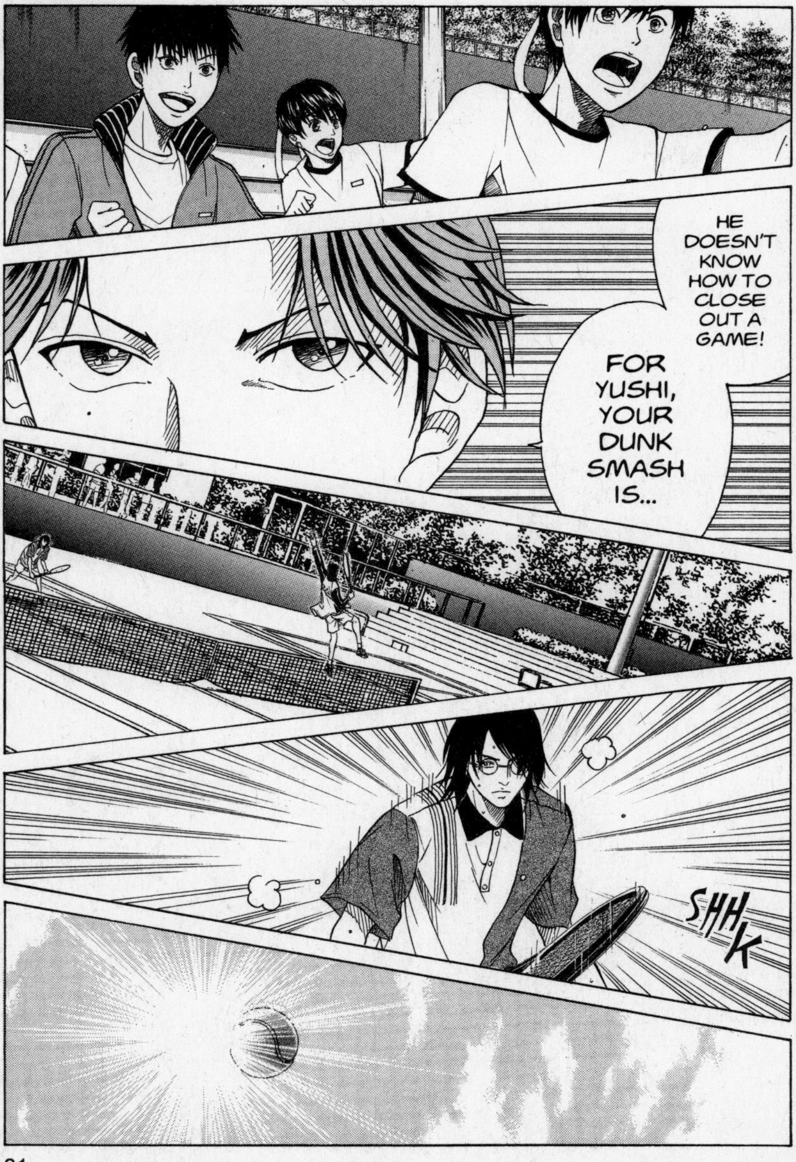
HE DOESN'T KNOW HOW TO CLOSE OUT A GAME!
FOR YUSHI, YOUR DUNK SMASH IS...
SHHK

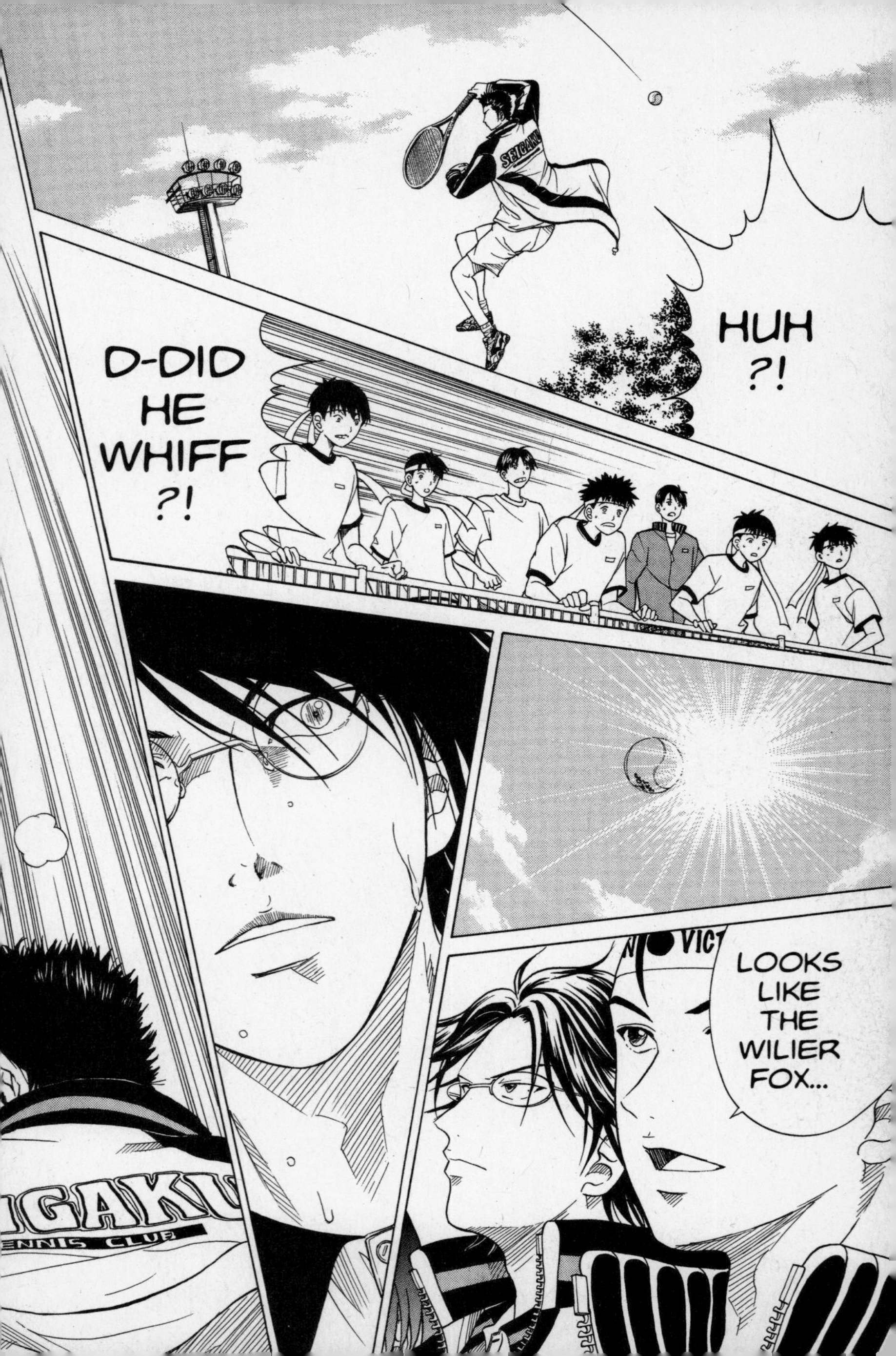
HUH ?!
D-DID HE WHIFF ?!
LOOKS LIKE THE WILIER FOX...

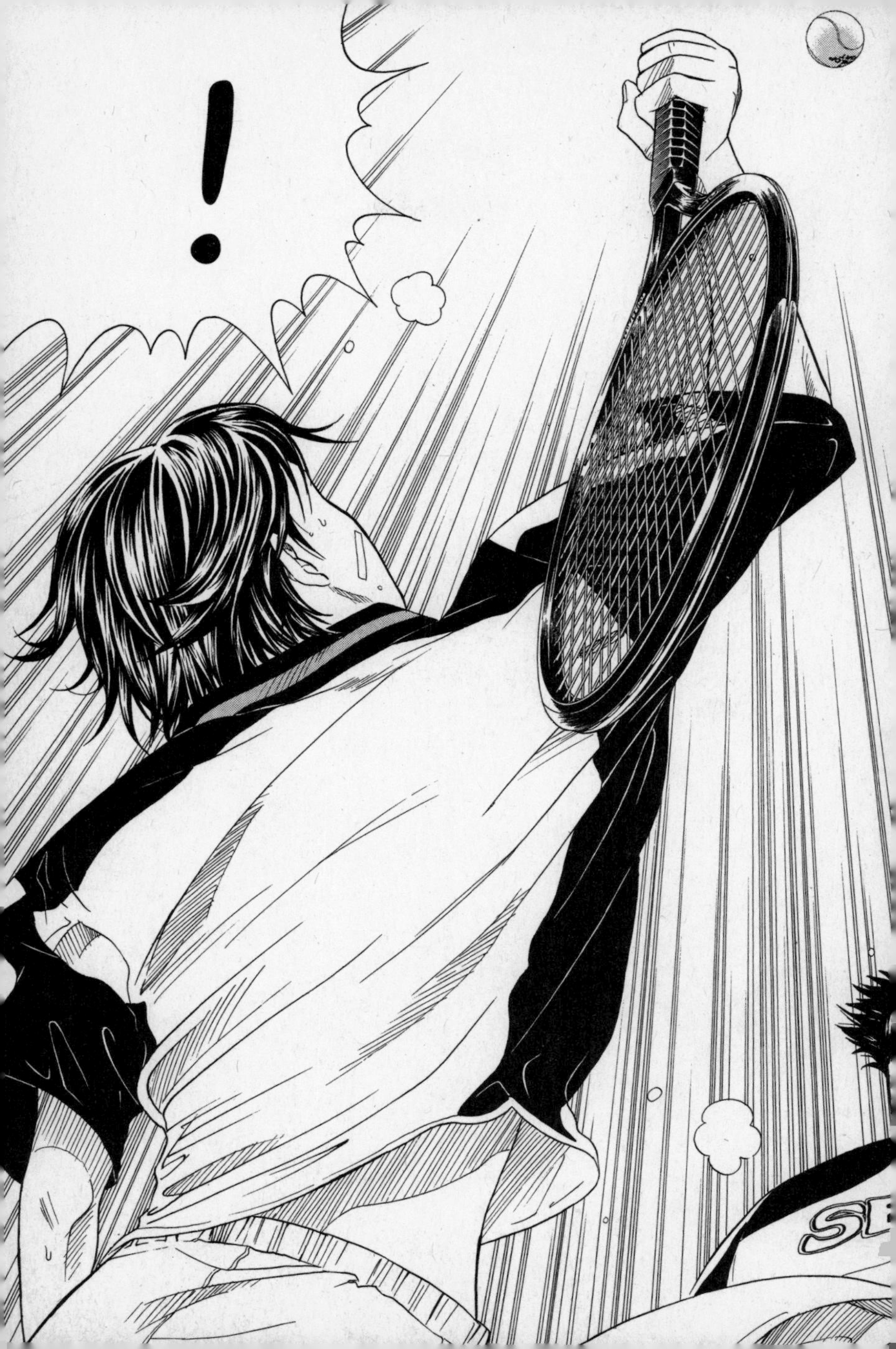
!

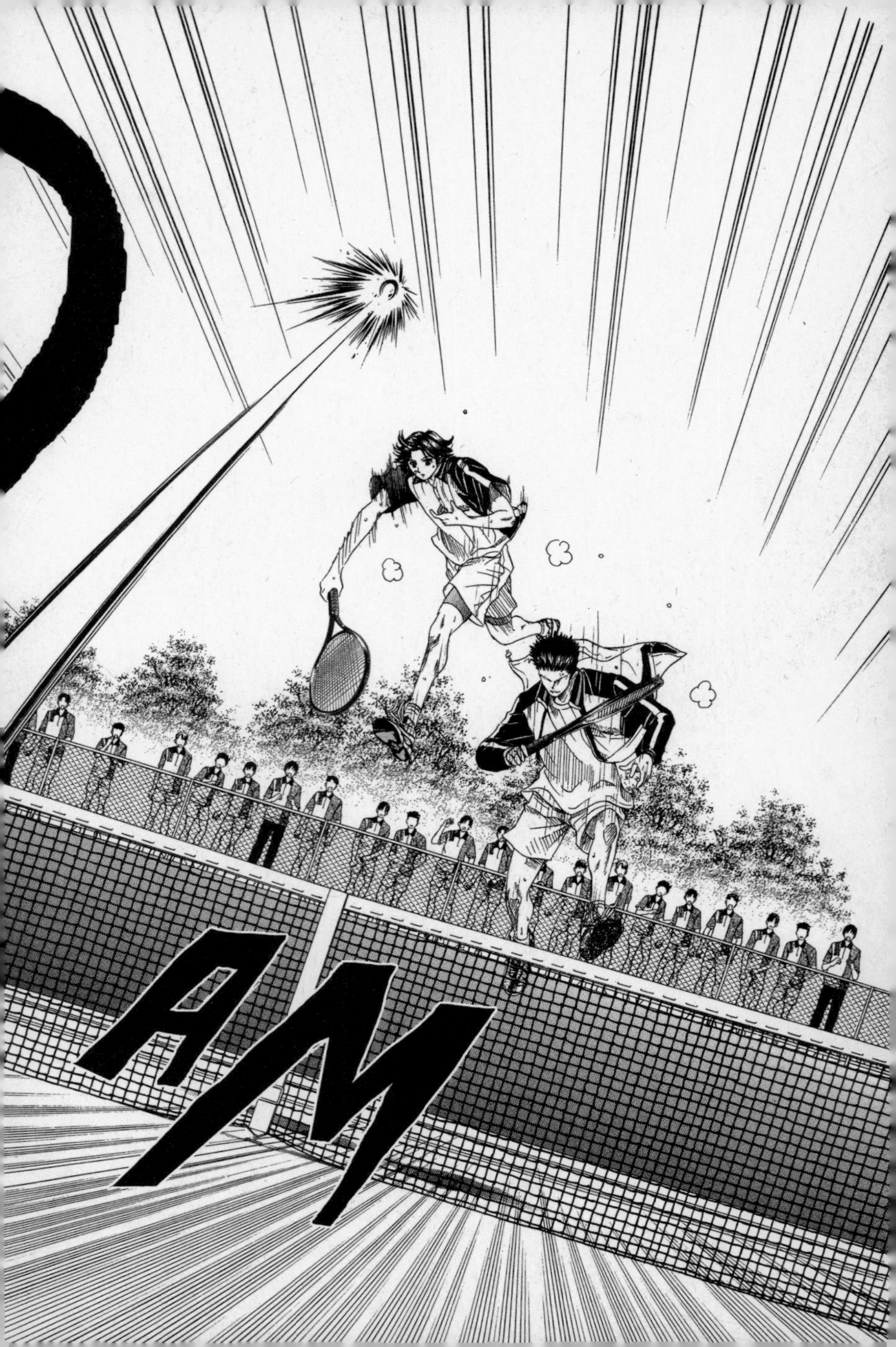
AM

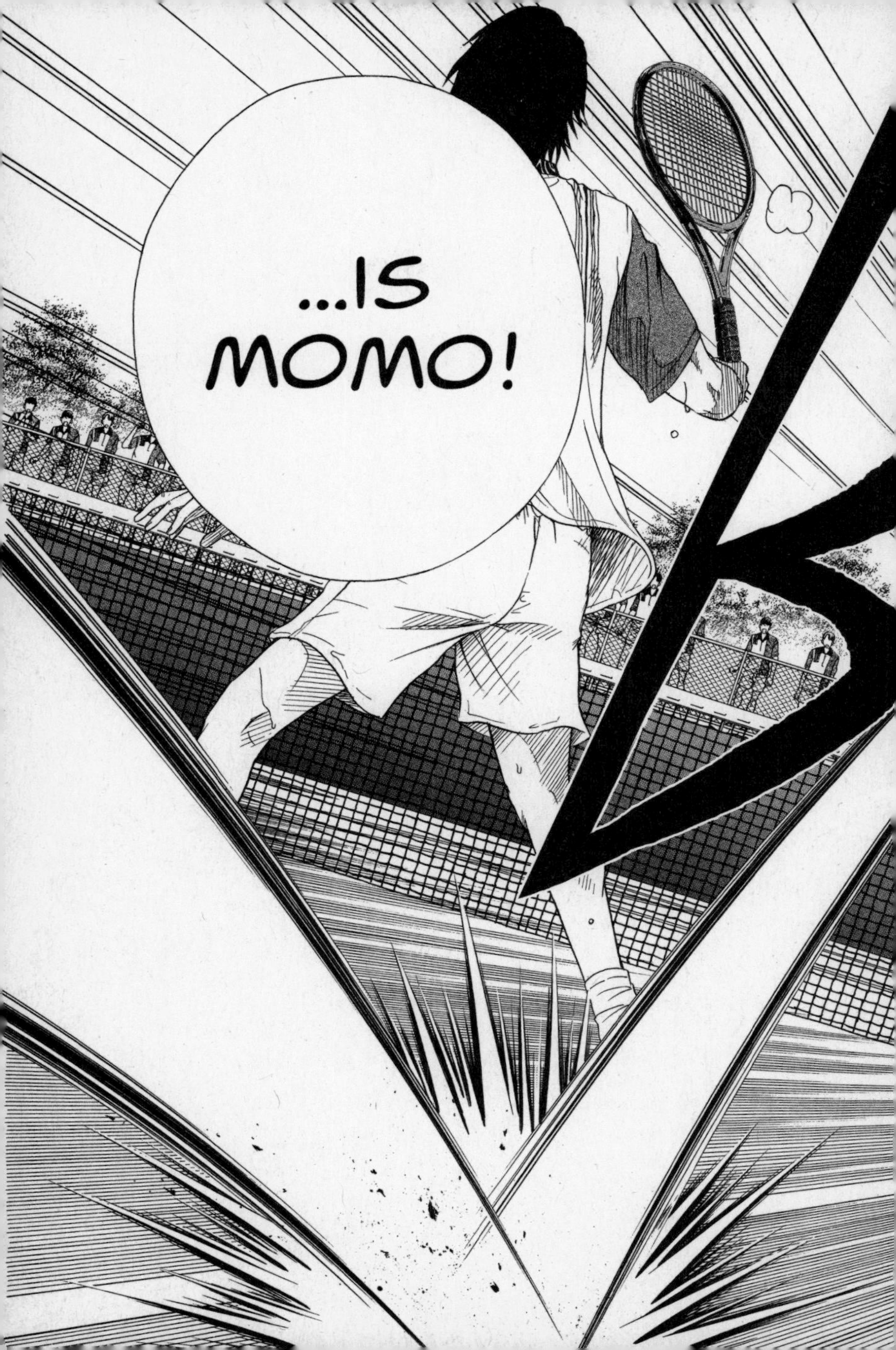
...IS MOMO!

An Early Lunch with Takeshi Momoshiro!

8th Grade Class 8 Classmates!

We received a tremendous amount of submissions for Momo's class! Thank you so much! Each one of them was truly heartfelt, so it was hard to choose. I was surprised that Kimeru, who sings the ending theme song for the anime, entered the contest! Thanks! (Momo) "You can't be depressed just because you weren't selected, okay?"

(some of them came with really good pictures, too!)

8th Grade Class 8 Attendance Sheet

(Boys)	(Girls)
1 Masashi Arai	1 Epo Aihara
2 Masaya Ikeda	2 Kaori Ichikawa
3 Koji Uchikoshi	3 Humi Iwase
4 Hiroya Umeki	4 Yukako Oohama
5 Senri Okada	5 Chihiro Okabe
6 Takuya Okachi	6 Aki Kamijo
7 Hiromu Ozawa	7 Michi Kotani
8 Masashi Kikuchi	8 Yui Kubota
9 Hirosato Kitano	9 Mayuko Sakurai
10 Yuya Koga	10 Tokuko Sakuraba
11 Yuji Satsukibi	11 Hitomi Takada
12 Yuta Kondo	12 Ayano Fujita
13 Koshichi Tanaka	13 Sayuri Fujino
14 Genta Shintame	14 Akane Miyazaka
15 Akihiro Noda	15 Masami Morihashi
16 Daisuke Hayashi	16 Yuna Nagakura
17 Shoji Horii	17 Mayu Nakajima
18 Daisuke Mitake	18 Yuriko Yamazaki
19 Takeshi Momoshiro	
20 Shoshi Yamamoto	
21 Nao Yokoda	
22 Yokota Nao	

Total: 40 (Titles omitted from name)

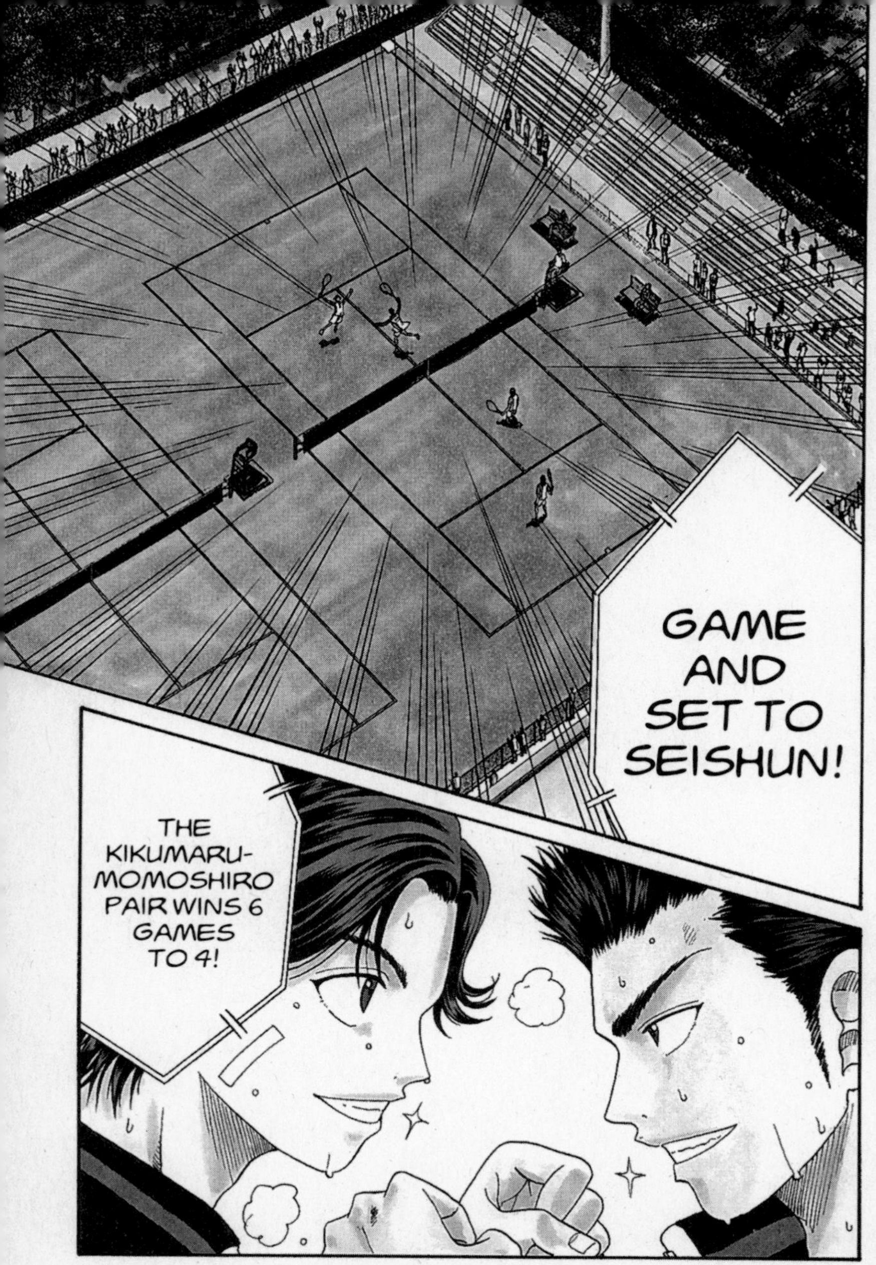
GAME AND SET TO SEISHUN!
THE KIKUMARU-MOMOSHIRO PAIR WINS 6 GAMES TO 4!

GENIUS 128: THE SADAHARU-KAORU PAIR

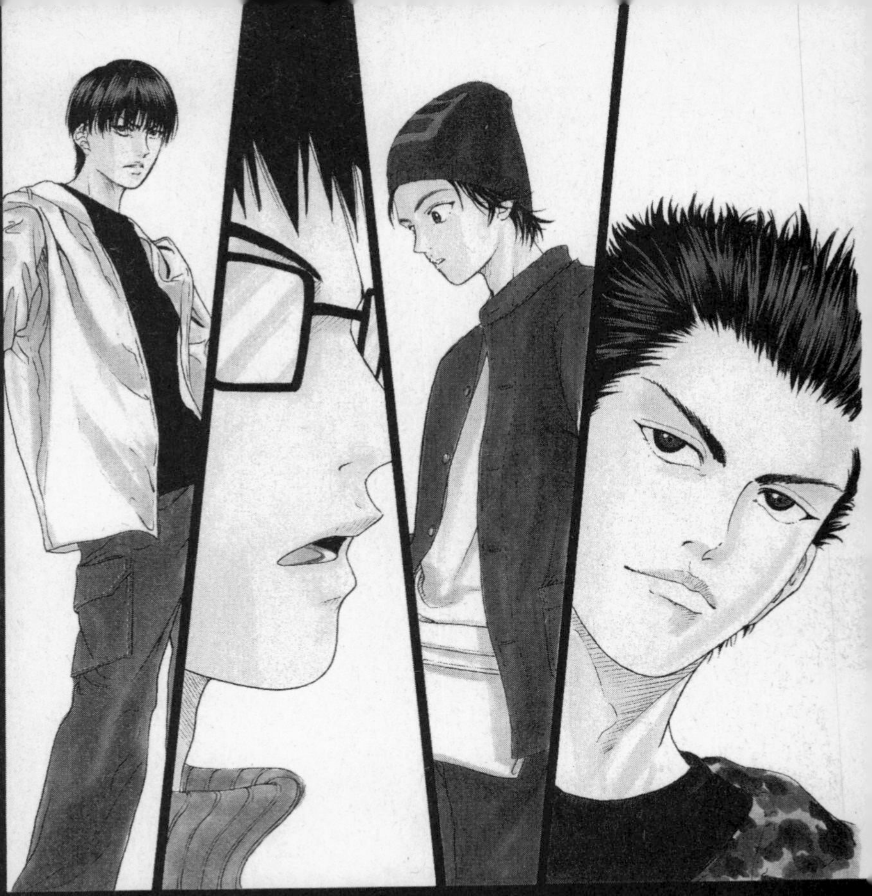

THE SADAHARU-KAORU PAIR

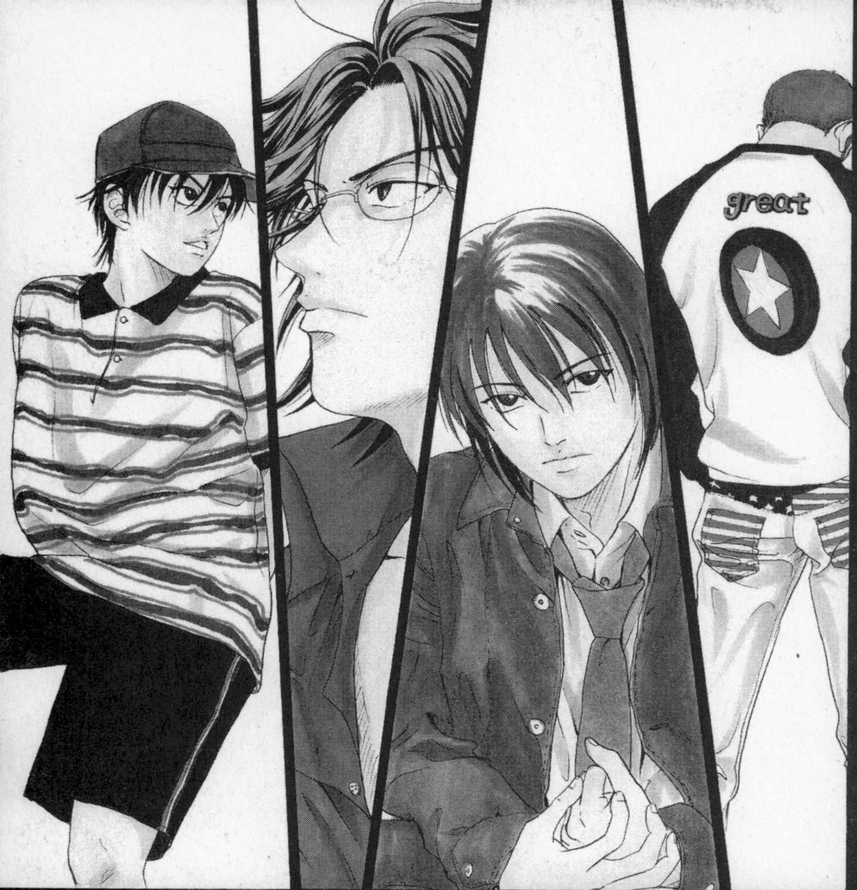
great

GENIUS 128:

テニスの王子様

THE PRINCE OF TENNIS™

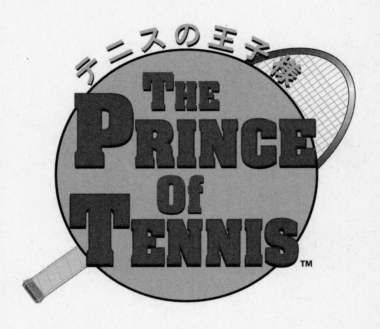

READ THIS WAY

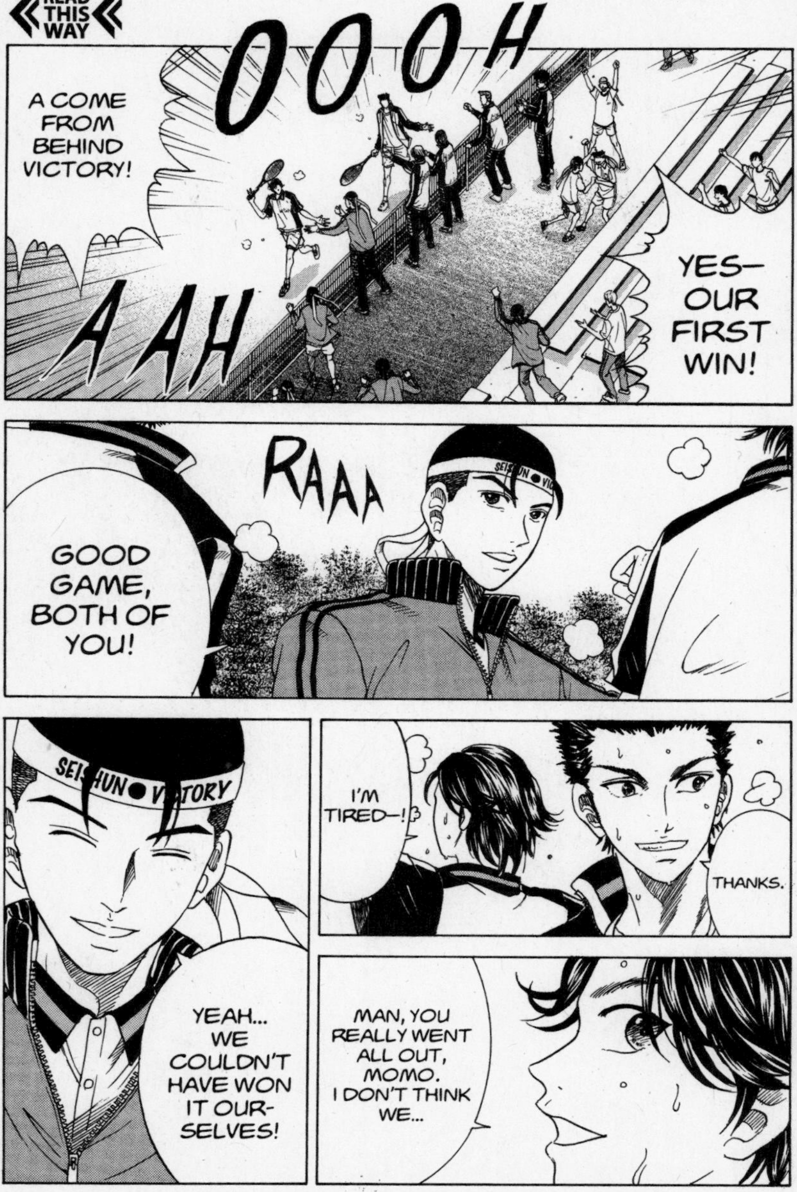
OOOH
YES—OUR FIRST WIN!
A COME FROM BEHIND VICTORY!
AAH
RAAA
GOOD GAME, BOTH OF YOU!
THANKS.
I'M TIRED—!
MAN, YOU REALLY WENT ALL OUT, MOMO. I DON'T THINK WE...
YEAH... WE COULDN'T HAVE WON IT OURSELVES!

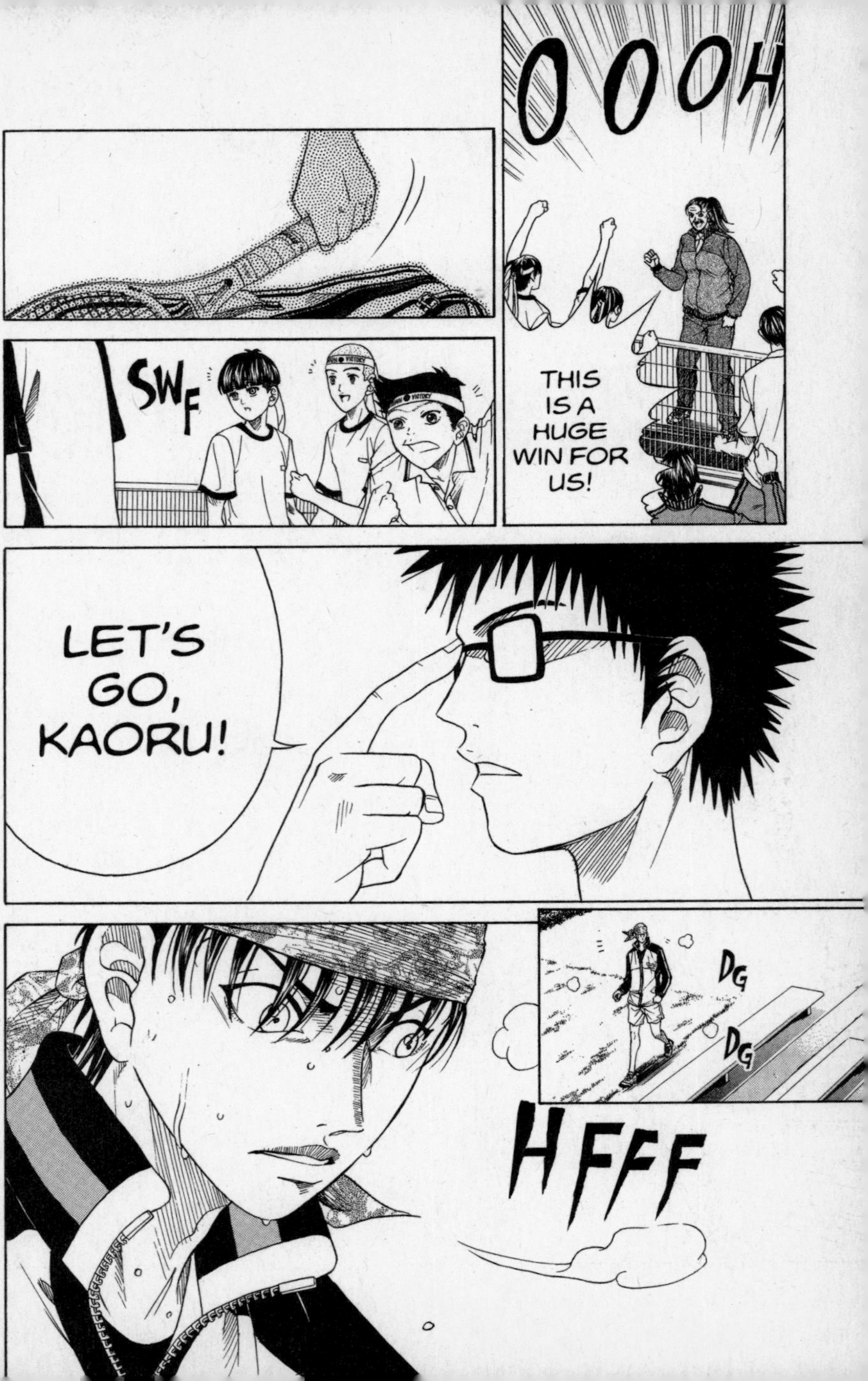
OOOH
THIS IS A HUGE WIN FOR US!
SWF
LET'S GO, KAORU!
DG
DG
HFFF

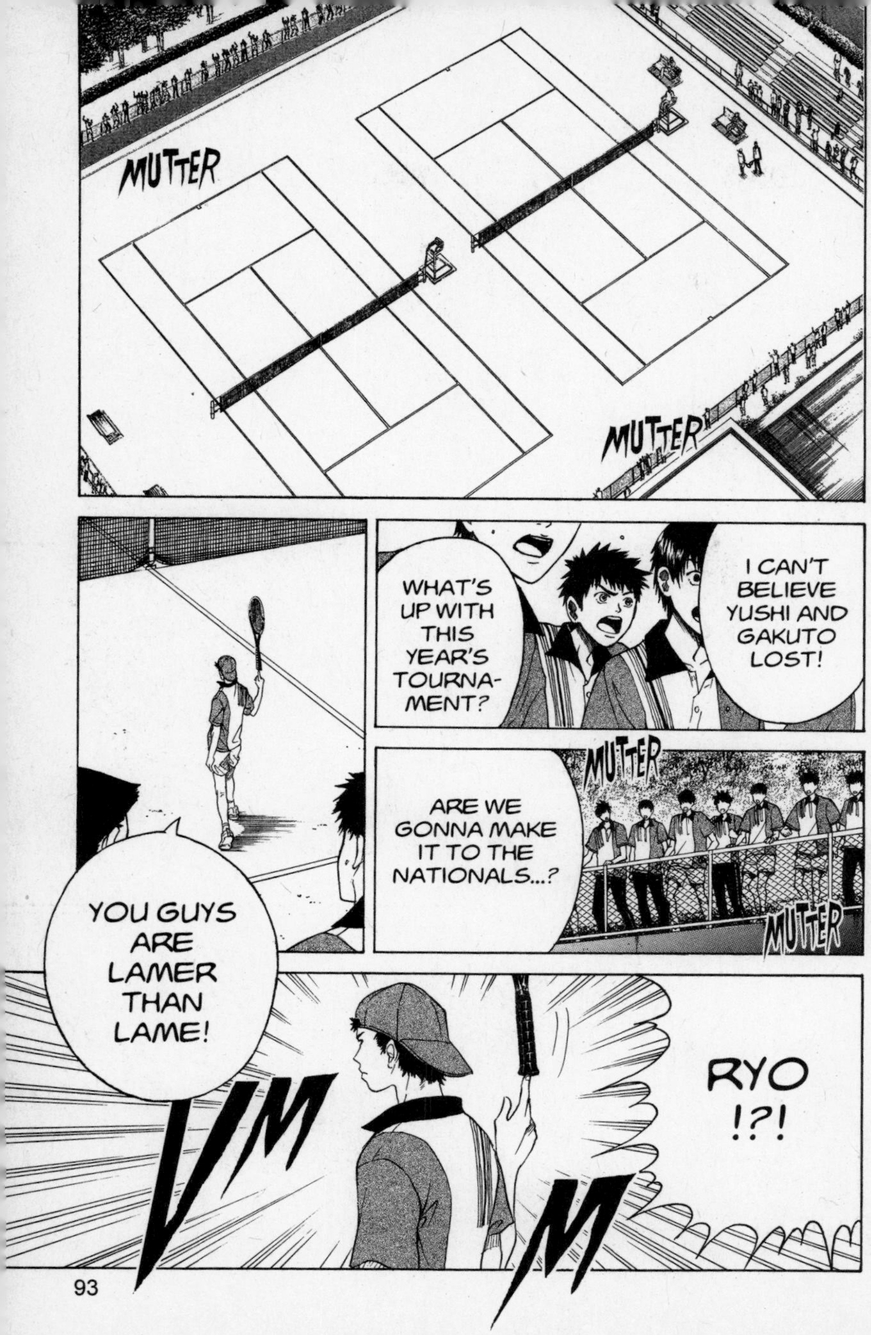
MUTTER
MUTTER
I CAN'T BELIEVE YUSHI AND GAKUTO LOST!
WHAT'S UP WITH THIS YEAR'S TOURNA-MENT?
MUTTER
ARE WE GONNA MAKE IT TO THE NATIONALS...?
MUTTER
YOU GUYS ARE LAMER THAN LAME!
RYO !?!
VIMM

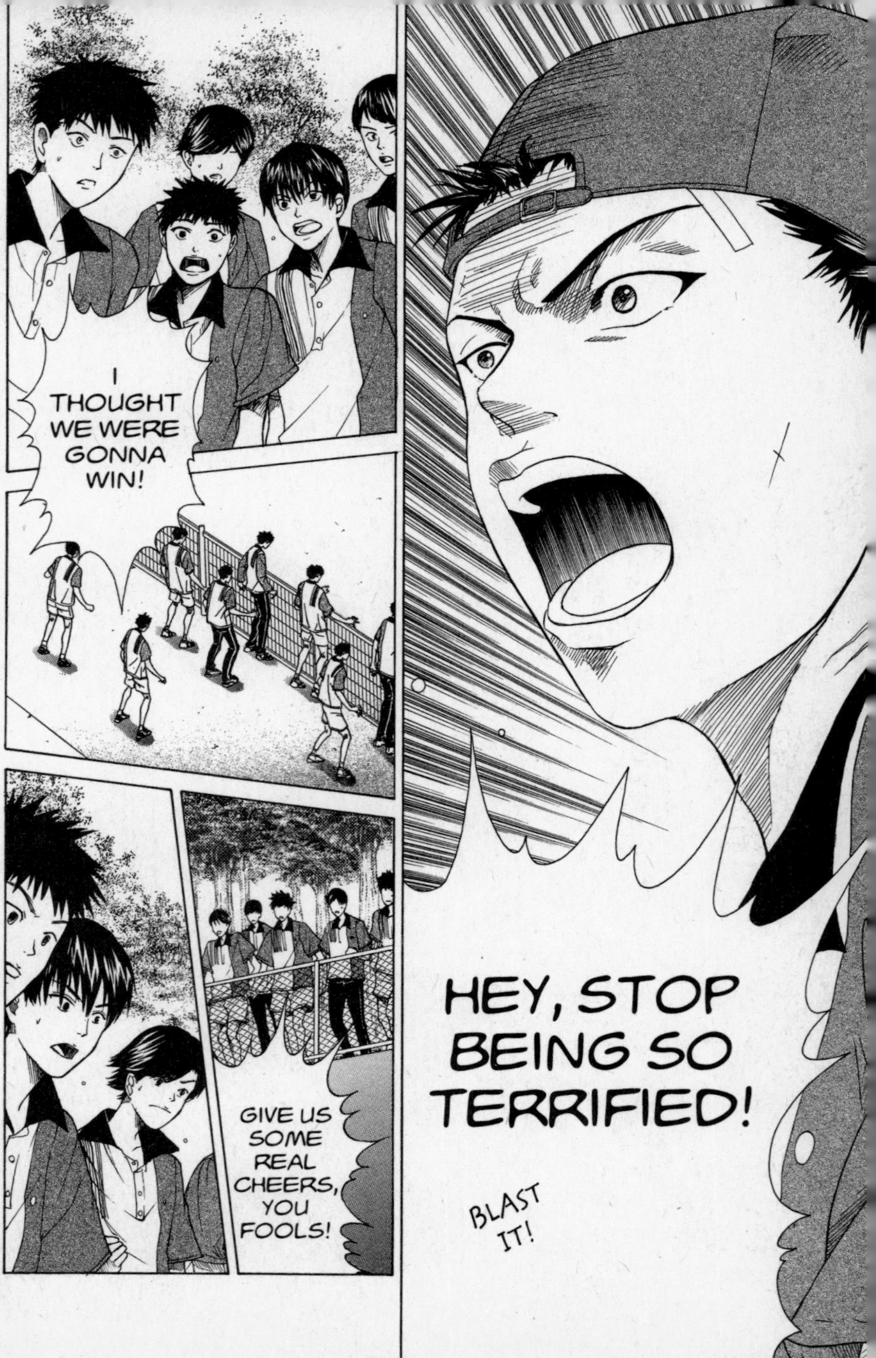
HEY, STOP BEING SO TERRIFIED!
BLAST IT!
I THOUGHT WE WERE GONNA WIN!
GIVE US SOME REAL CHEERS, YOU FOOLS!

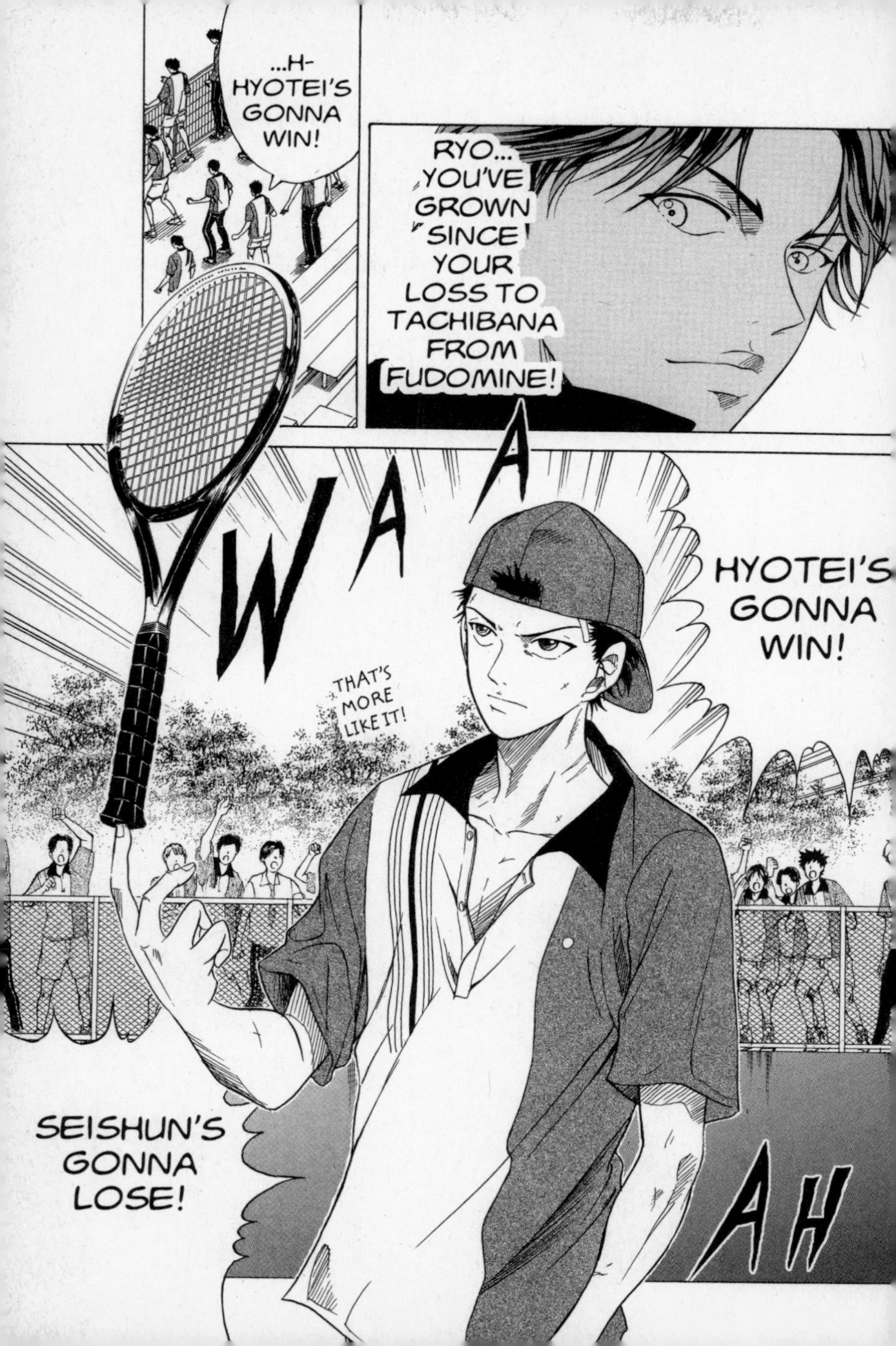
RYO... YOU'VE GROWN SINCE YOUR LOSS TO TACHIBANA FROM FUDOMINE!
...H- HYOTEI'S GONNA WIN!
HYOTEI'S GONNA WIN!
WAAA
THAT'S MORE LIKE IT!
SEISHUN'S GONNA LOSE!
AH

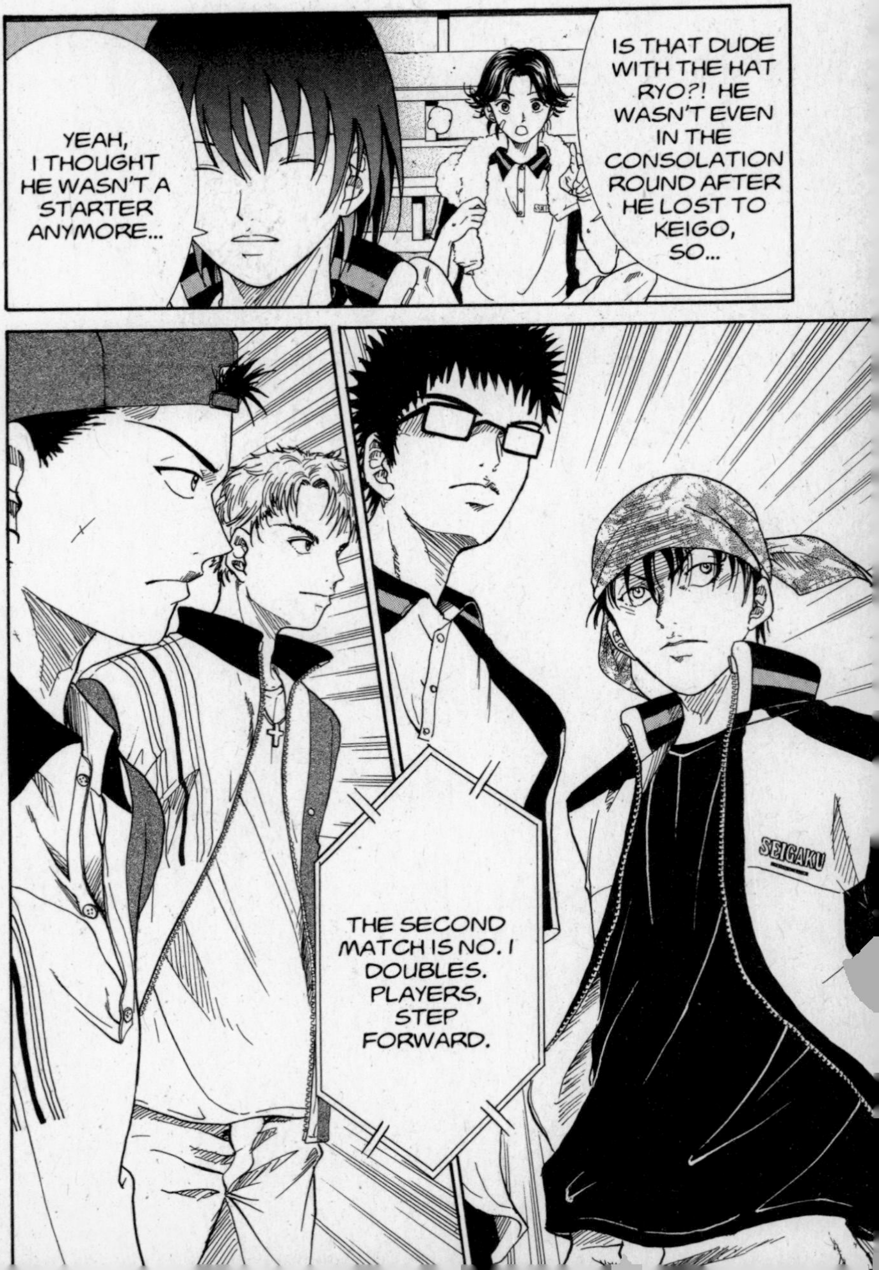
IS THAT DUDE WITH THE HAT RYO?! HE WASN'T EVEN IN THE CONSOLATION ROUND AFTER HE LOST TO KEIGO, SO...
YEAH, I THOUGHT HE WASN'T A STARTER ANYMORE...
THE SECOND MATCH IS NO. 1 DOUBLES. PLAYERS, STEP FORWARD.

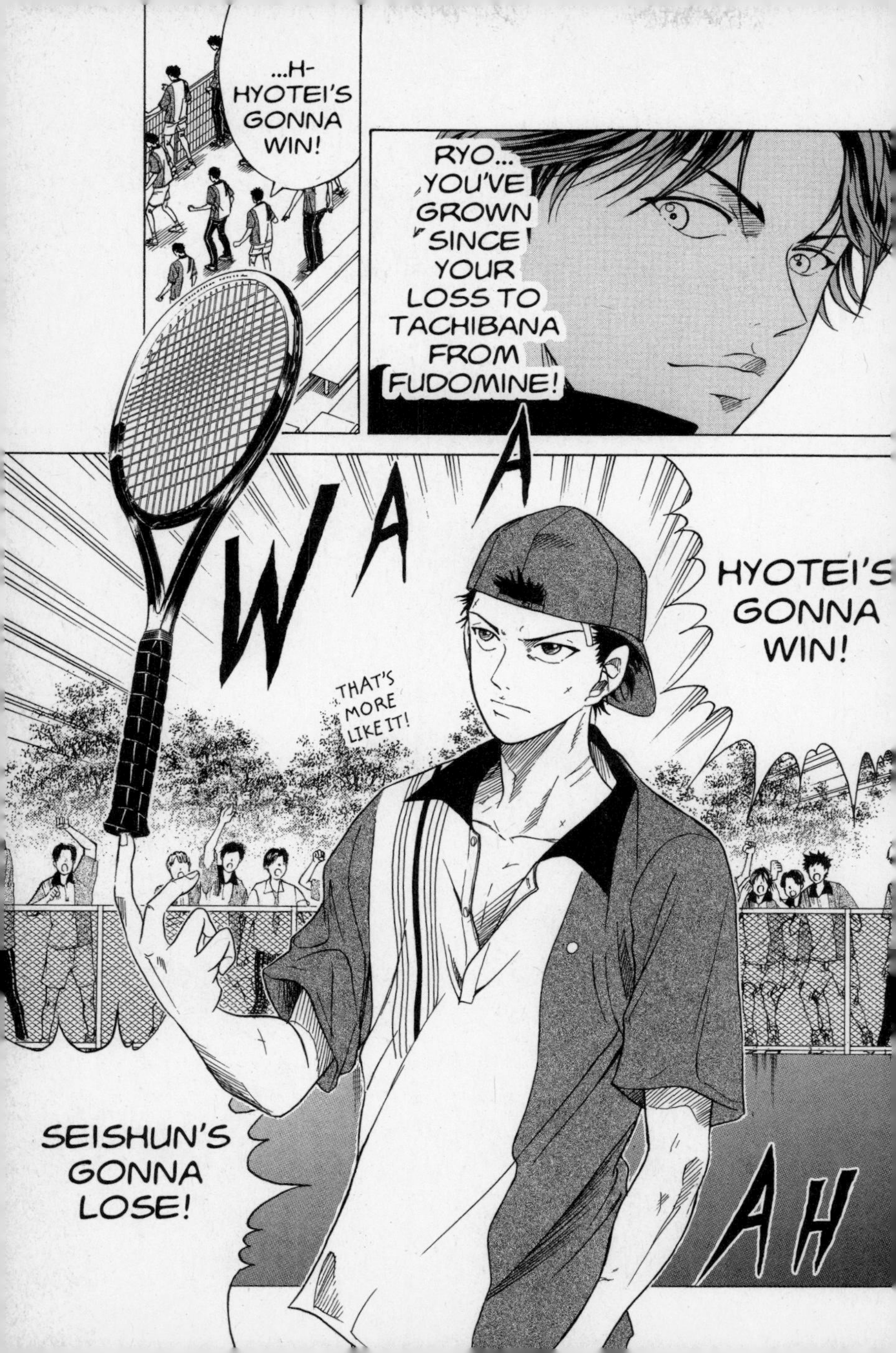
RYO... YOU'VE GROWN SINCE YOUR LOSS TO TACHIBANA FROM FUDOMINE!
...H- HYOTEI'S GONNA WIN!
WAA
HYOTEI'S GONNA WIN!
THAT'S MORE LIKE IT!
AH
SEISHUN'S GONNA LOSE!

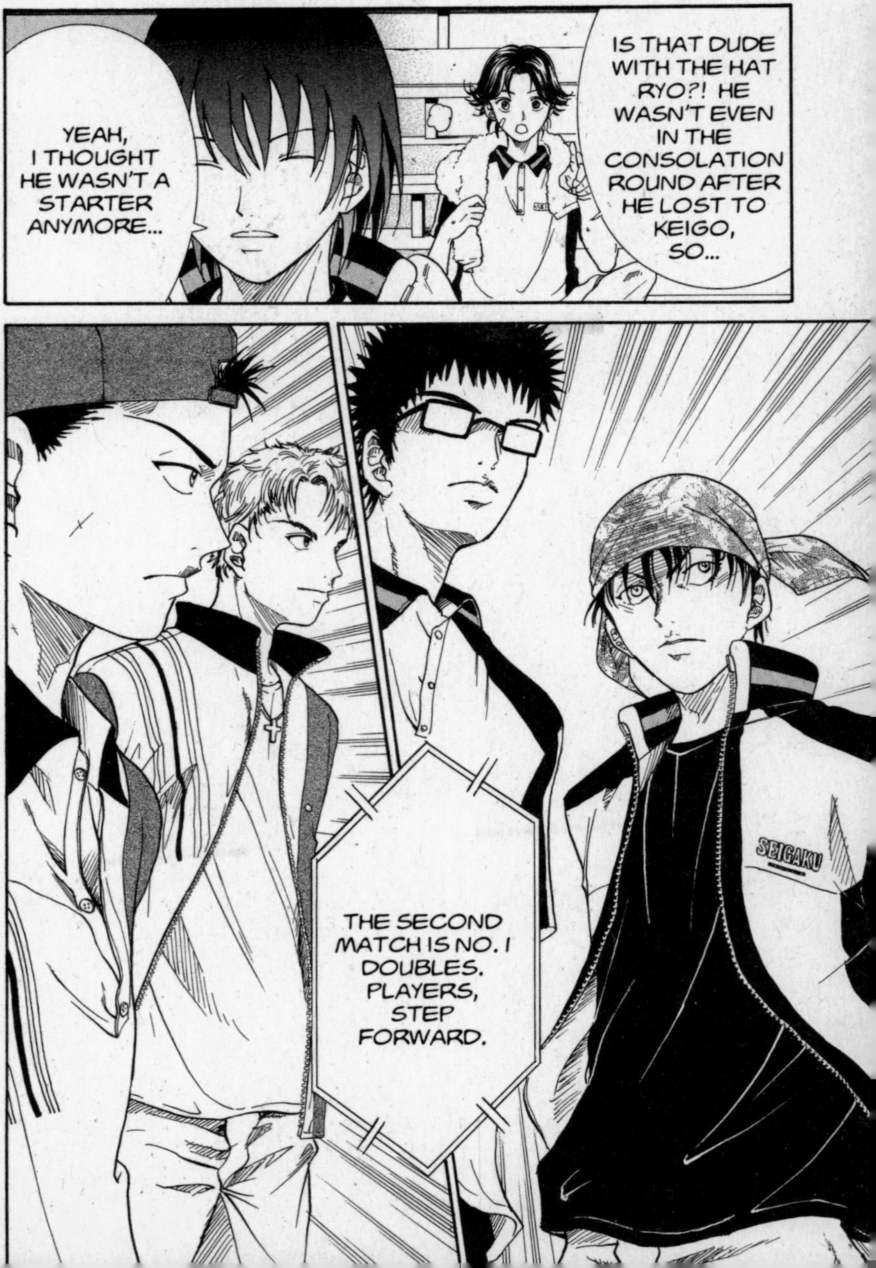
IS THAT DUDE WITH THE HAT RYO?! HE WASN'T EVEN IN THE CONSOLATION ROUND AFTER HE LOST TO KEIGO, SO...
YEAH, I THOUGHT HE WASN'T A STARTER ANYMORE...
SEIGAKU
THE SECOND MATCH IS NO. 1 DOUBLES. PLAYERS, STEP FORWARD.

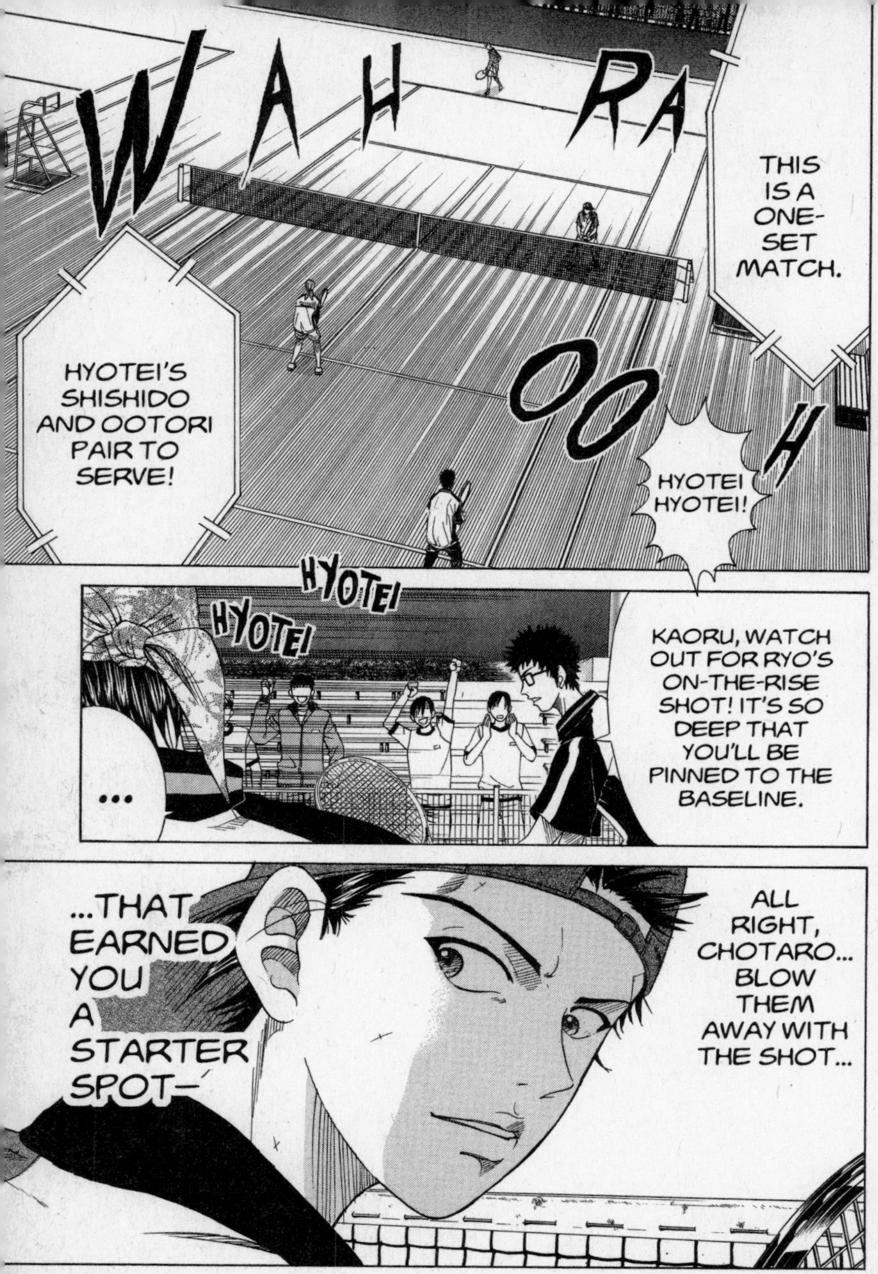
WAH RA
THIS IS A ONE-SET MATCH.
HYOTEI'S SHISHIDO AND OOTORI PAIR TO SERVE!
OOOH
HYOTEI HYOTEI!
KAORU, WATCH OUT FOR RYO'S ON-THE-RISE SHOT! IT'S SO DEEP THAT YOU'LL BE PINNED TO THE BASELINE.
HYOTEI
HYOTEI
...
ALL RIGHT, CHOTARO... BLOW THEM AWAY WITH THE SHOT...
...THAT EARNED YOU A STARTER SPOT—

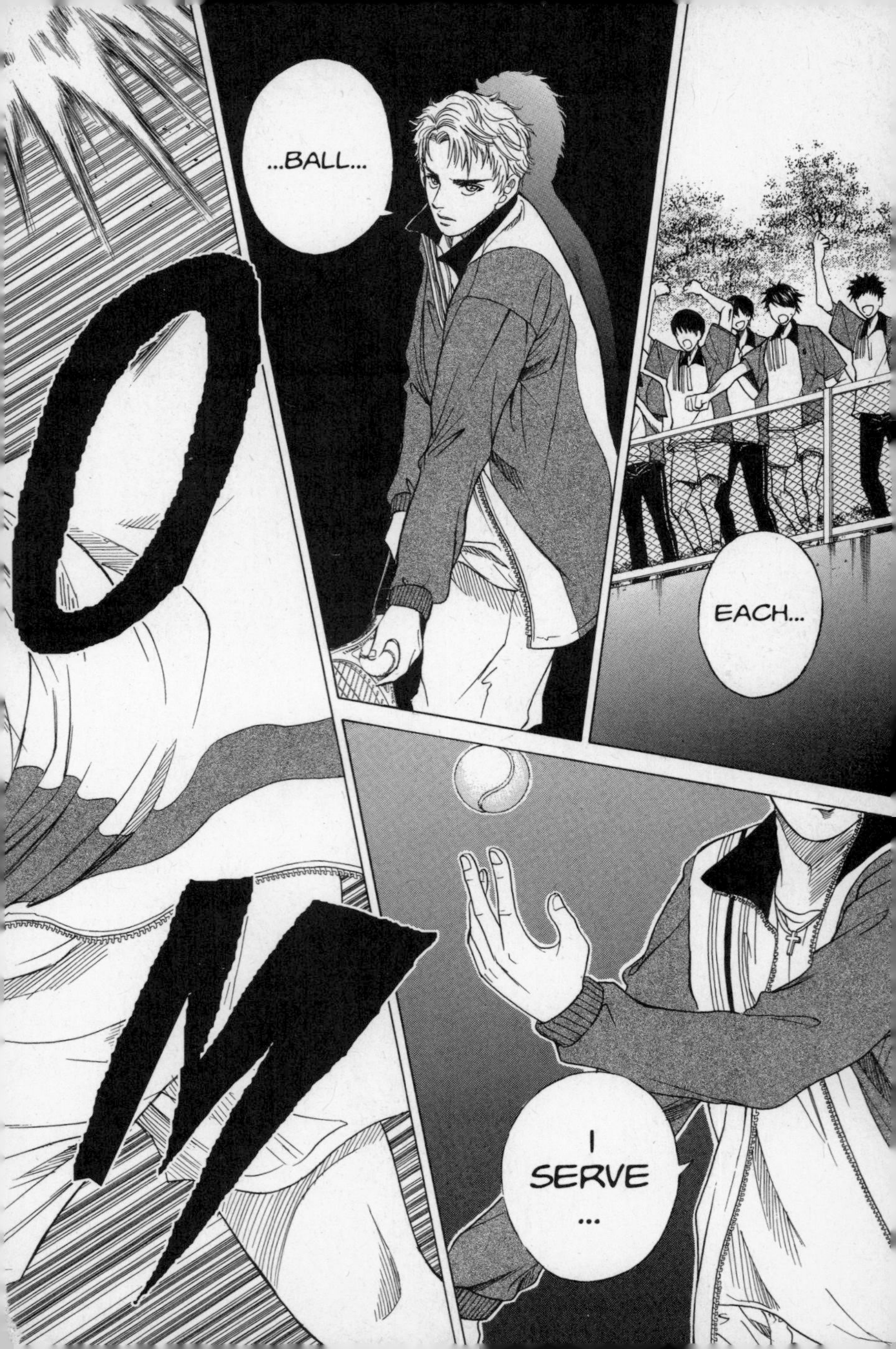
EACH...
...BALL...
I SERVE ...

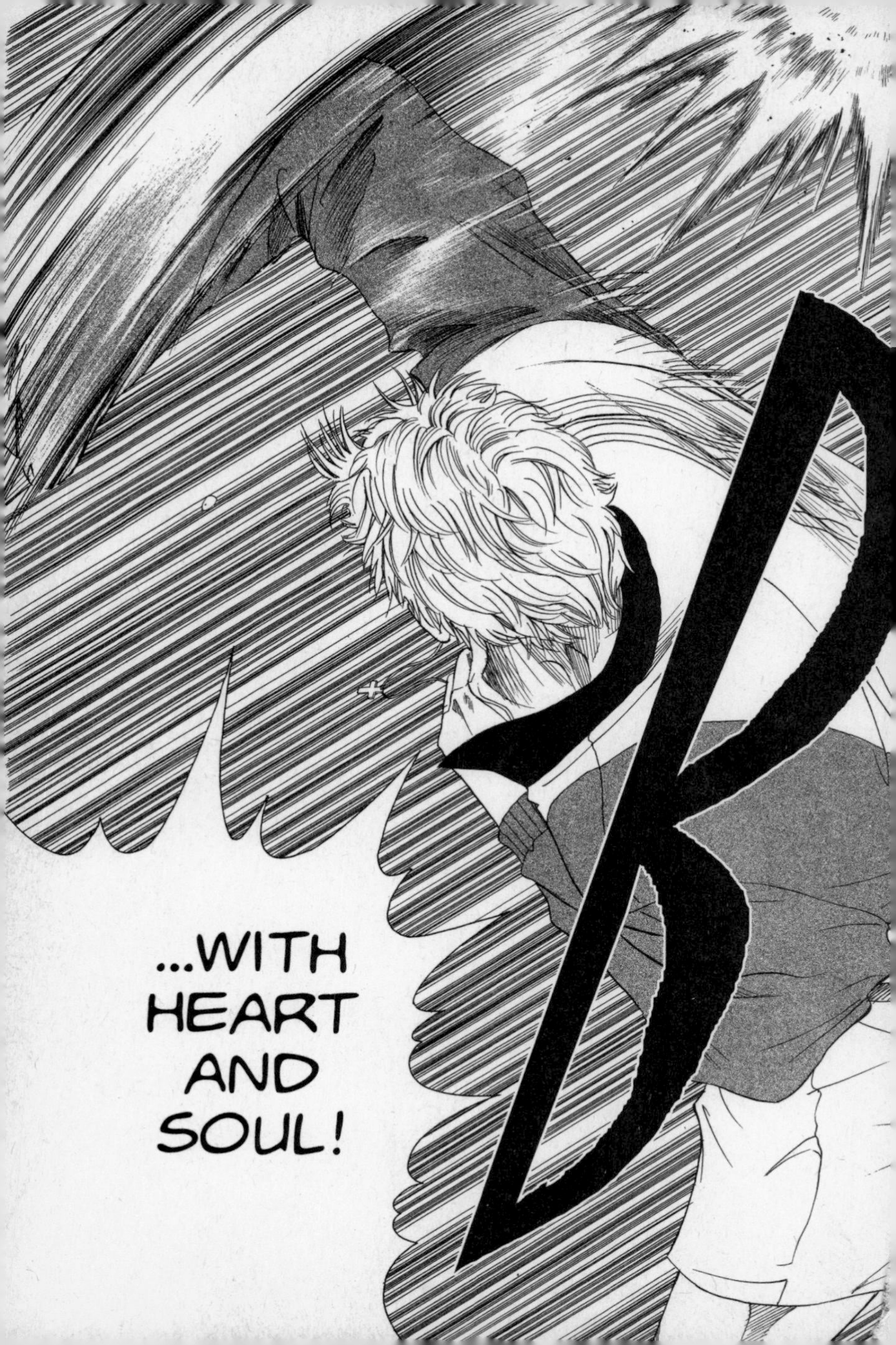
...WITH HEART AND SOUL!

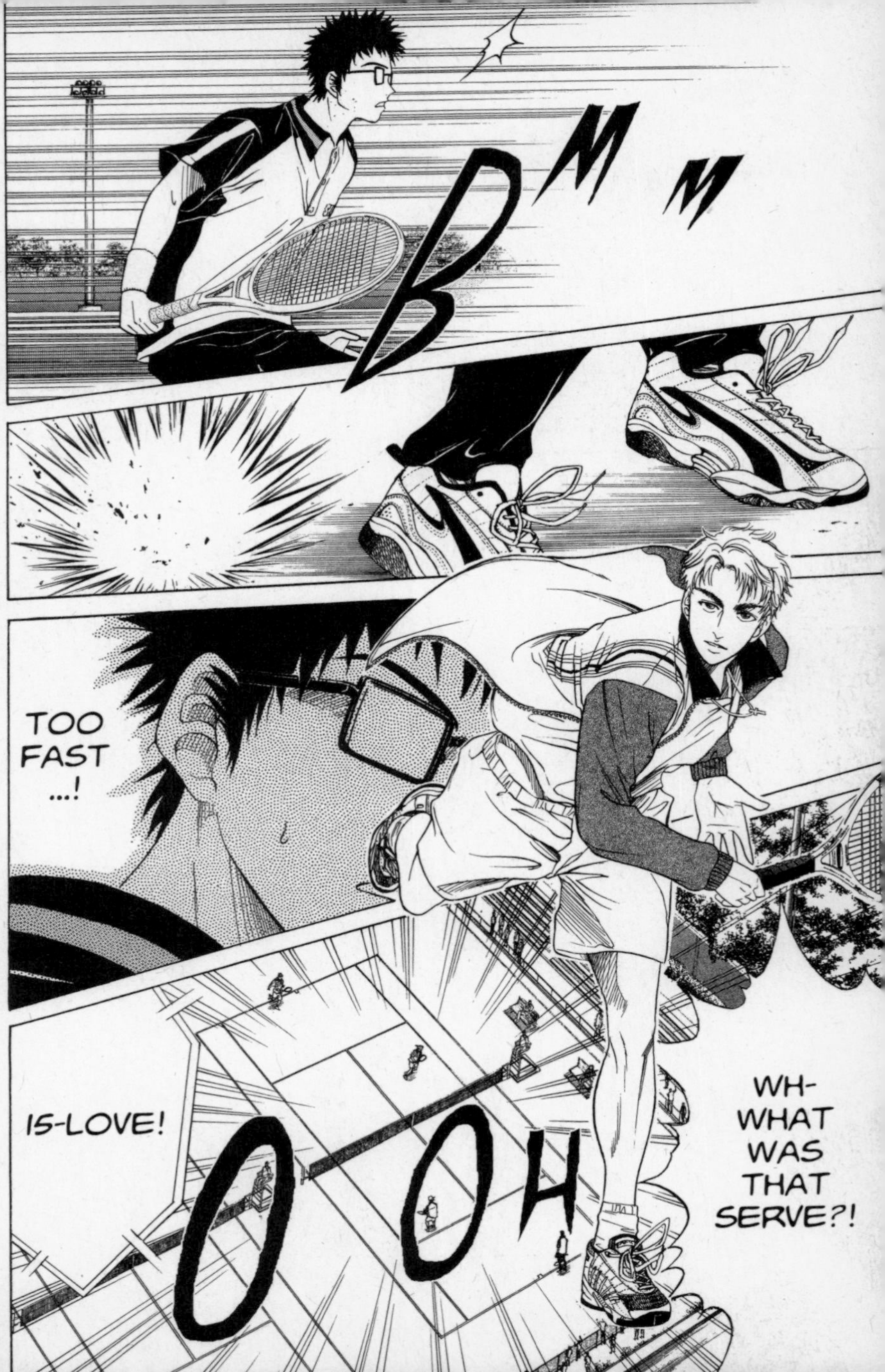
BMM
TOO FAST ...!
WH- WHAT WAS THAT SERVE?!
OOH
15-LOVE!

READ THIS WAY

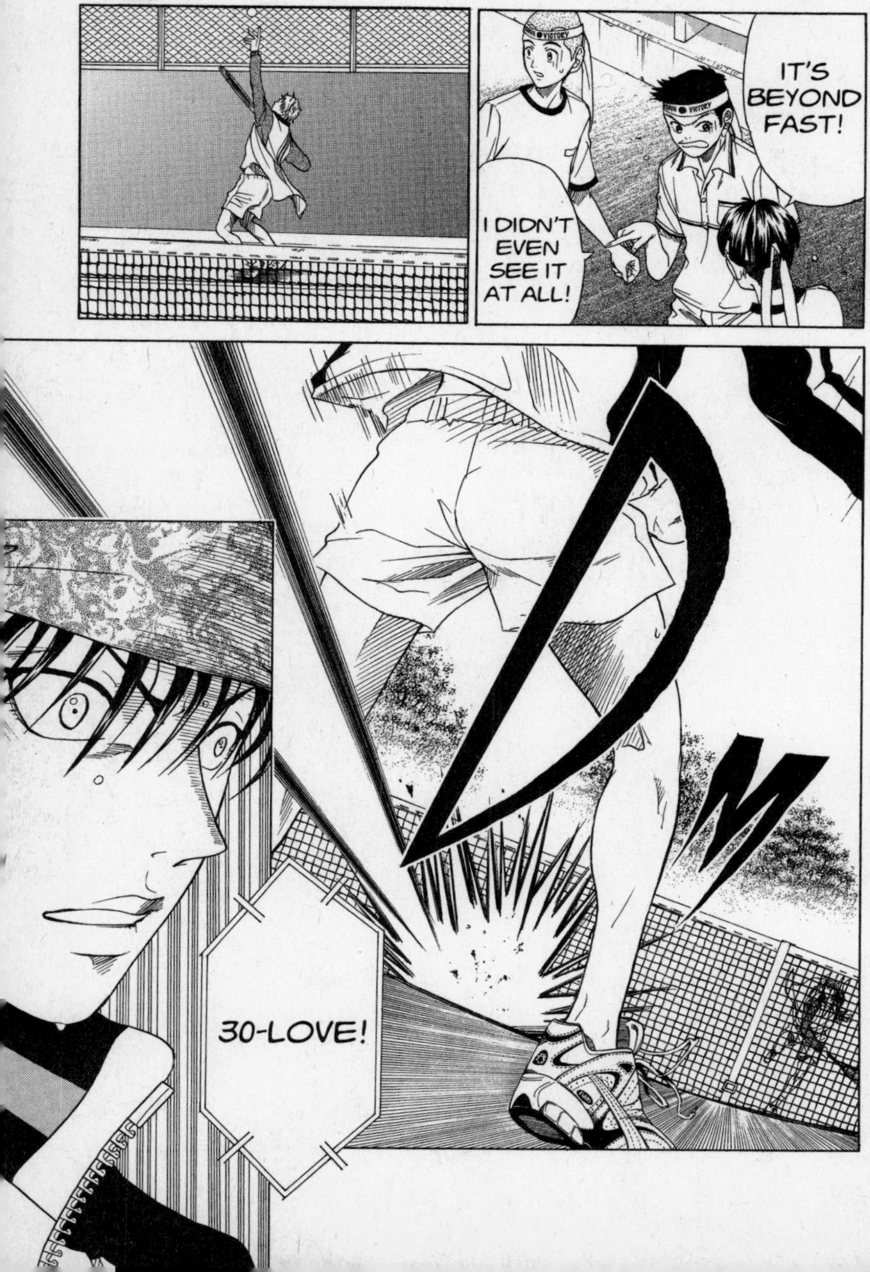
IT'S BEYOND FAST!
I DIDN'T EVEN SEE IT AT ALL!
30-LOVE!

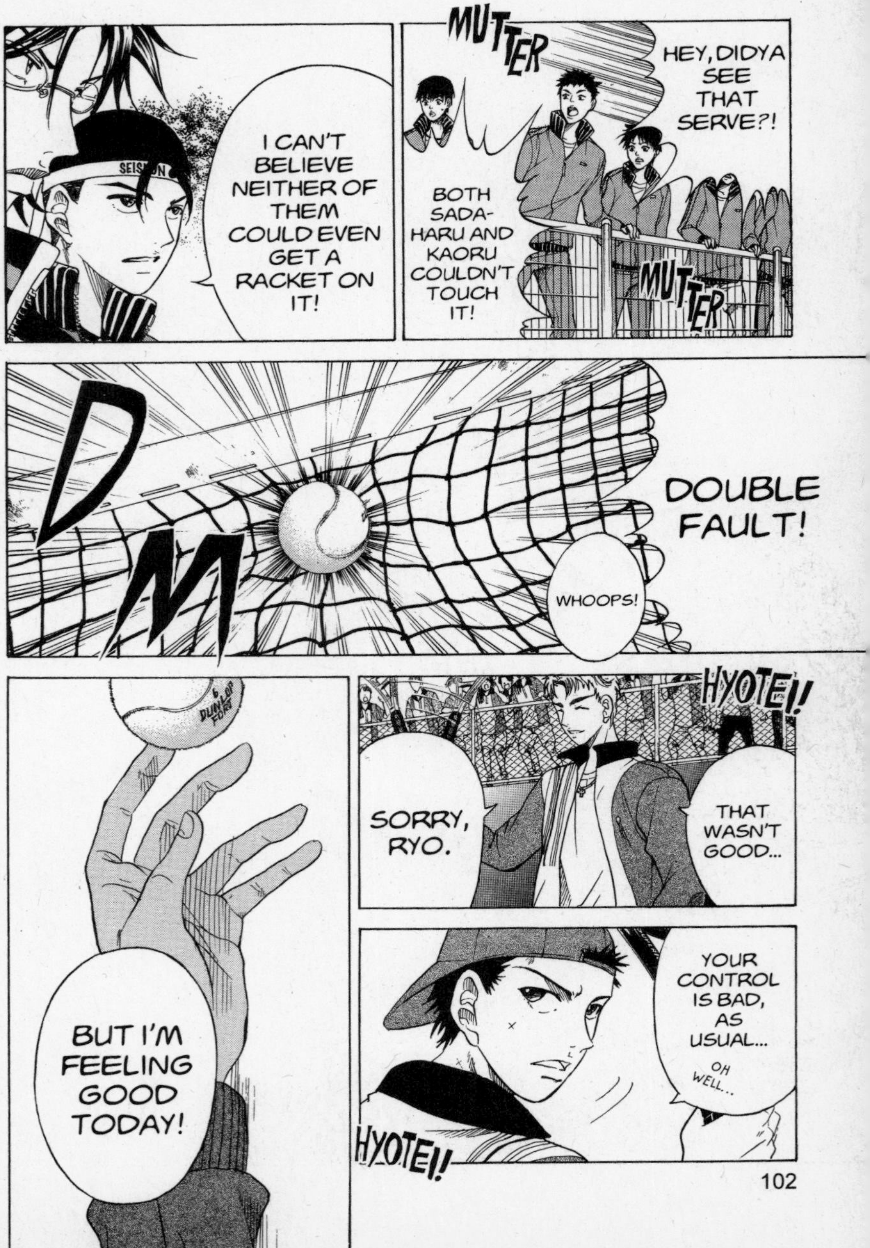
MUTTER
HEY, DIDYA SEE THAT SERVE?!
BOTH SADA-HARU AND KAORU COULDN'T TOUCH IT!
MUTTER
I CAN'T BELIEVE NEITHER OF THEM COULD EVEN GET A RACKET ON IT!
DOUBLE FAULT!
WHOOPS!
DM
HYOTEI!
THAT WASN'T GOOD...
SORRY, RYO.
YOUR CONTROL IS BAD, AS USUAL...
OH WELL...
HYOTEI!
BUT I'M FEELING GOOD TODAY!

IT'S BEYOND FAST!

I DIDN'T EVEN SEE IT AT ALL!

30-LOVE!

I CAN'T BELIEVE NEITHER OF THEM COULD EVEN GET A RACKET ON IT!

MUTTER

BOTH SADAHARU AND KAORU COULDN'T TOUCH IT!

HEY, DIDYA SEE THAT SERVE?!

MUTTER

DOUBLE FAULT!

WHOOPS!

BUT I'M FEELING GOOD TODAY!

SORRY, RYO.

HYOTEI!!

THAT WASN'T GOOD...

YOUR CONTROL IS BAD, AS USUAL...

OH WELL...

HYOTEI!!

102

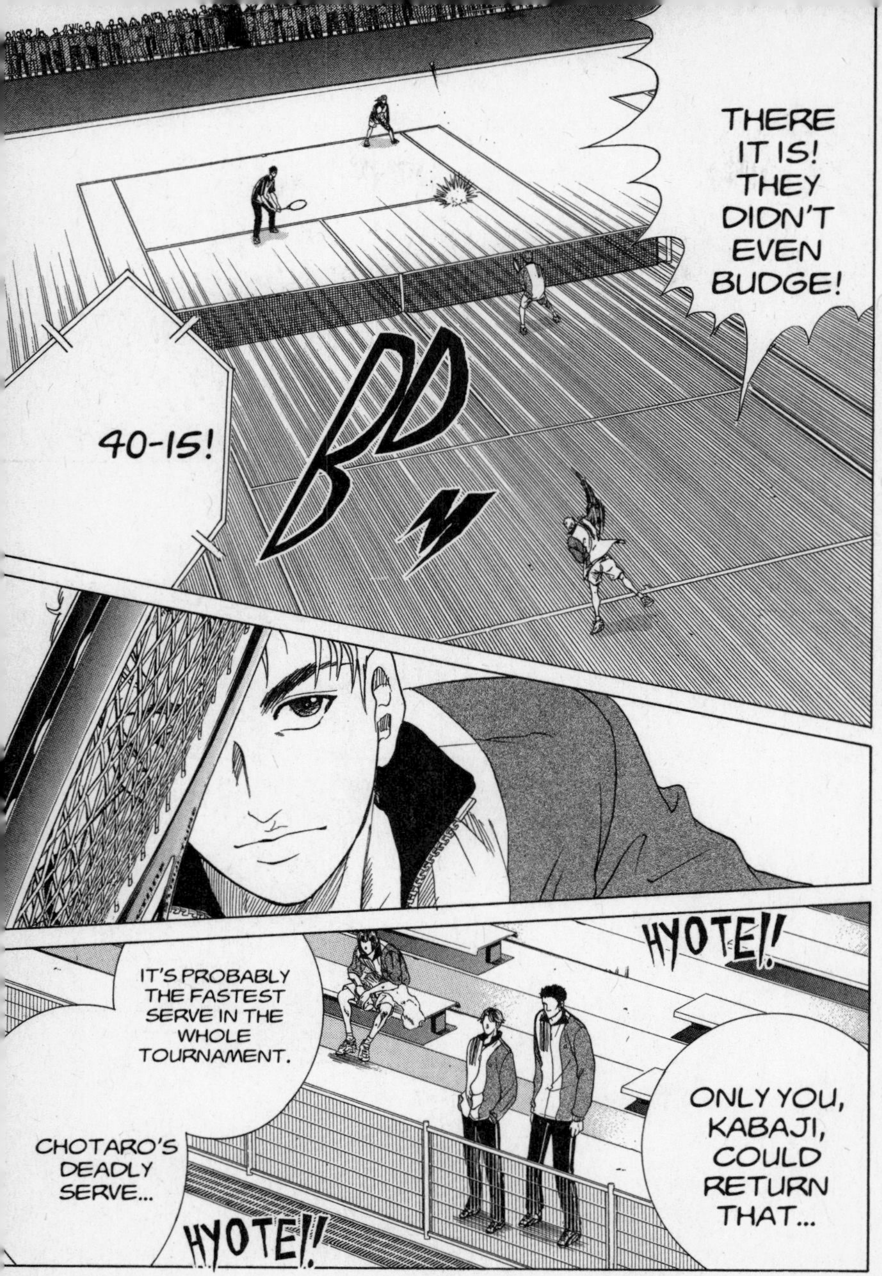
THERE IT IS! THEY DIDN'T EVEN BUDGE!
40-15!
HYOTEI!
IT'S PROBABLY THE FASTEST SERVE IN THE WHOLE TOURNAMENT.
ONLY YOU, KABAJI, COULD RETURN THAT...
CHOTARO'S DEADLY SERVE...
HYOTEI!

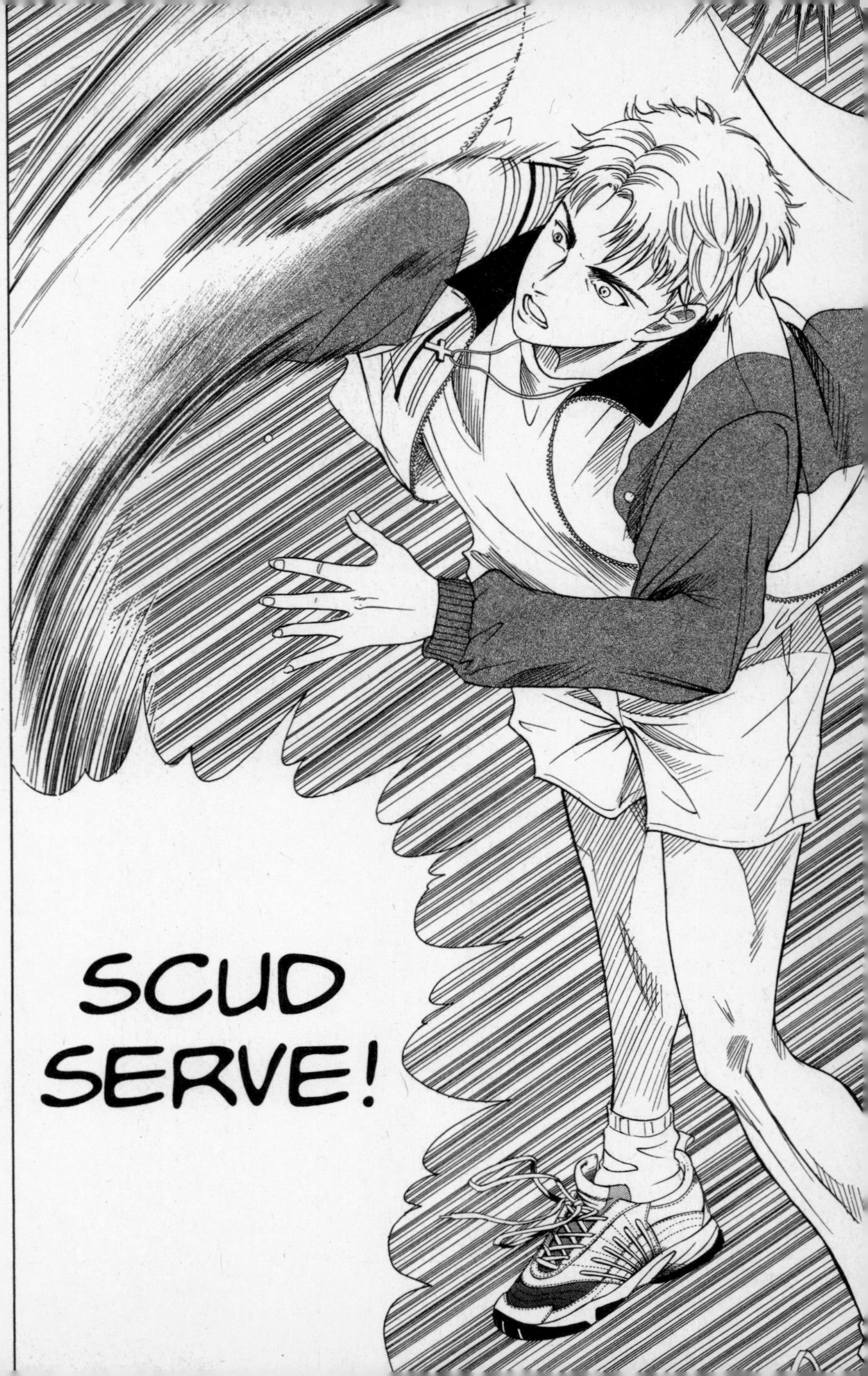
SCUD
SERVE!

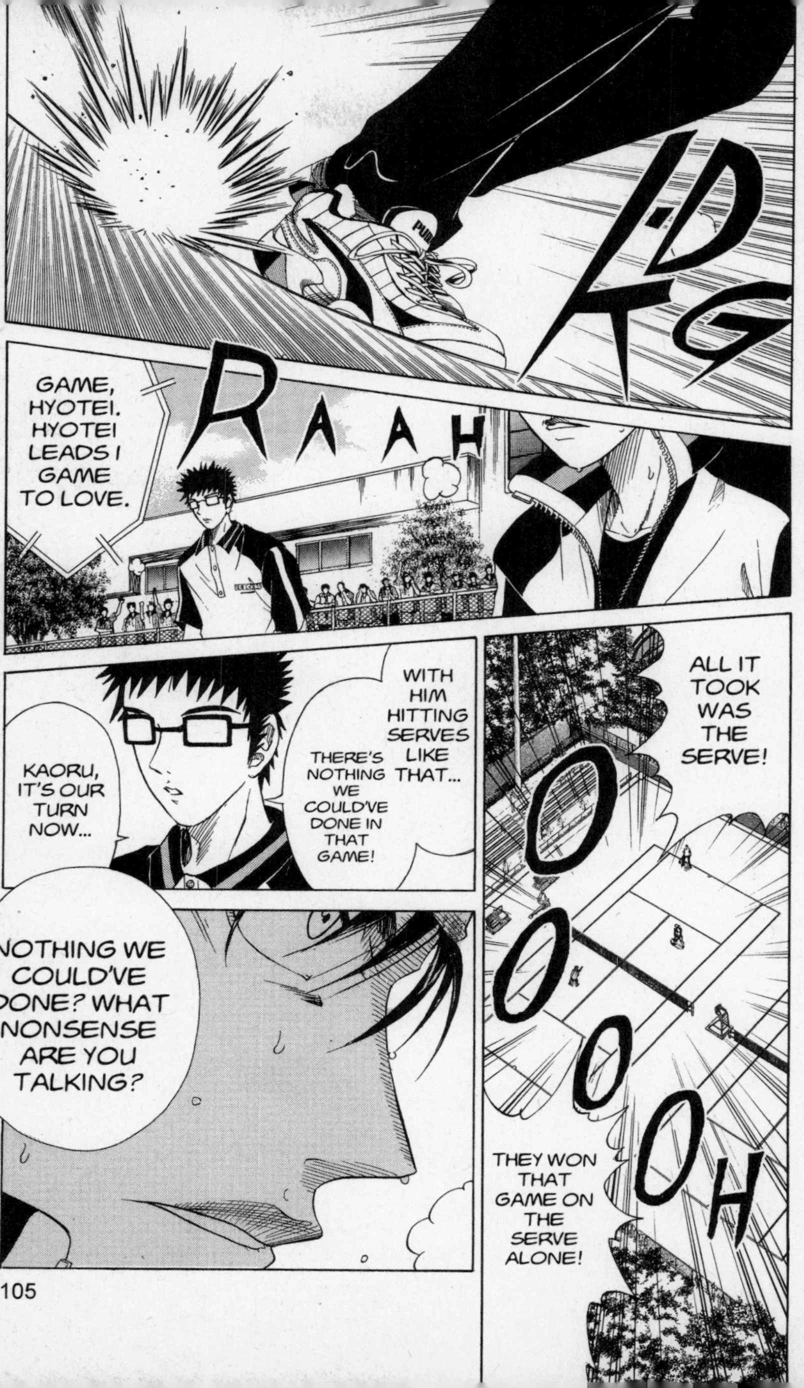
DKG
RAAH
GAME, HYOTEI. HYOTEI LEADS 1 GAME TO LOVE.
OOOOOH
ALL IT TOOK WAS THE SERVE!
THEY WON THAT GAME ON THE SERVE ALONE!
WITH HIM HITTING SERVES LIKE THAT...
THERE'S NOTHING WE COULD'VE DONE IN THAT GAME!
KAORU, IT'S OUR TURN NOW...
NOTHING WE COULD'VE DONE? WHAT NONSENSE ARE YOU TALKING?

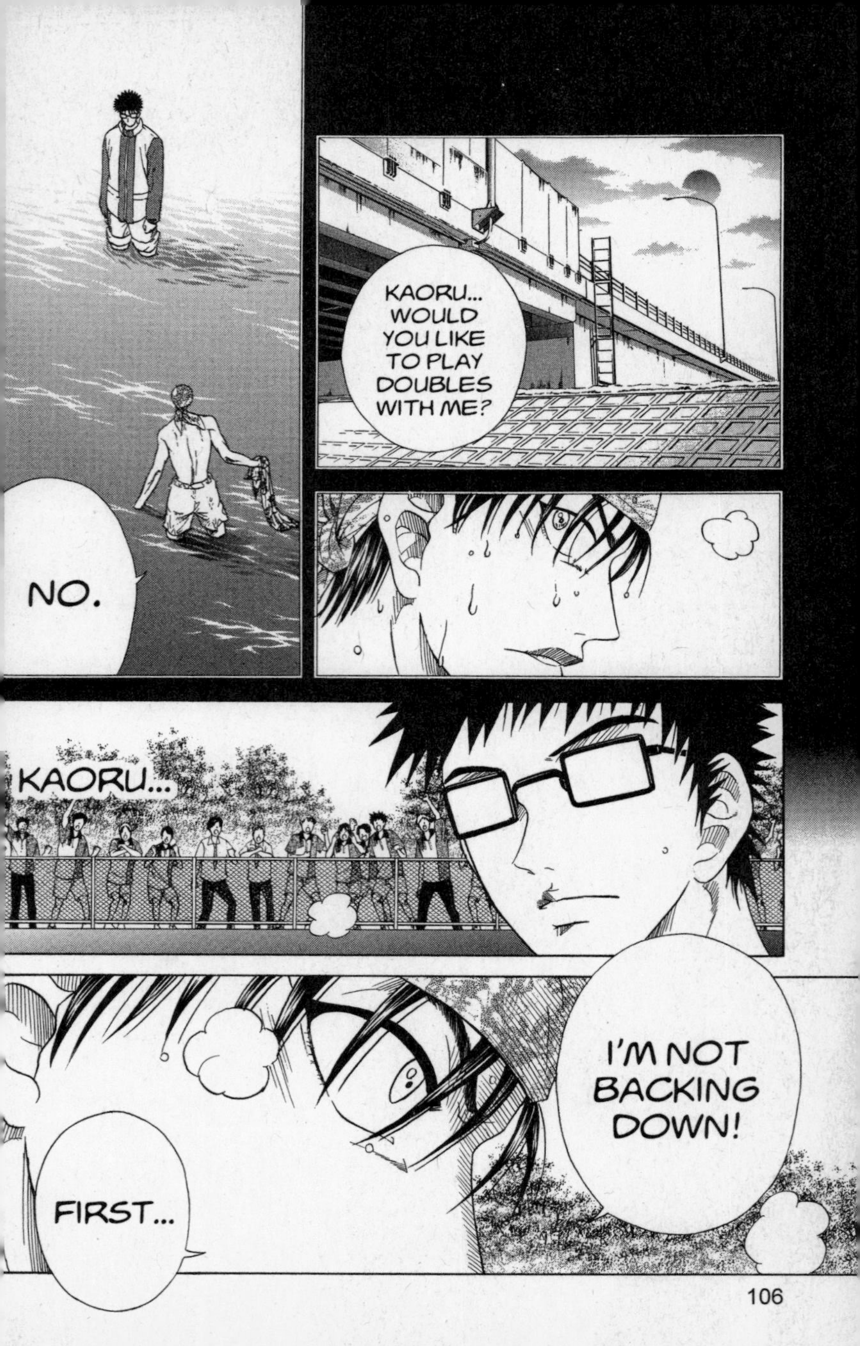
KAORU... WOULD YOU LIKE TO PLAY DOUBLES WITH ME?
NO.
KAORU...
I'M NOT BACKING DOWN!
FIRST...

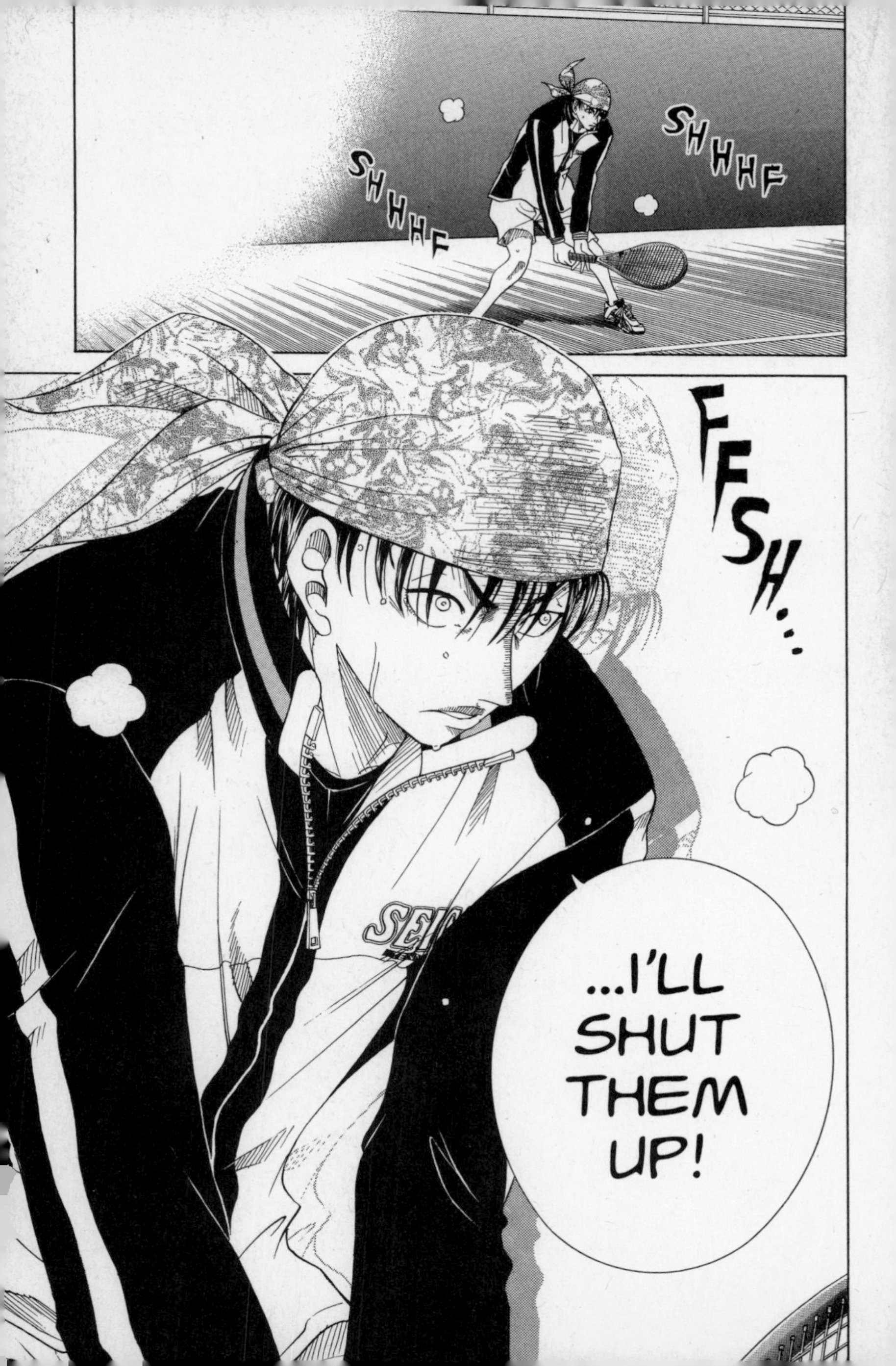
SHHHF
SHHHF
FFSH...
...I'LL SHUT THEM UP!

Thank you for reading The Prince of Tennis Volume 15. I'd like to talk about my participation in the dubbing of The Prince of Tennis anime.

Thursday morning after 10:00 a.m., a sweaty man came running into the booth while a meeting was being held. The booth went silent. The voice actors' sights were set on the intruder by the door. All of a sudden, the sweaty man's mouth opened and said, "I'm Konomi. Nice to meet you all—(laugh)!"

Everybody just gets along so well! They mimic each other's voices, and they sound like each other, too. Yuki Kaida, who plays Shusuke, was especially picked on. From either side of her, voices saying "I'll end it" or "I'll score"—fake Shusuke dialogues—were thrown around... (to her right, Mr. Okiayu, and to her left, Naru).
But once the tape started rolling, everybody got serious. I was impressed to see their expressions change as they got into character. They would even say, "This part was okay, but can I try it again?" I was very happy to see them work until they themselves were satisfied. It was a beautiful and very educational day. I don't think I'll ever forget a parfait called Strawberry Chocolate Super Deluxe. To the director and all the staff, thank you for a wonderful experience!

テニスの王子様☆
T. Konomi
2002.8.5

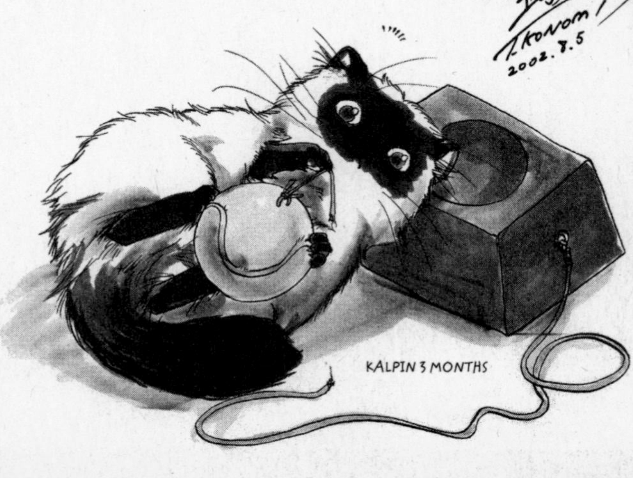

KALPIN 3 MONTHS

GENIUS 129: MENTAL STRENGTH x MENTAL STRENGTH

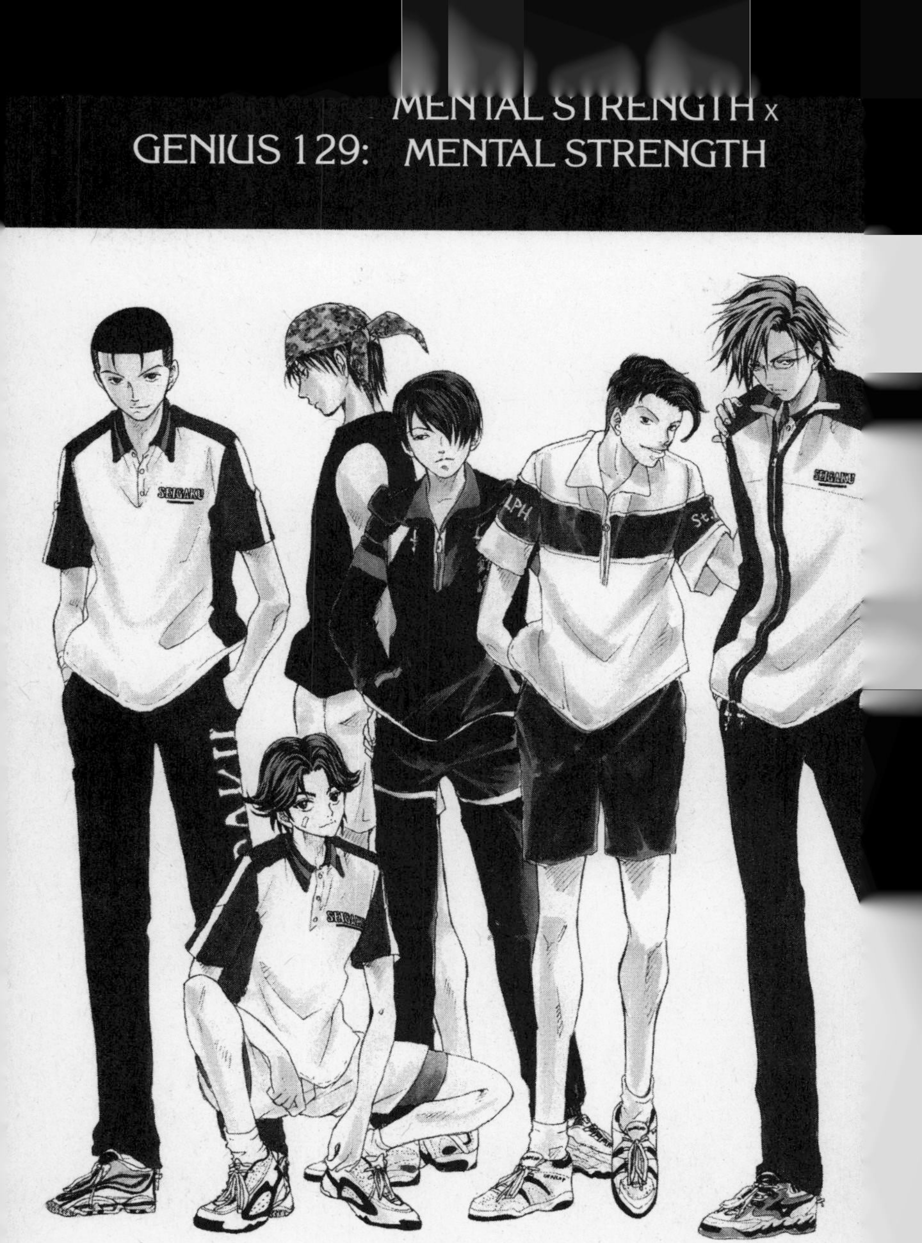
SEIGAKU
SEIGAKU
SEIGAKU

MENTAL STRENGTH x MENTAL STRENGTH

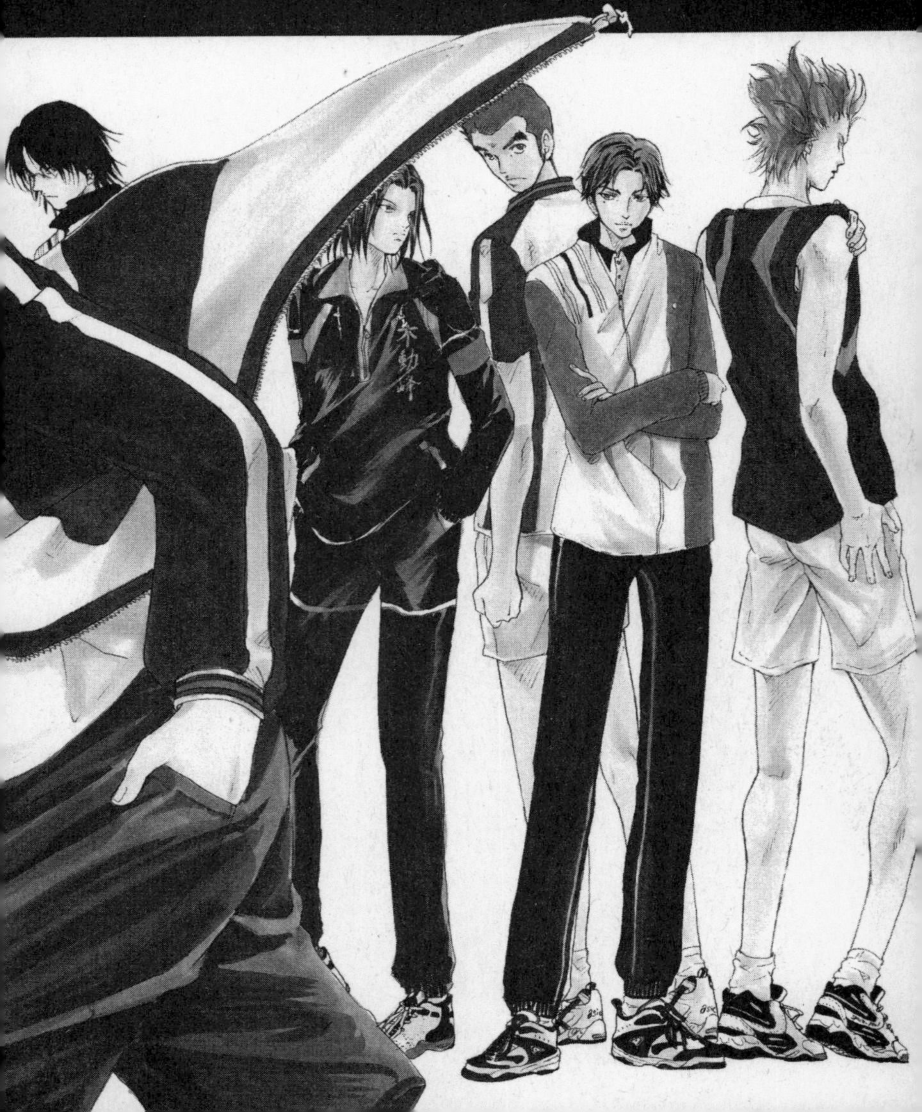

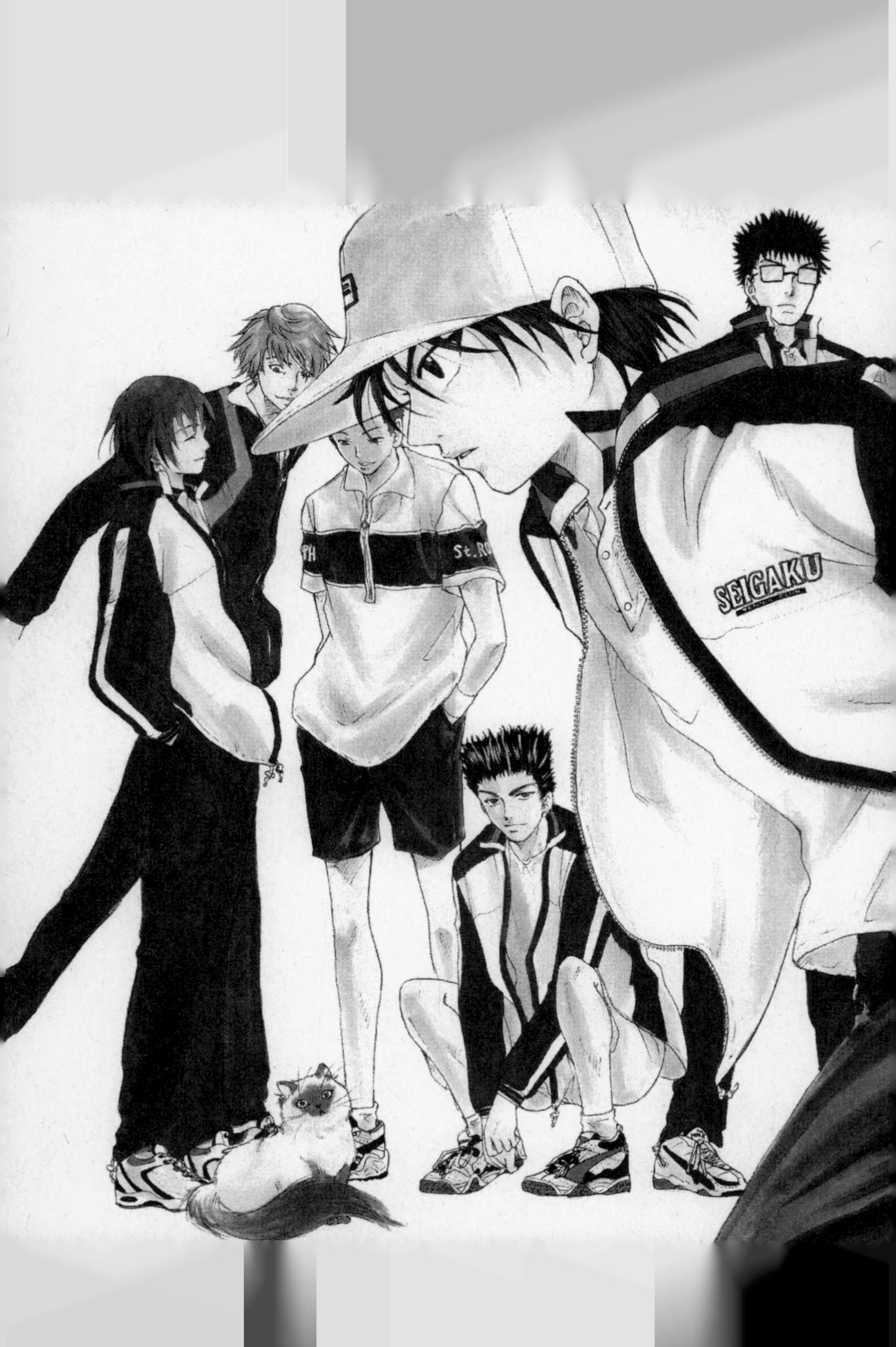
SEIGAKU

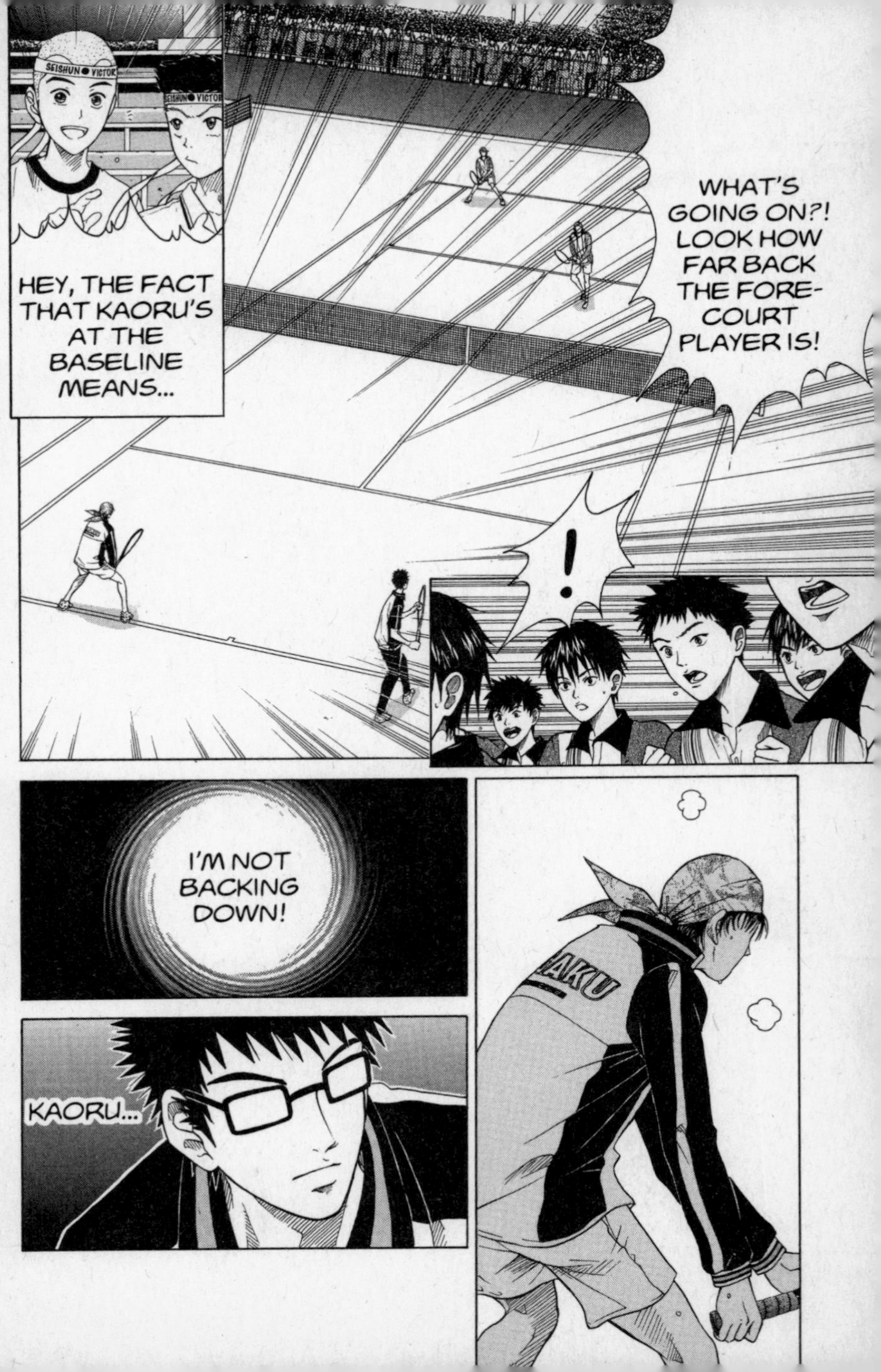
WHAT'S GOING ON?! LOOK HOW FAR BACK THE FORE-COURT PLAYER IS!
HEY, THE FACT THAT KAORU'S AT THE BASELINE MEANS...
!
I'M NOT BACKING DOWN!
KAORU...

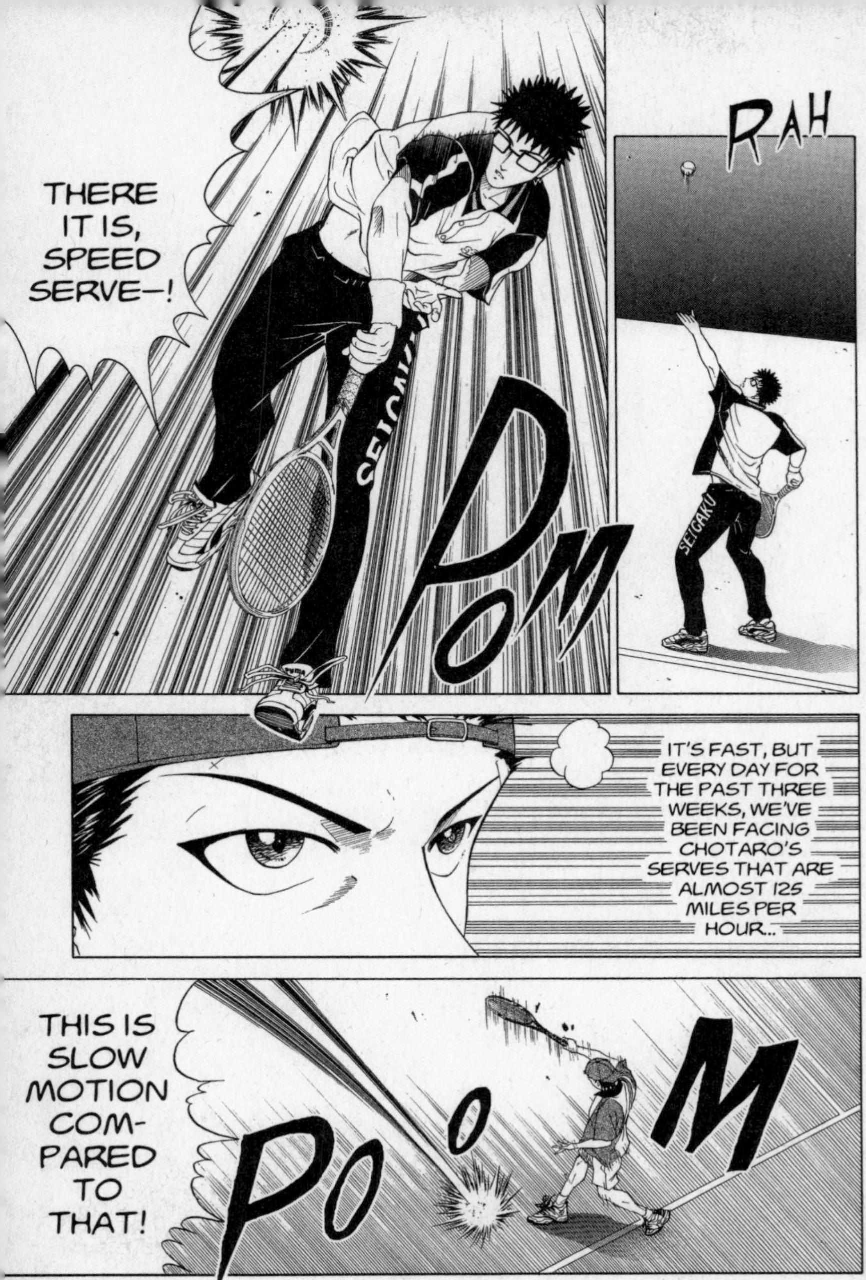
RAH
SEIGAKU
THERE IT IS, SPEED SERVE–!
POM
IT'S FAST, BUT EVERY DAY FOR THE PAST THREE WEEKS, WE'VE BEEN FACING CHOTARO'S SERVES THAT ARE ALMOST 125 MILES PER HOUR...
THIS IS SLOW MOTION COM-PARED TO THAT!
POOM

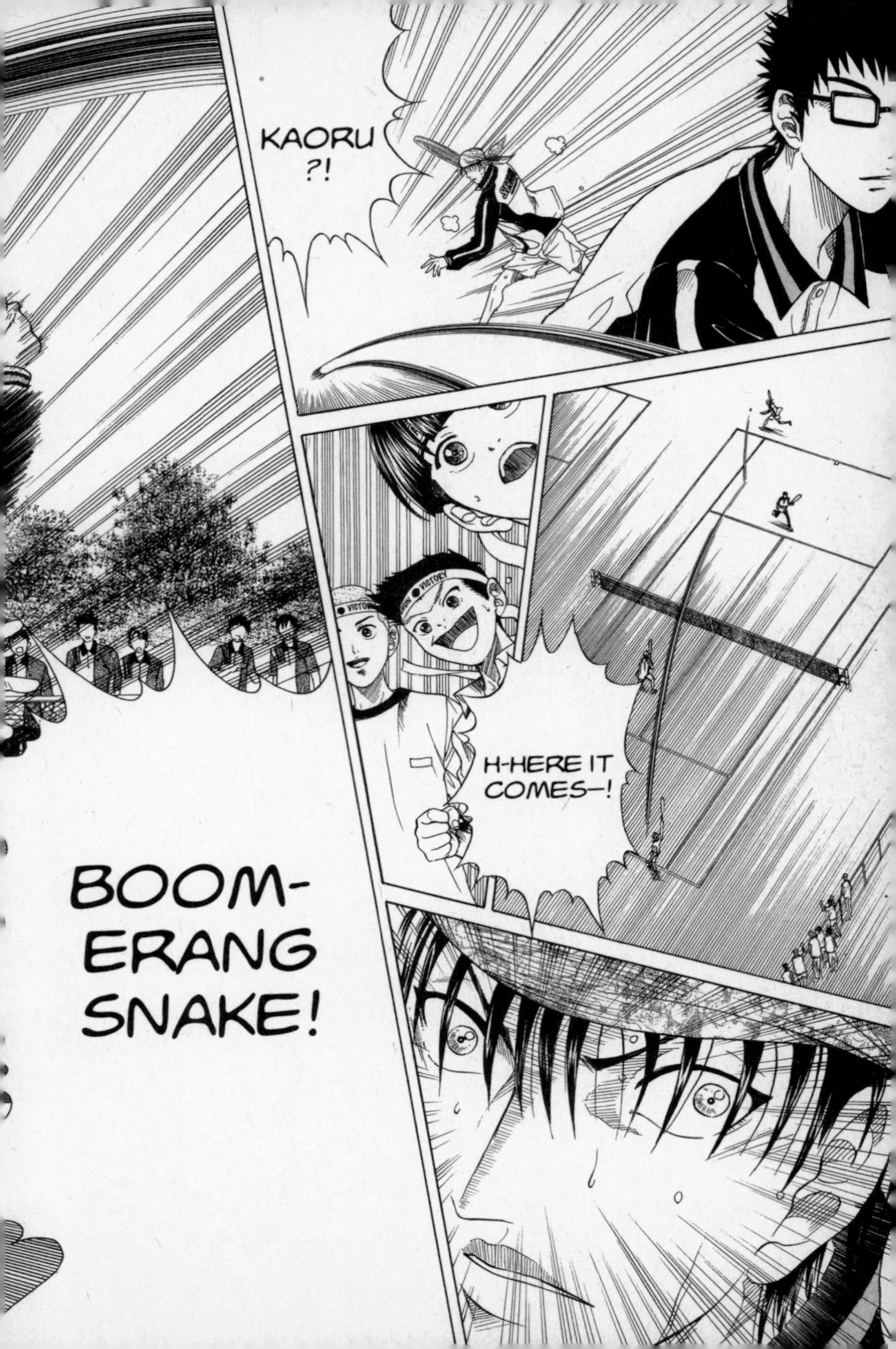
KAORU ?!
H-HERE IT COMES—!
BOOM-ERANG SNAKE!

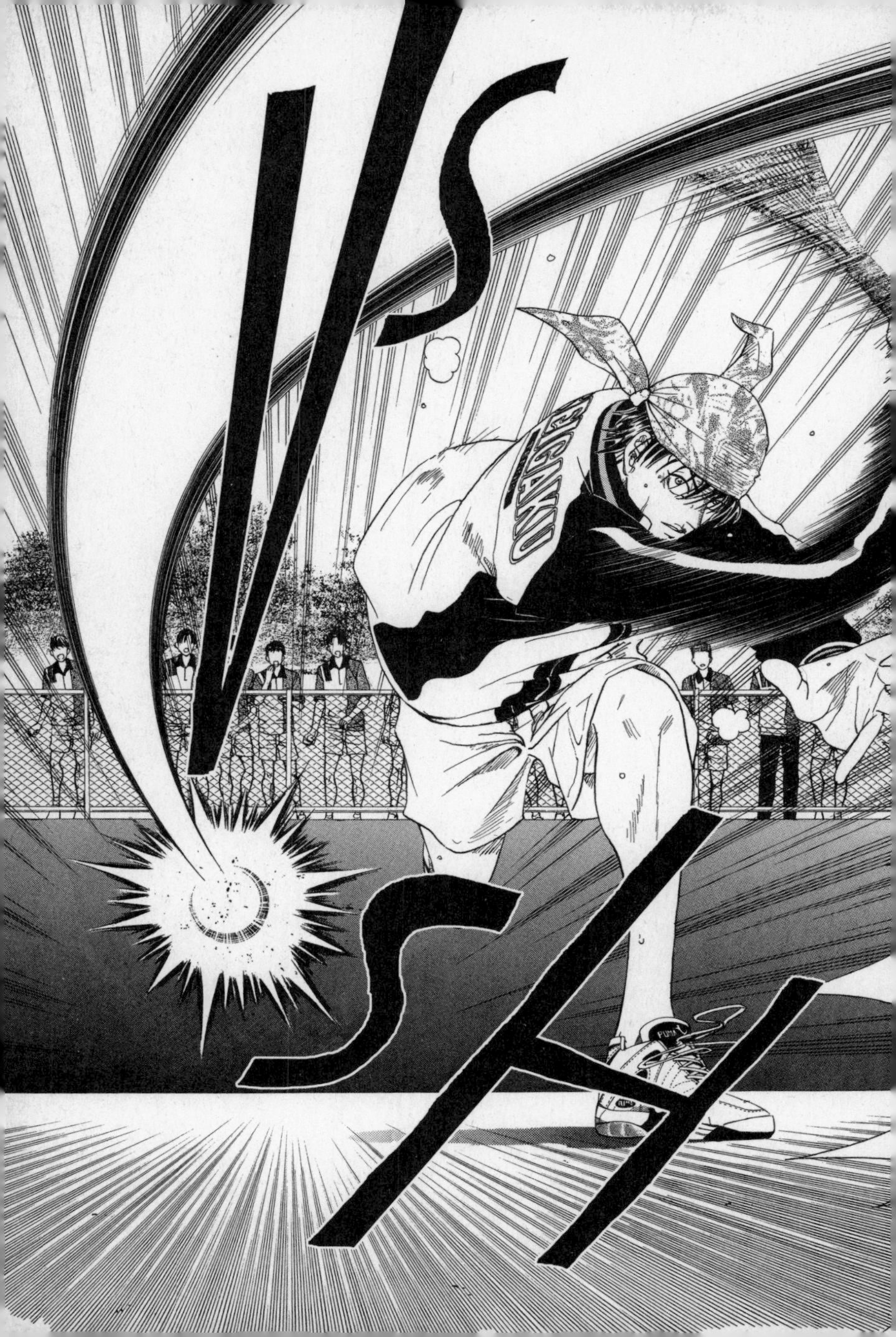
VSSH

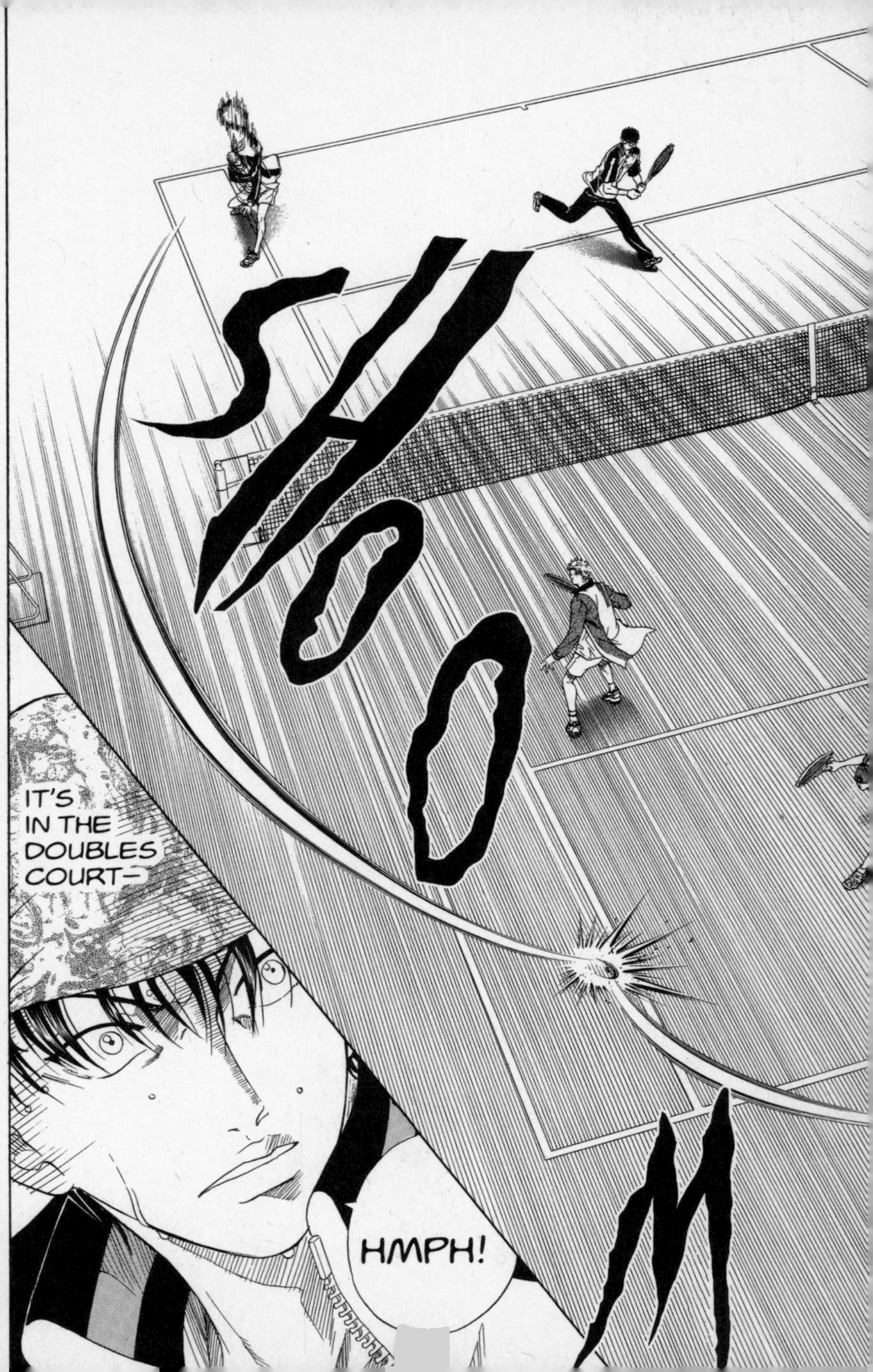
SHOOM
HMPH!
IT'S IN THE DOUBLES COURT—

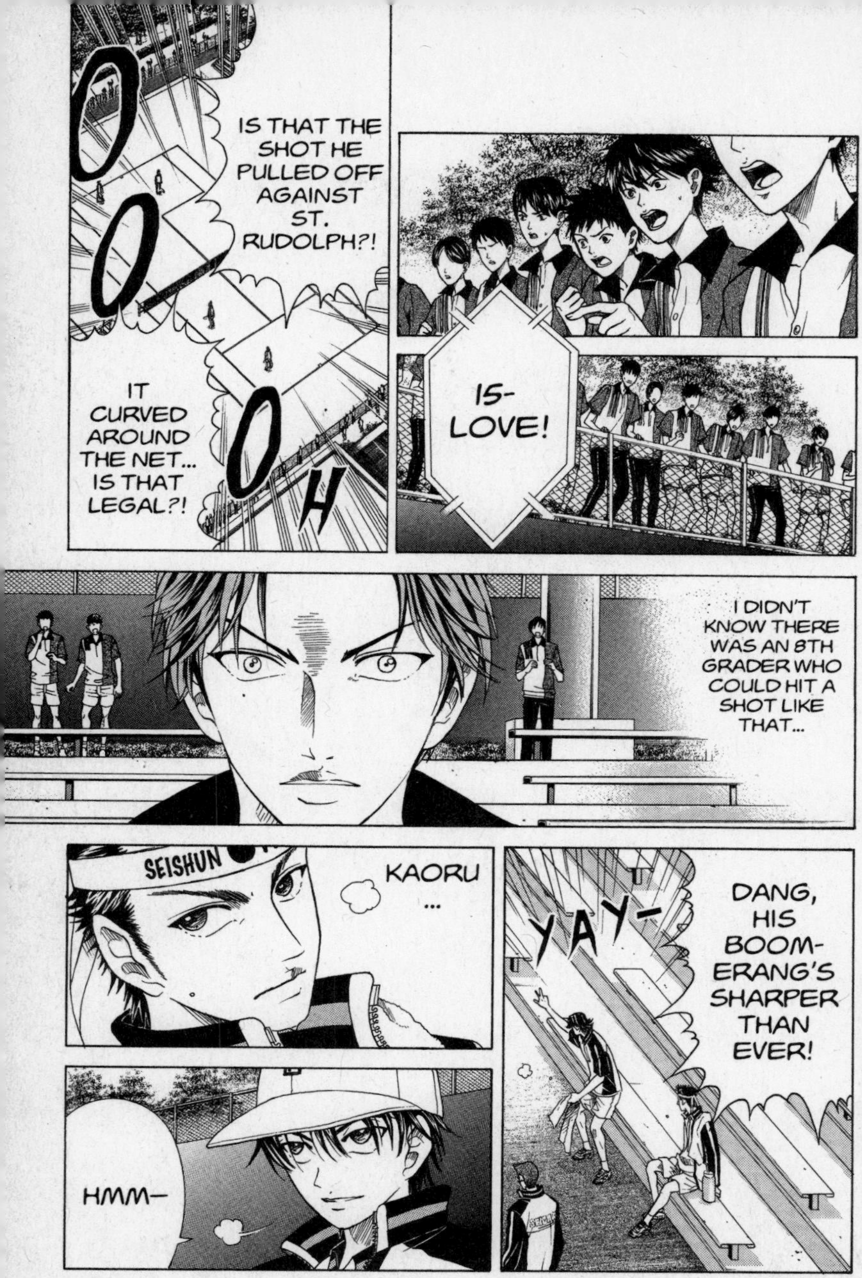
15-LOVE!
IS THAT THE SHOT HE PULLED OFF AGAINST ST. RUDOLPH?!
OOOH
IT CURVED AROUND THE NET... IS THAT LEGAL?!
I DIDN'T KNOW THERE WAS AN 8TH GRADER WHO COULD HIT A SHOT LIKE THAT...
YAY-
DANG, HIS BOOMERANG'S SHARPER THAN EVER!
SEISHUN
KAORU ...
HMM-

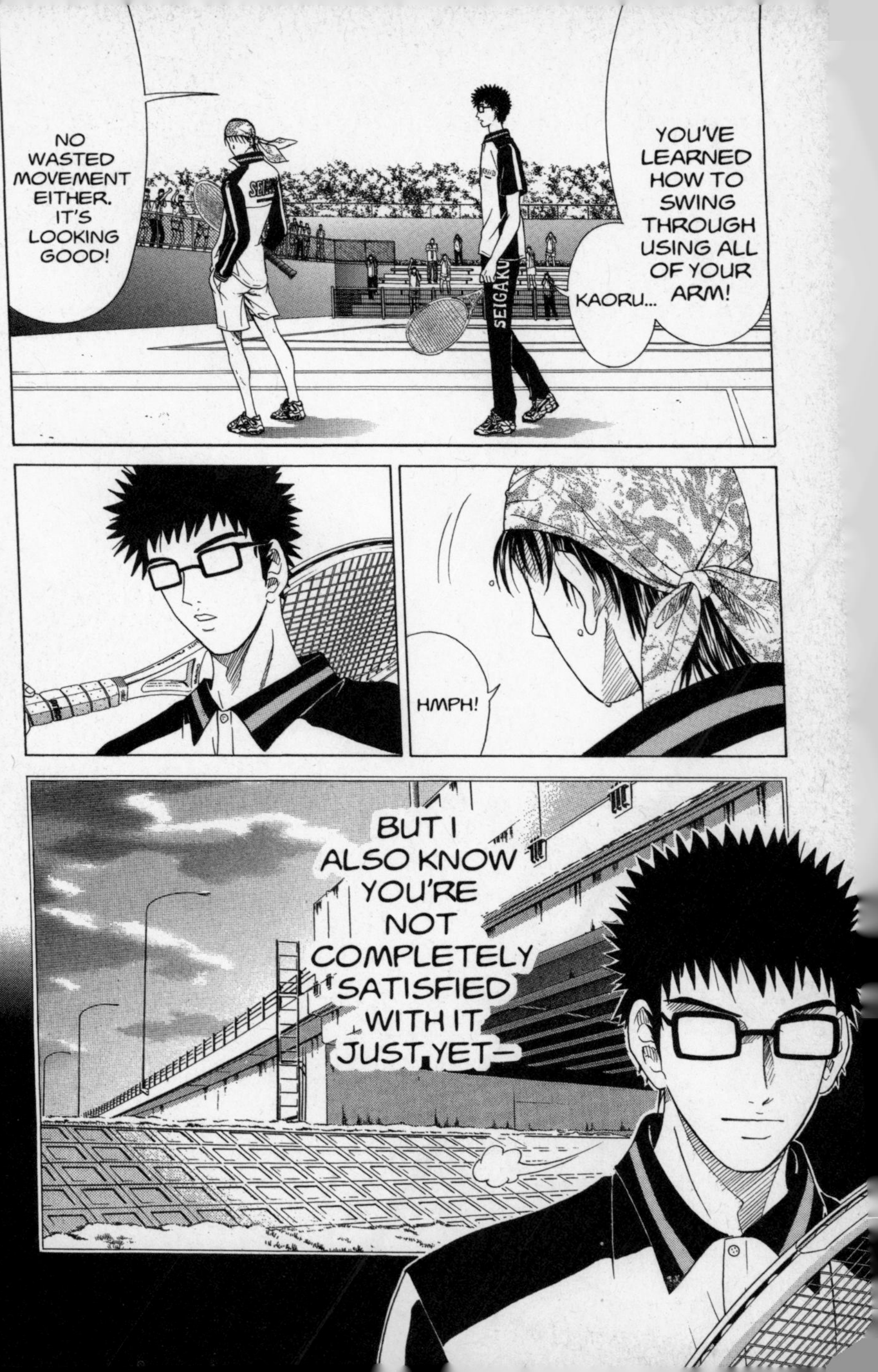

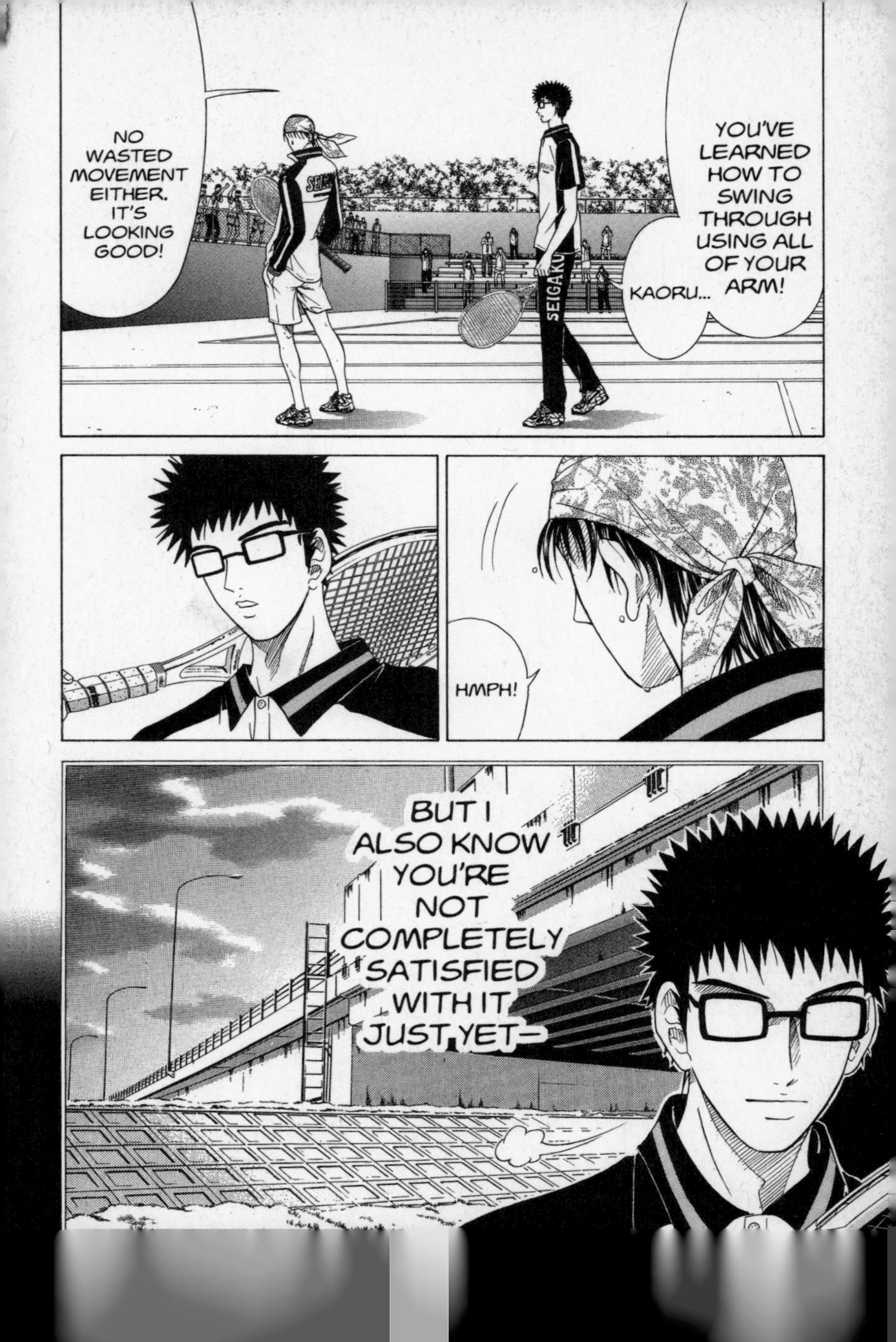
YOU'VE LEARNED HOW TO SWING THROUGH USING ALL OF YOUR ARM!
KAORU...
NO WASTED MOVEMENT EITHER. IT'S LOOKING GOOD!
HMPH!
BUT I ALSO KNOW YOU'RE NOT COMPLETELY SATISFIED WITH IT JUST YET—

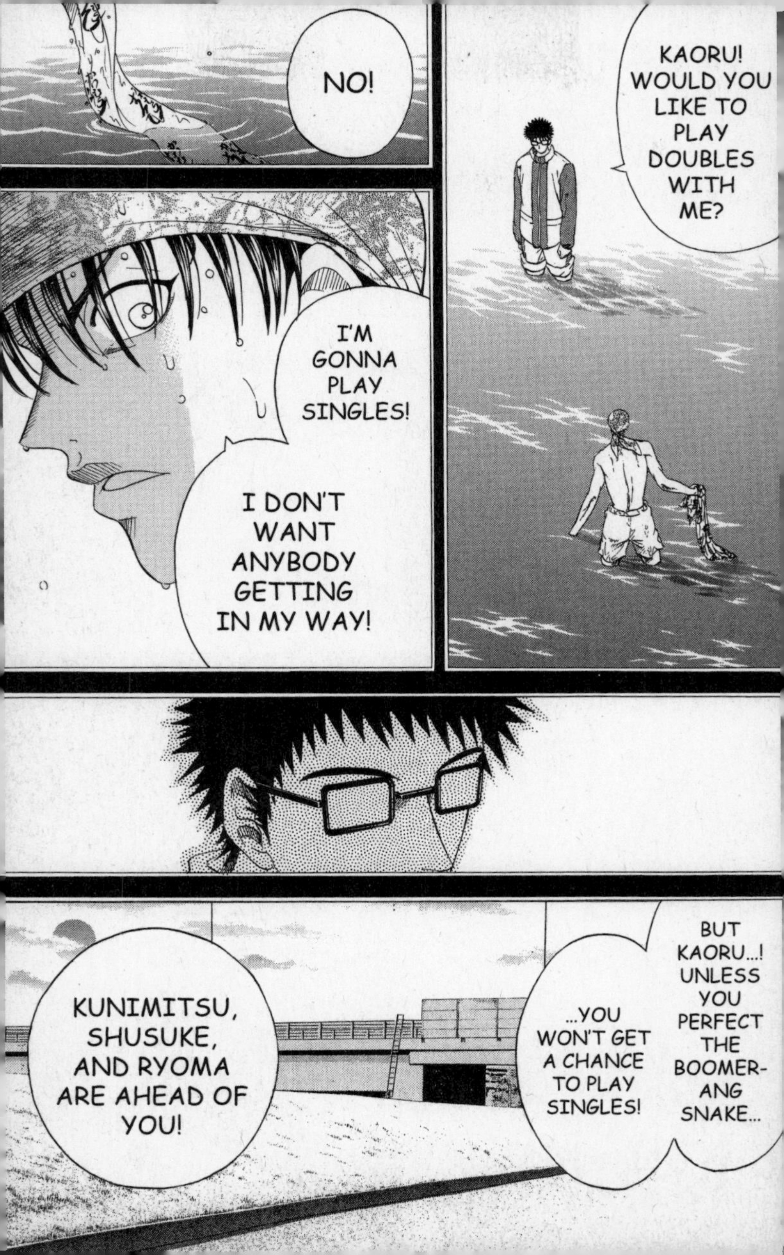
KAORU! WOULD YOU LIKE TO PLAY DOUBLES WITH ME?
NO!
I'M GONNA PLAY SINGLES!
I DON'T WANT ANYBODY GETTING IN MY WAY!
BUT KAORU...! UNLESS YOU PERFECT THE BOOMER-ANG SNAKE...
...YOU WON'T GET A CHANCE TO PLAY SINGLES!
KUNIMITSU, SHUSUKE, AND RYOMA ARE AHEAD OF YOU!

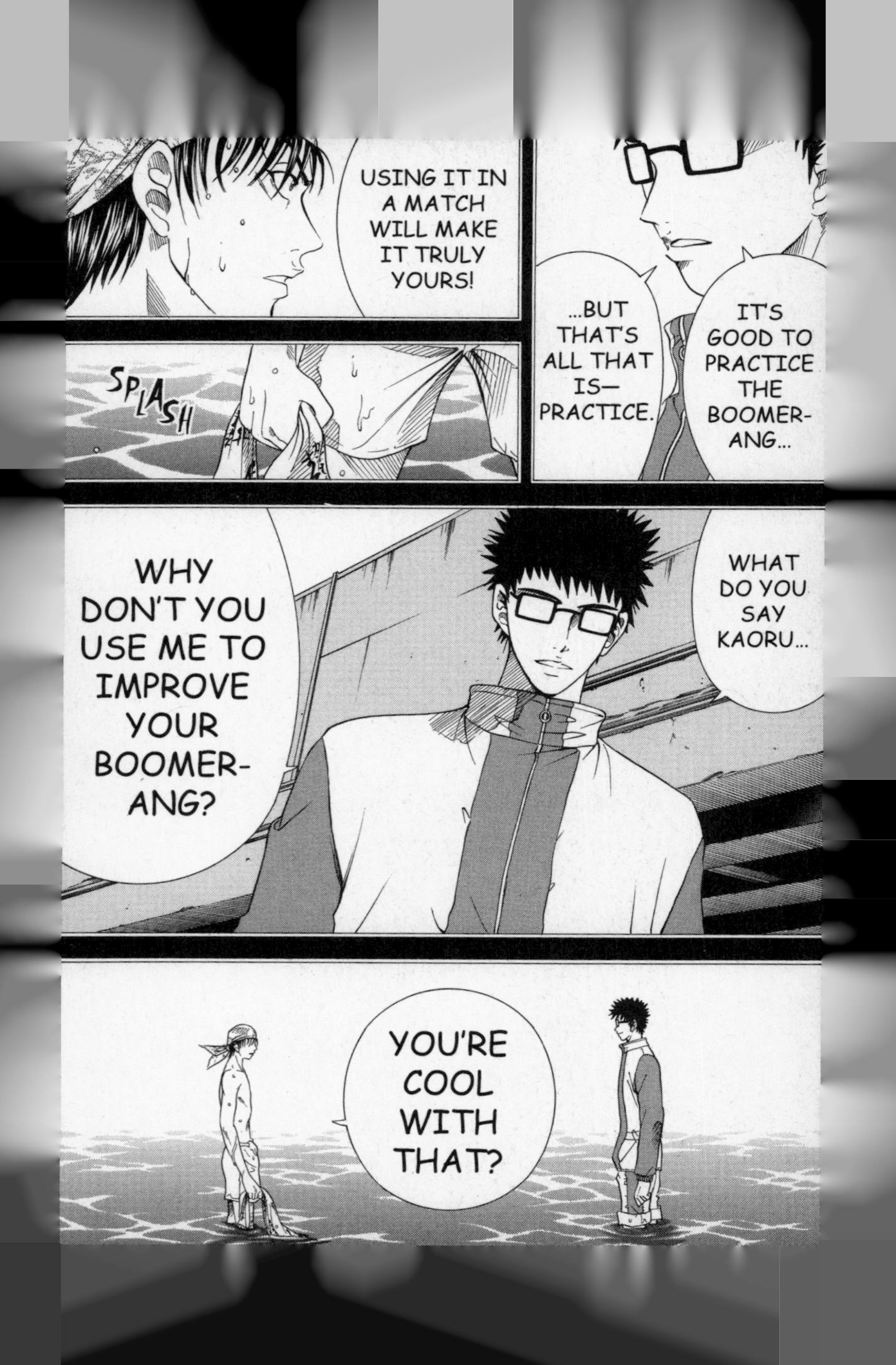
IT'S GOOD TO PRACTICE THE BOOMER-ANG...
...BUT THAT'S ALL THAT IS— PRACTICE.
USING IT IN A MATCH WILL MAKE IT TRULY YOURS!
SPLASH
WHAT DO YOU SAY KAORU...
WHY DON'T YOU USE ME TO IMPROVE YOUR BOOMER-ANG?
YOU'RE COOL WITH THAT?

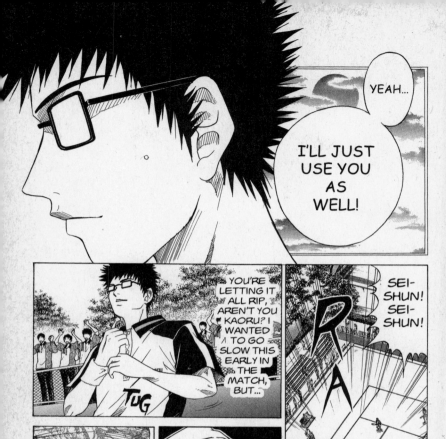

YEAH...
I'LL JUST USE YOU AS WELL!
SEI-SHUN! SEI-SHUN!
RAAAH
BOOMER-ANG! BOOMER-ANG!
YOU'RE LETTING IT ALL RIP, AREN'T YOU KAORU? I WANTED TO GO SLOW THIS EARLY IN THE MATCH, BUT...
TUG
I'LL START ATTACKING TOO!
...?!

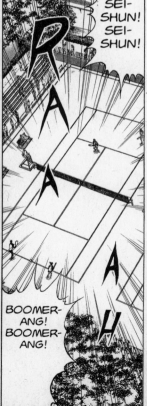

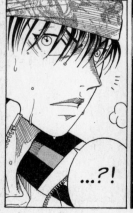

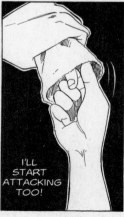

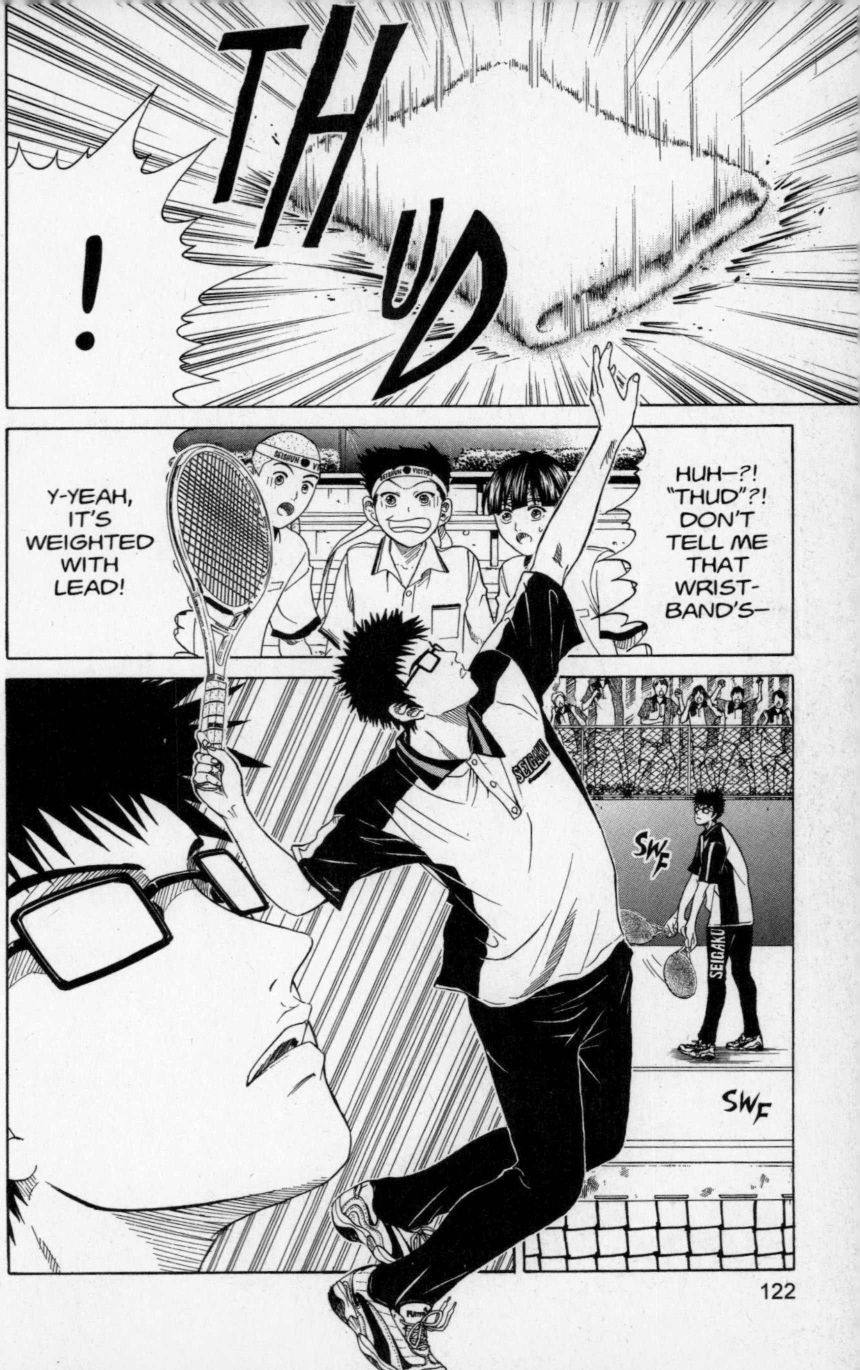
THUD
!
HUH—?! "THUD"?! DON'T TELL ME THAT WRIST-BAND'S—
Y-YEAH, IT'S WEIGHTED WITH LEAD!
SWF
SWF

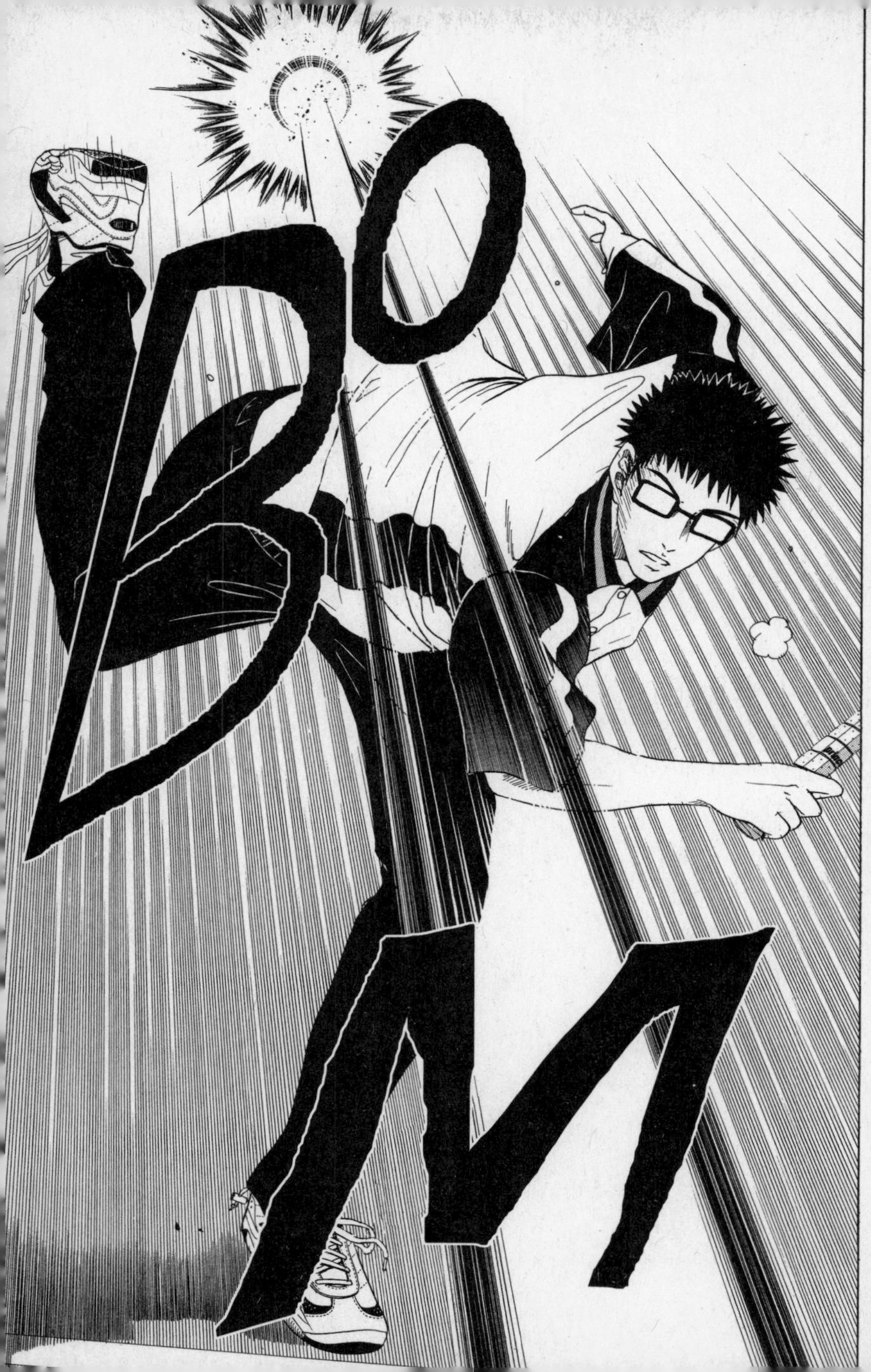
BOM

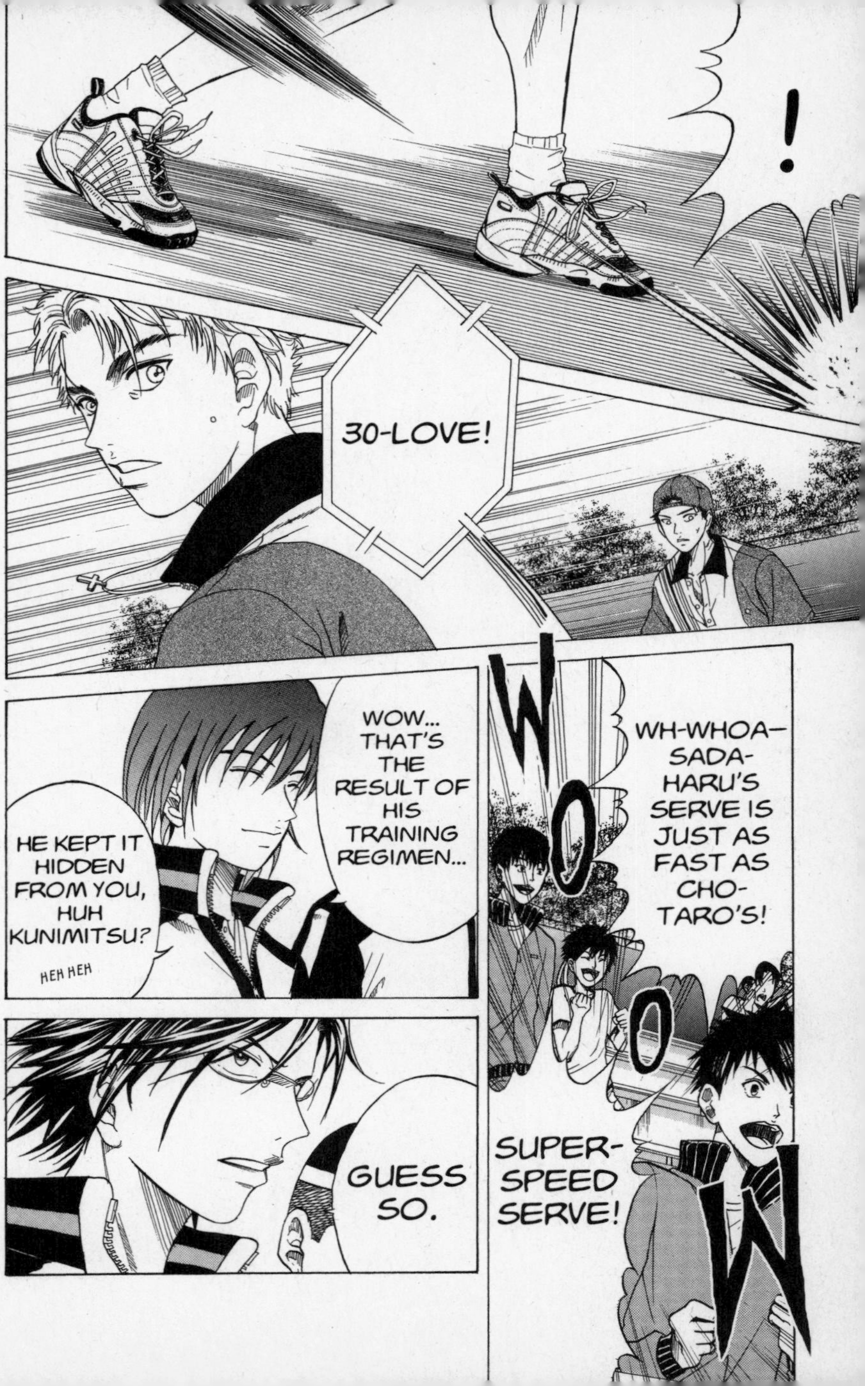
!
30-LOVE!
WOW
WOW... THAT'S THE RESULT OF HIS TRAINING REGIMEN...
HE KEPT IT HIDDEN FROM YOU, HUH KUNIMITSU?
HEH HEH
WH-WHOA-SADA-HARU'S SERVE IS JUST AS FAST AS CHO-TARO'S!
SUPER-SPEED SERVE!
GUESS SO.

READ THIS WAY

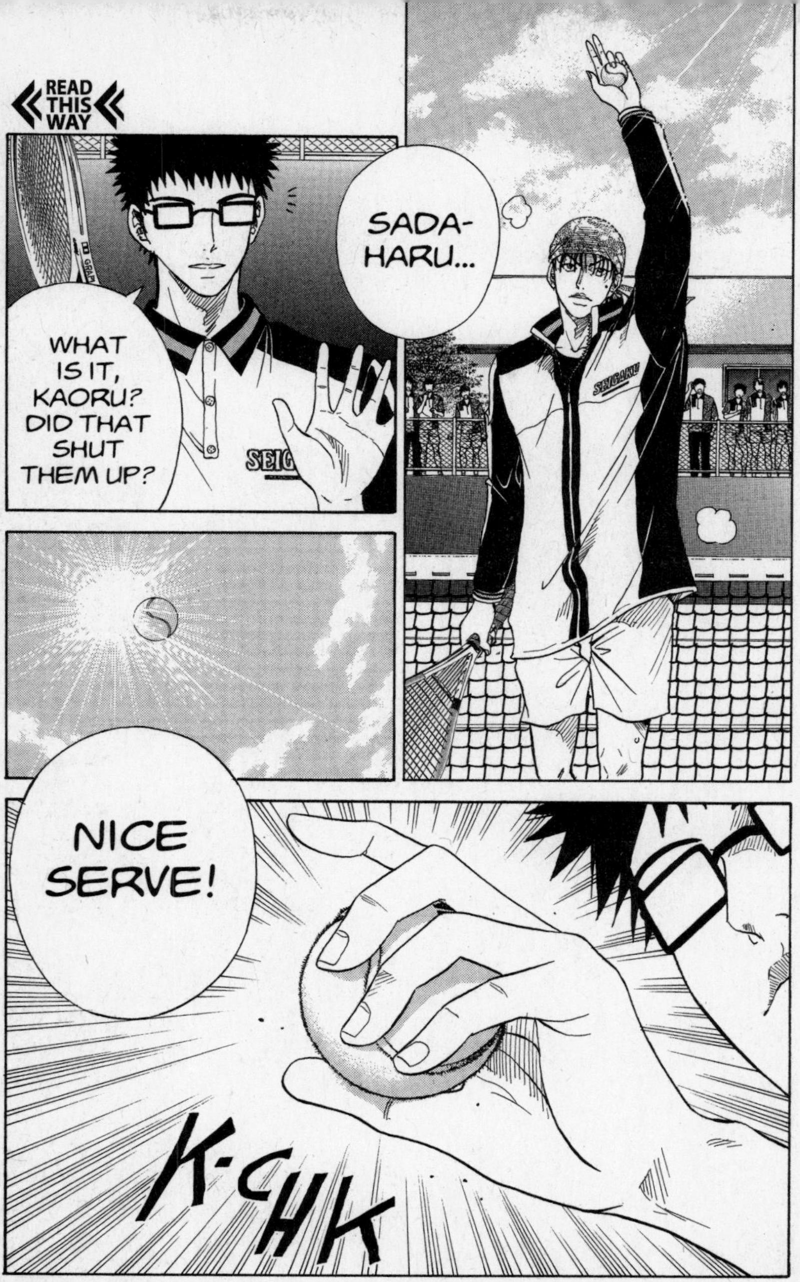
SADA-HARU...
WHAT IS IT, KAORU? DID THAT SHUT THEM UP?
NICE SERVE!
K-CHK

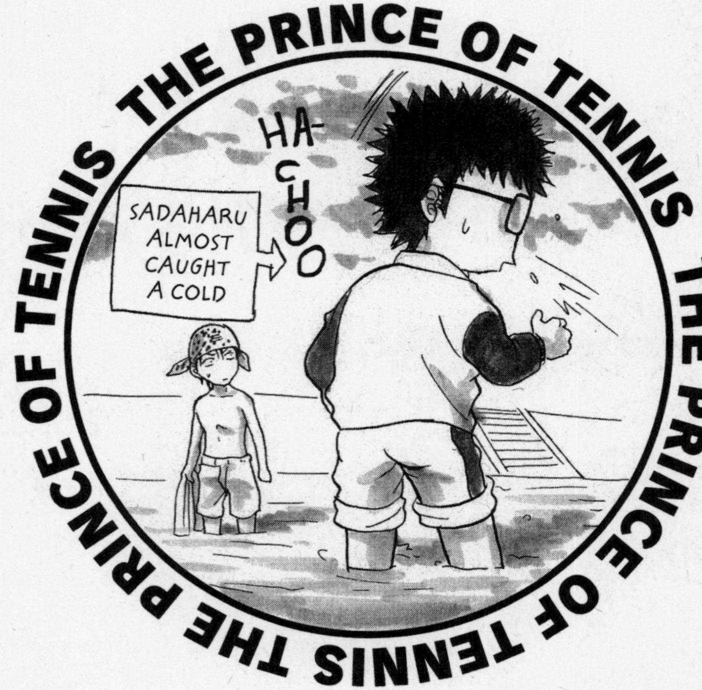
THE PRINCE OF TENNIS THE PRINCE OF TENNIS THE PRINCE OF TENNIS
SADAHARU ALMOST CAUGHT A COLD
HA-CHOO

GENIUS 130: REACTION TIME

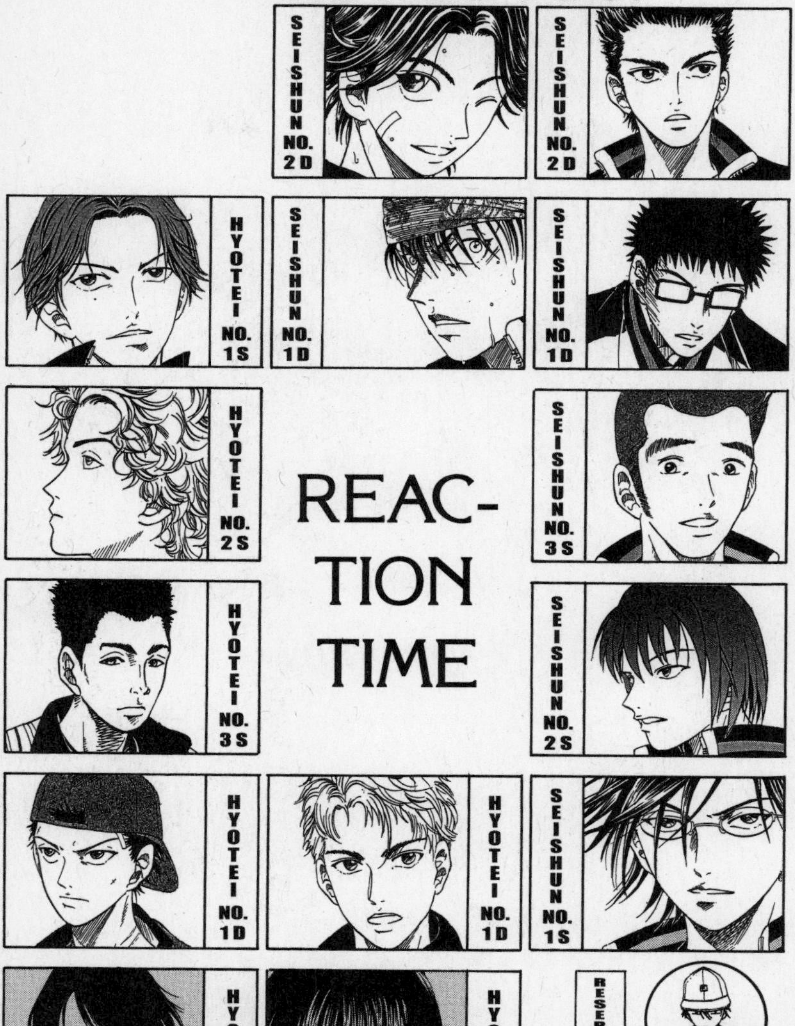
SEISHUN NO. 2D
SEISHUN NO. 2D
SEISHUN NO. 1D
SEISHUN NO. 1D
HYOTEI NO. 1S
SEISHUN NO. 3S
HYOTEI NO. 2S
SEISHUN NO. 2S
HYOTEI NO. 3S
SEISHUN NO. 1S
HYOTEI NO. 1D
HYOTEI NO. 1D
RESERVE
HYOTEI NO. 2D
HYOTEI NO. 2D

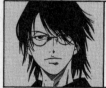

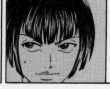

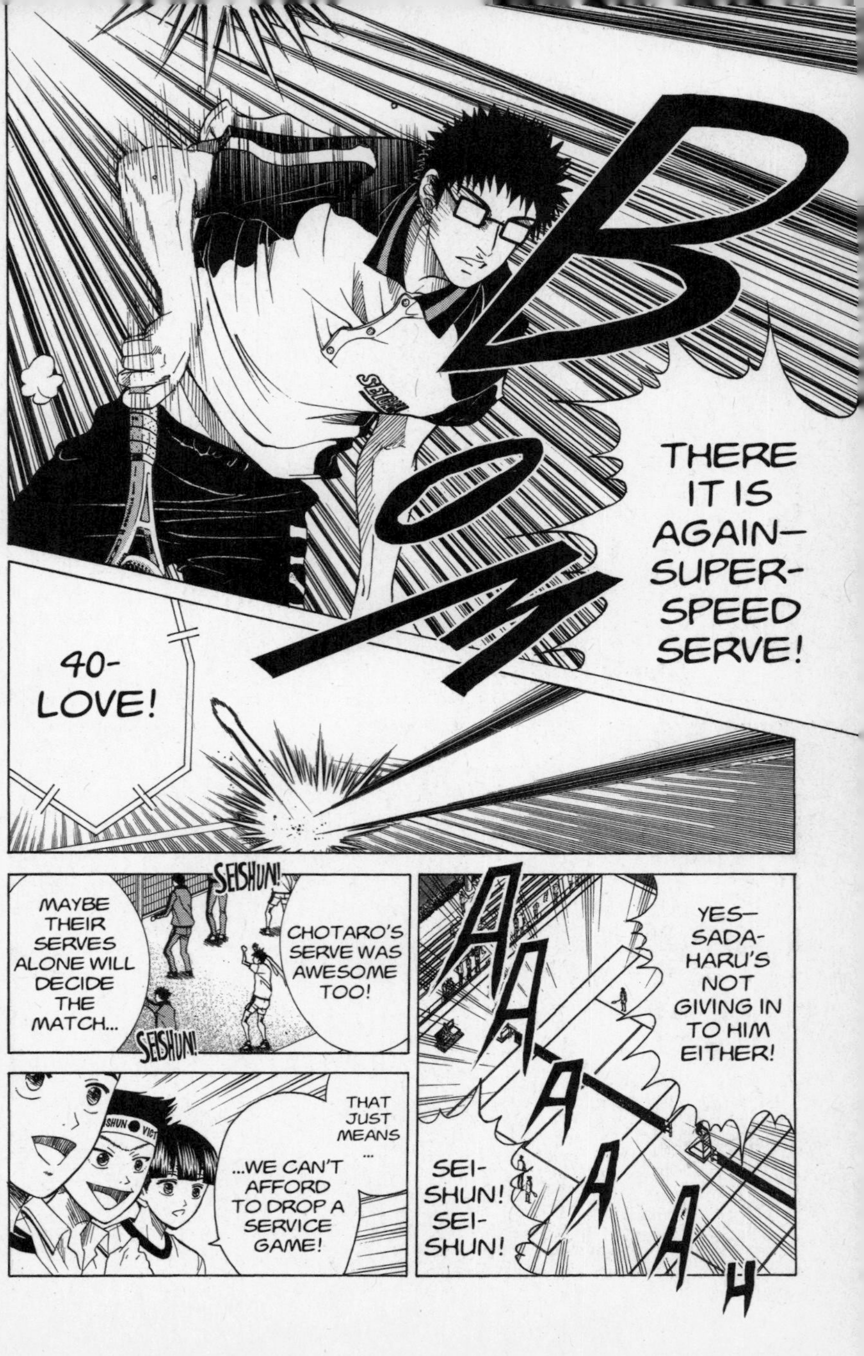
BOOM
THERE IT IS AGAIN—SUPER-SPEED SERVE!
40-LOVE!
AAAAAH
YES—SADAHARU'S NOT GIVING IN TO HIM EITHER!
SEI-SHUN! SEI-SHUN!
SEISHUN!
CHOTARO'S SERVE WAS AWESOME TOO!
MAYBE THEIR SERVES ALONE WILL DECIDE THE MATCH...
SEISHUN!
THAT JUST MEANS...
...WE CAN'T AFFORD TO DROP A SERVICE GAME!

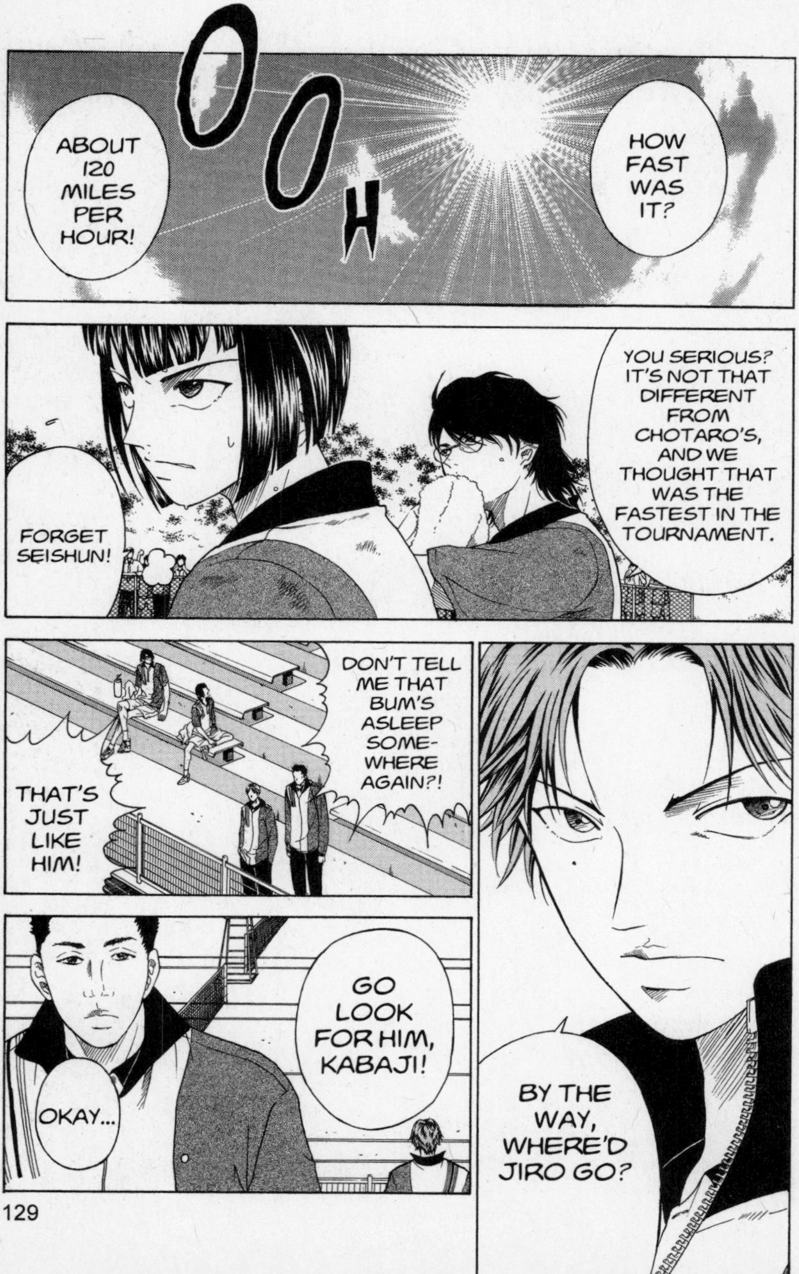
HOW FAST WAS IT?
OOH
ABOUT 120 MILES PER HOUR!
YOU SERIOUS? IT'S NOT THAT DIFFERENT FROM CHOTARO'S, AND WE THOUGHT THAT WAS THE FASTEST IN THE TOURNAMENT.
FORGET SEISHUN!
BY THE WAY, WHERE'D JIRO GO?
DON'T TELL ME THAT BUM'S ASLEEP SOME-WHERE AGAIN?!
THAT'S JUST LIKE HIM!
GO LOOK FOR HIM, KABAJI!
OKAY...

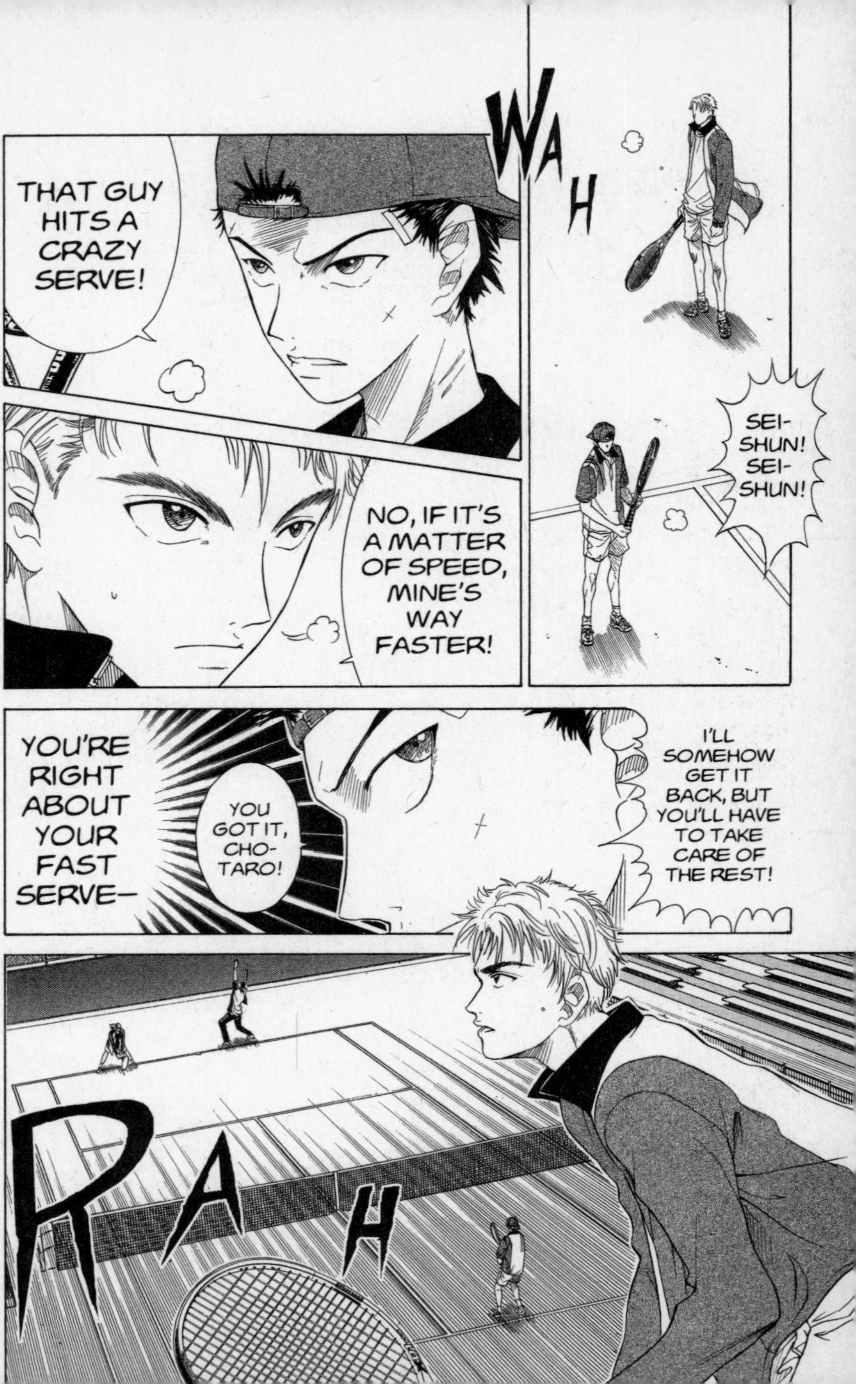
WAH
SEI-SHUN! SEI-SHUN!
THAT GUY HITS A CRAZY SERVE!
NO, IF IT'S A MATTER OF SPEED, MINE'S WAY FASTER!
I'LL SOMEHOW GET IT BACK, BUT YOU'LL HAVE TO TAKE CARE OF THE REST!
YOU GOT IT, CHO-TARO!
YOU'RE RIGHT ABOUT YOUR FAST SERVE—
RAH

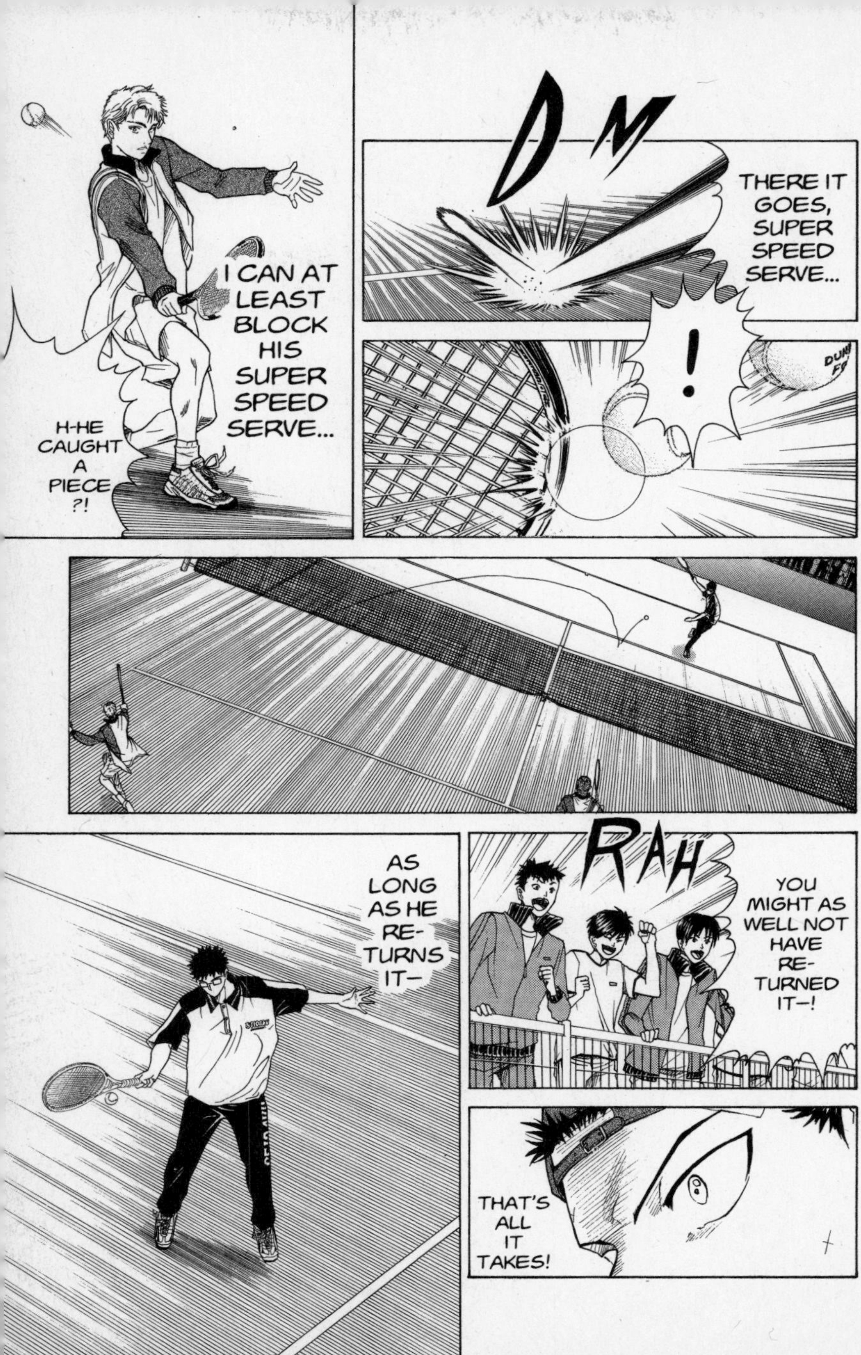
DM
THERE IT GOES, SUPER SPEED SERVE...
!
I CAN AT LEAST BLOCK HIS SUPER SPEED SERVE...
H-HE CAUGHT A PIECE?!
RAH
YOU MIGHT AS WELL NOT HAVE RE-TURNED IT—!
THAT'S ALL IT TAKES!
AS LONG AS HE RE-TURNS IT—

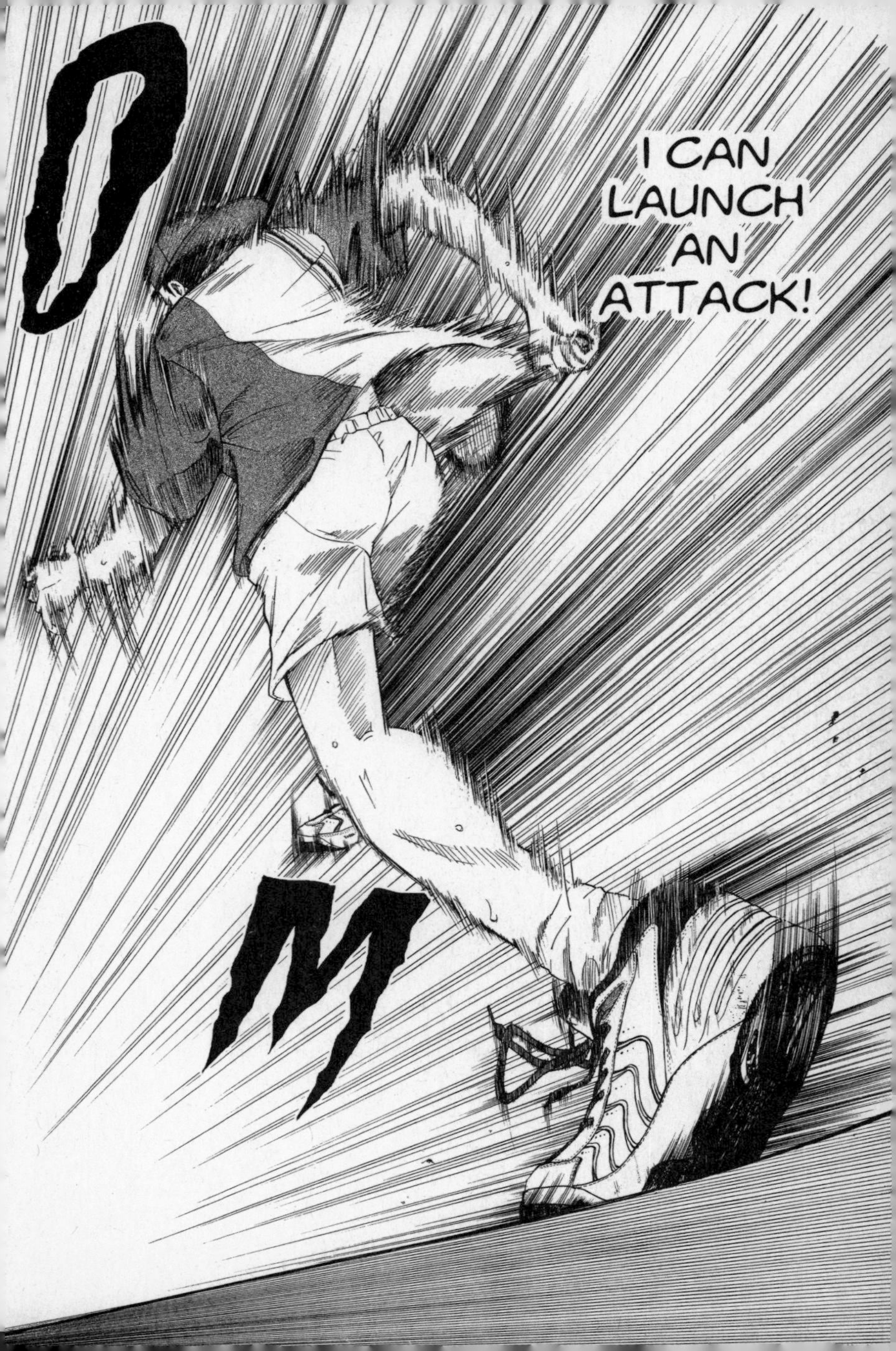
I CAN LAUNCH AN ATTACK!
DOM

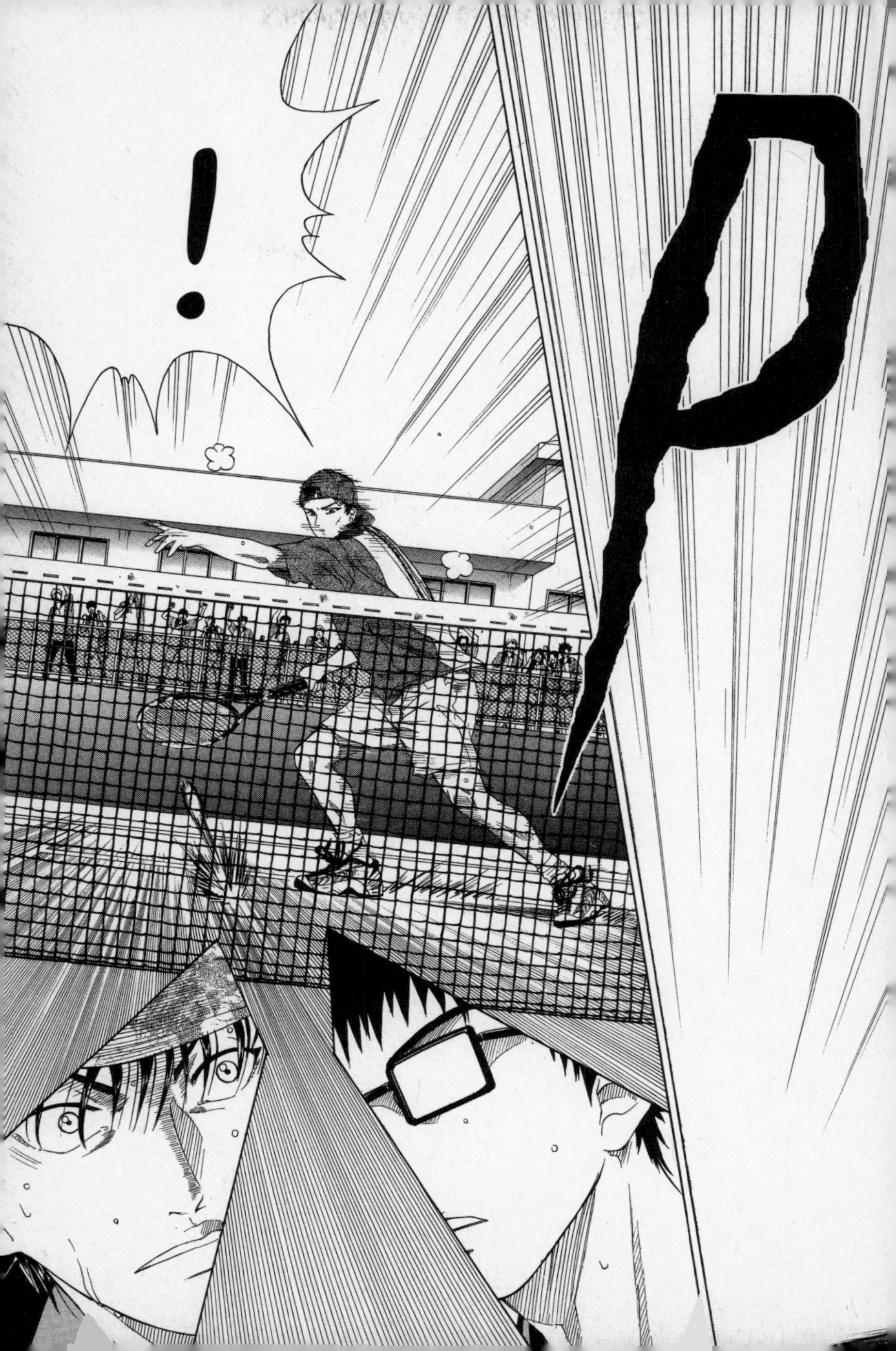
!
P

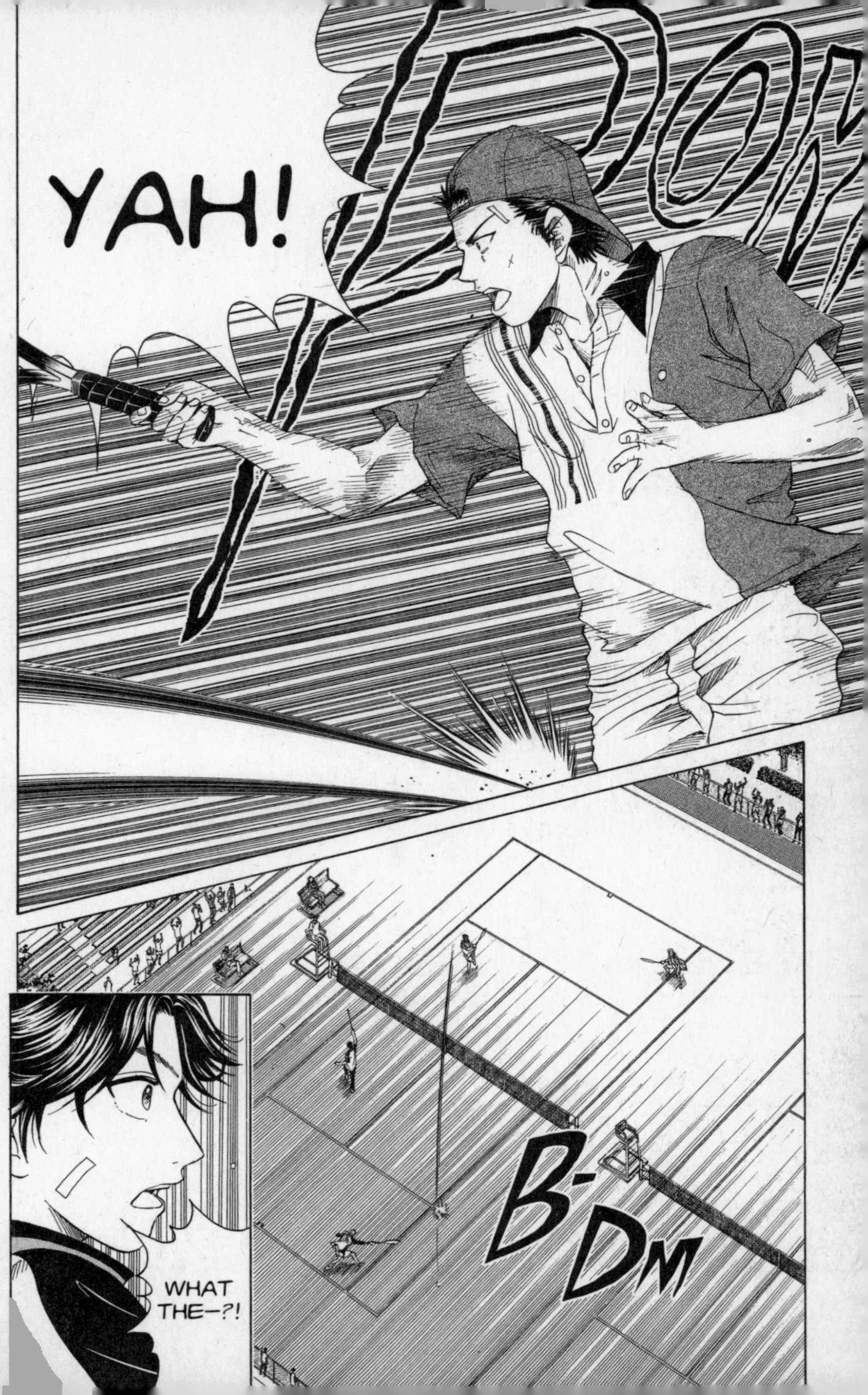
DO
YAH!
B-DM
WHAT THE-?!

READ THIS WAY

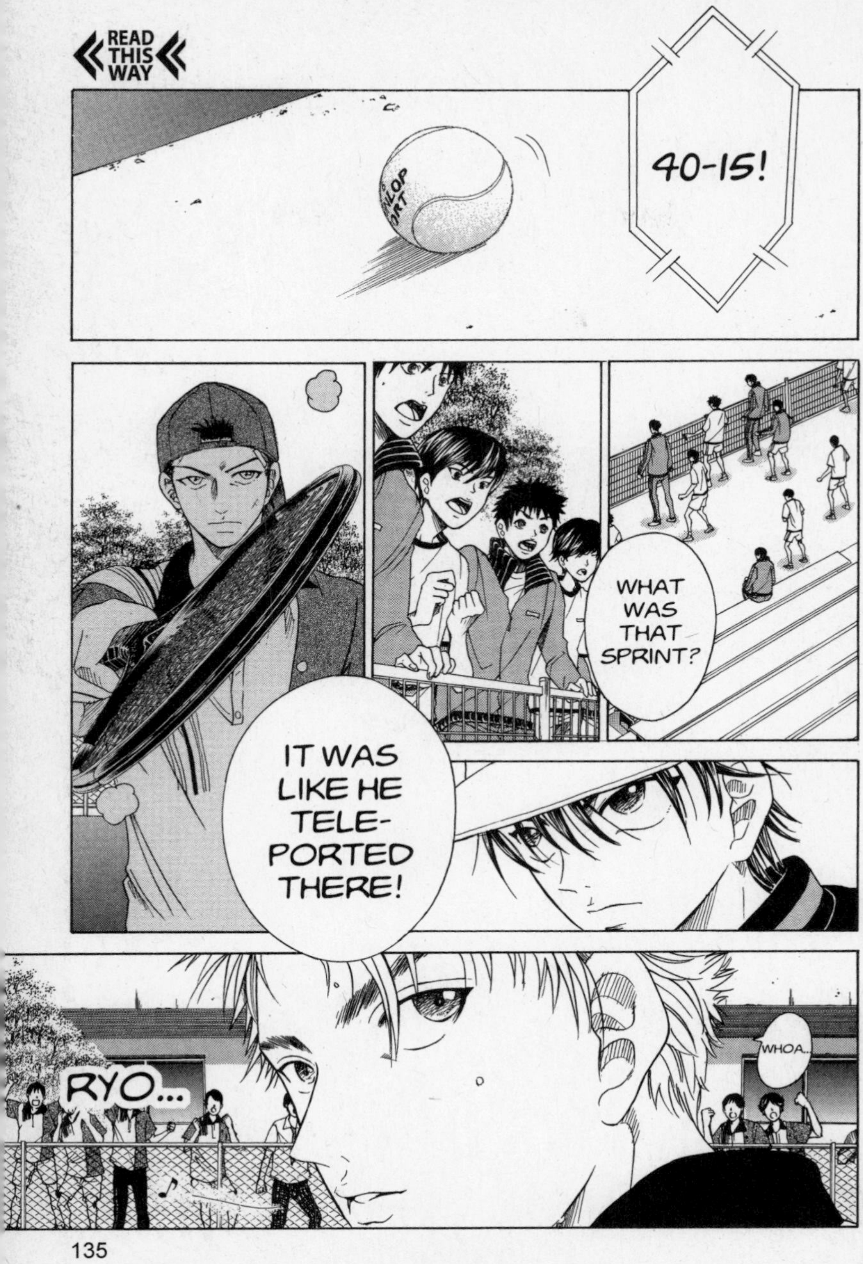

40-15!
WHAT WAS THAT SPRINT?
IT WAS LIKE HE TELE-PORTED THERE!
WHOA...
RYO...

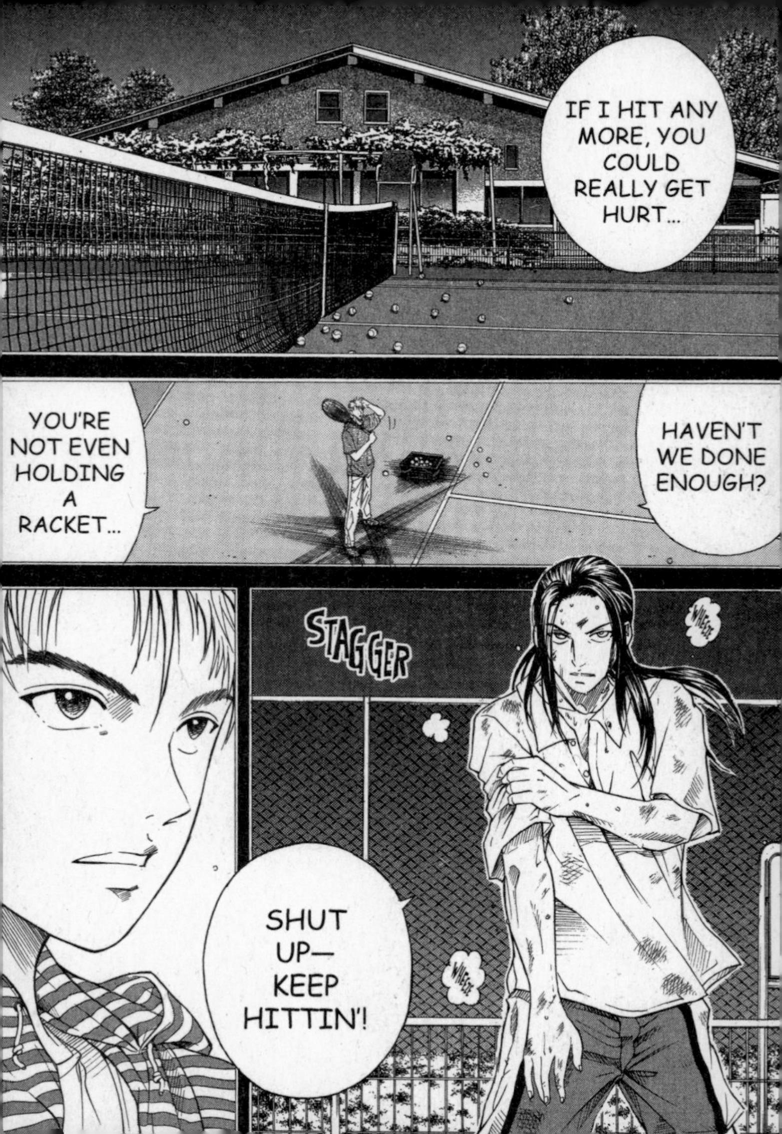
IF I HIT ANY MORE, YOU COULD REALLY GET HURT...
HAVEN'T WE DONE ENOUGH?
YOU'RE NOT EVEN HOLDING A RACKET...
STAGGER
WHEEZE
WHEEZE
SHUT UP— KEEP HITTIN'!

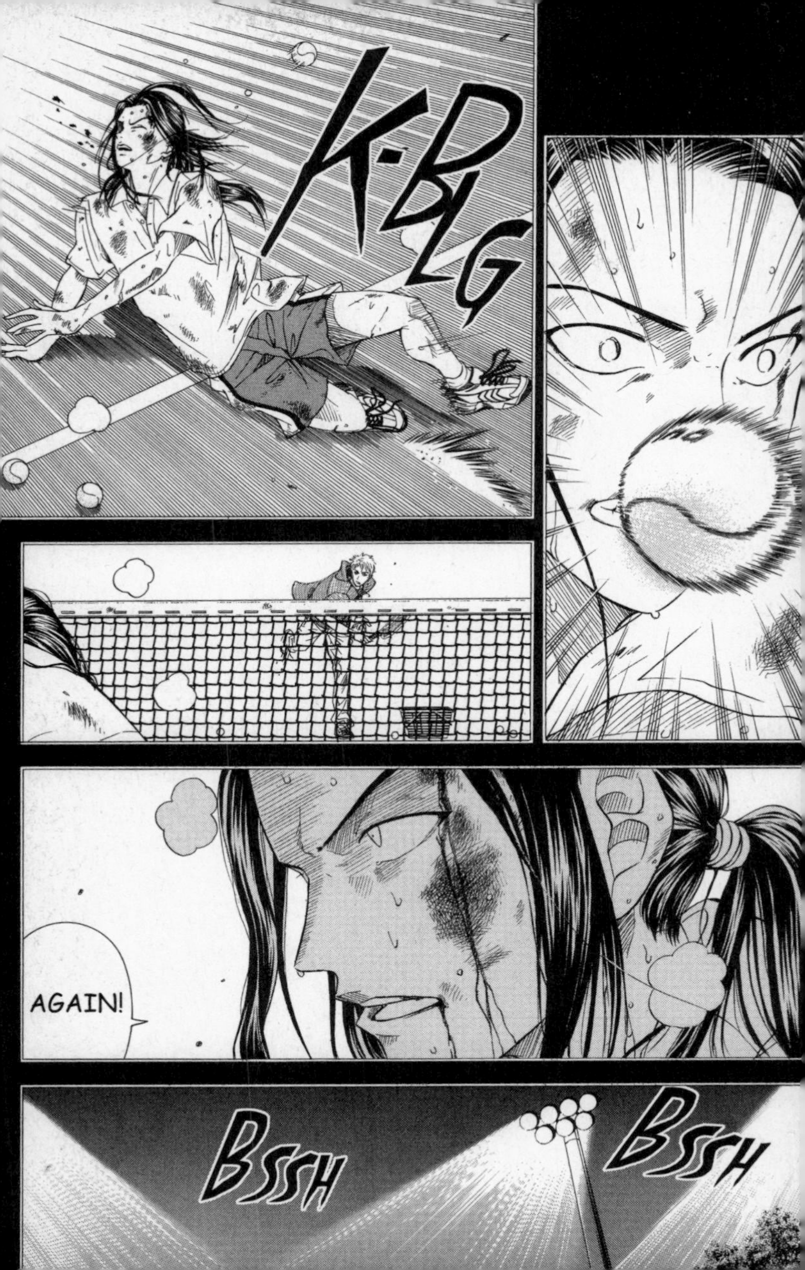
K-BLG
AGAIN!
BSSH
BSSH

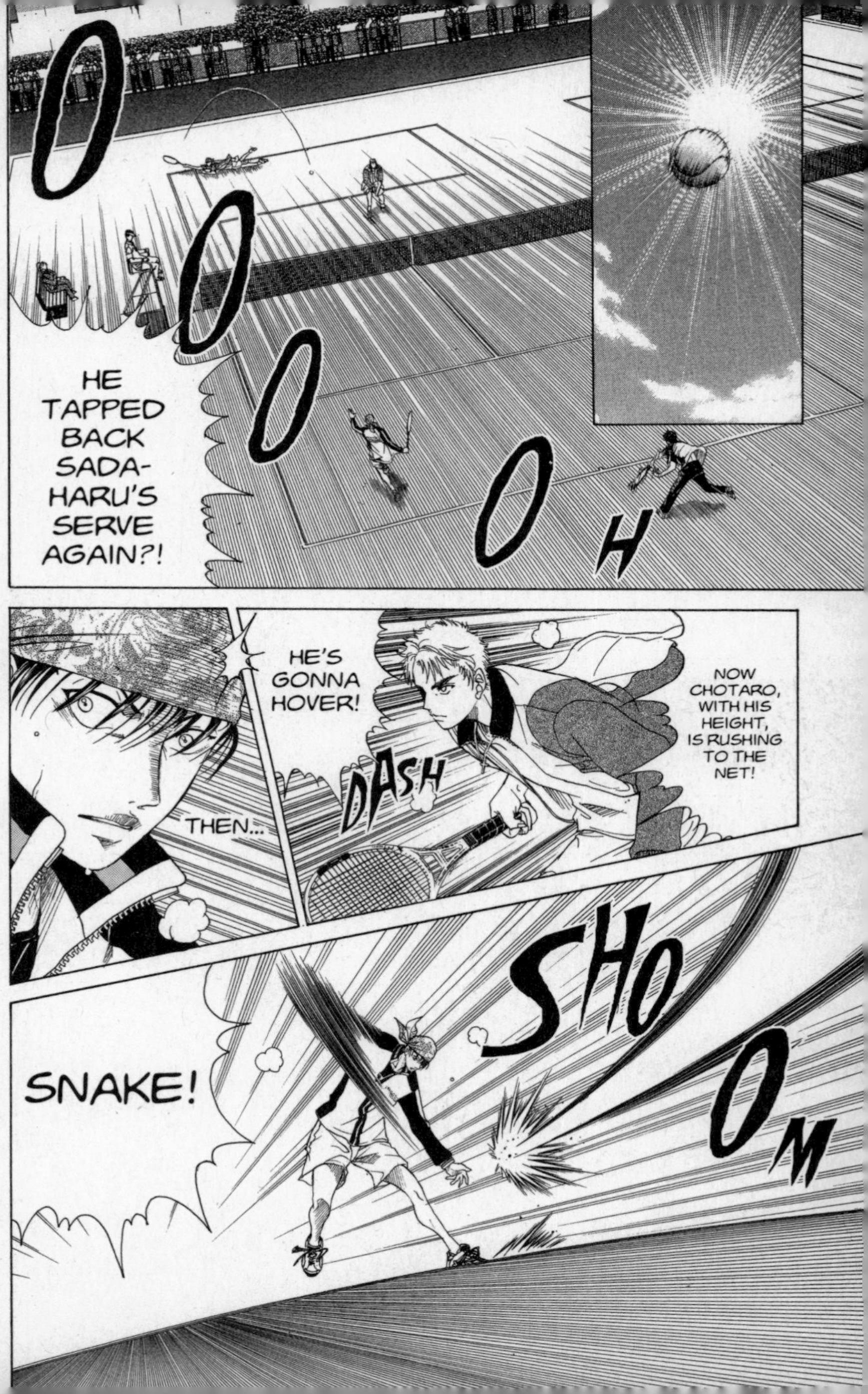
OOOOOH
HE TAPPED BACK SADAHARU'S SERVE AGAIN?!
NOW CHOTARO, WITH HIS HEIGHT, IS RUSHING TO THE NET!
DASH
HE'S GONNA HOVER!
THEN...
SHOOOM
SNAKE!

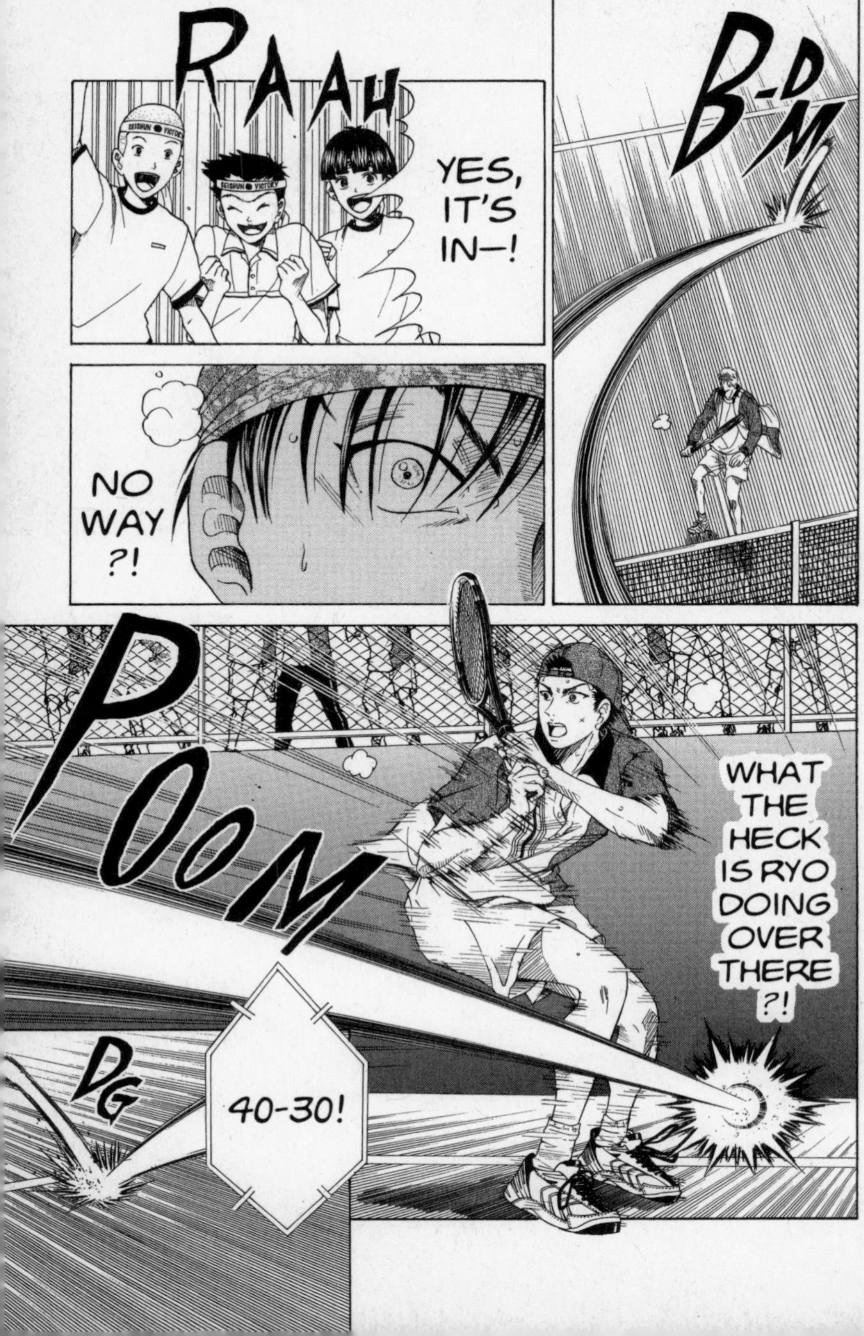
B-DM
RAAH
YES, IT'S IN—!
NO WAY?!
WHAT THE HECK IS RYO DOING OVER THERE?!
POOM
DG
40-30!

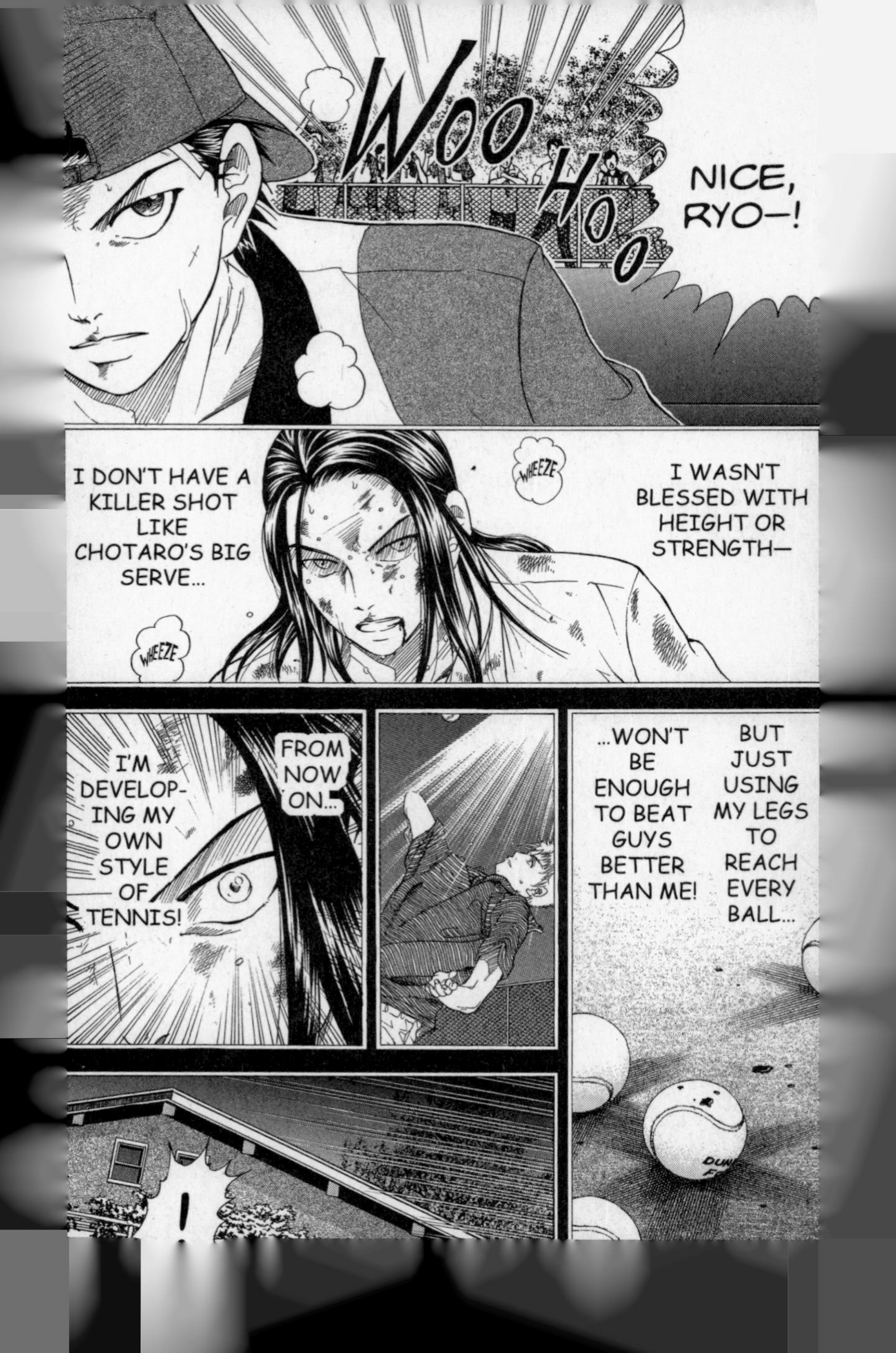
WOO HOO
NICE, RYO—!
I WASN'T BLESSED WITH HEIGHT OR STRENGTH—
WHEEZE
I DON'T HAVE A KILLER SHOT LIKE CHOTARO'S BIG SERVE...
WHEEZE
BUT JUST USING MY LEGS TO REACH EVERY BALL...
...WON'T BE ENOUGH TO BEAT GUYS BETTER THAN ME!
FROM NOW ON...
I'M DEVELOP-ING MY OWN STYLE OF TENNIS!
!

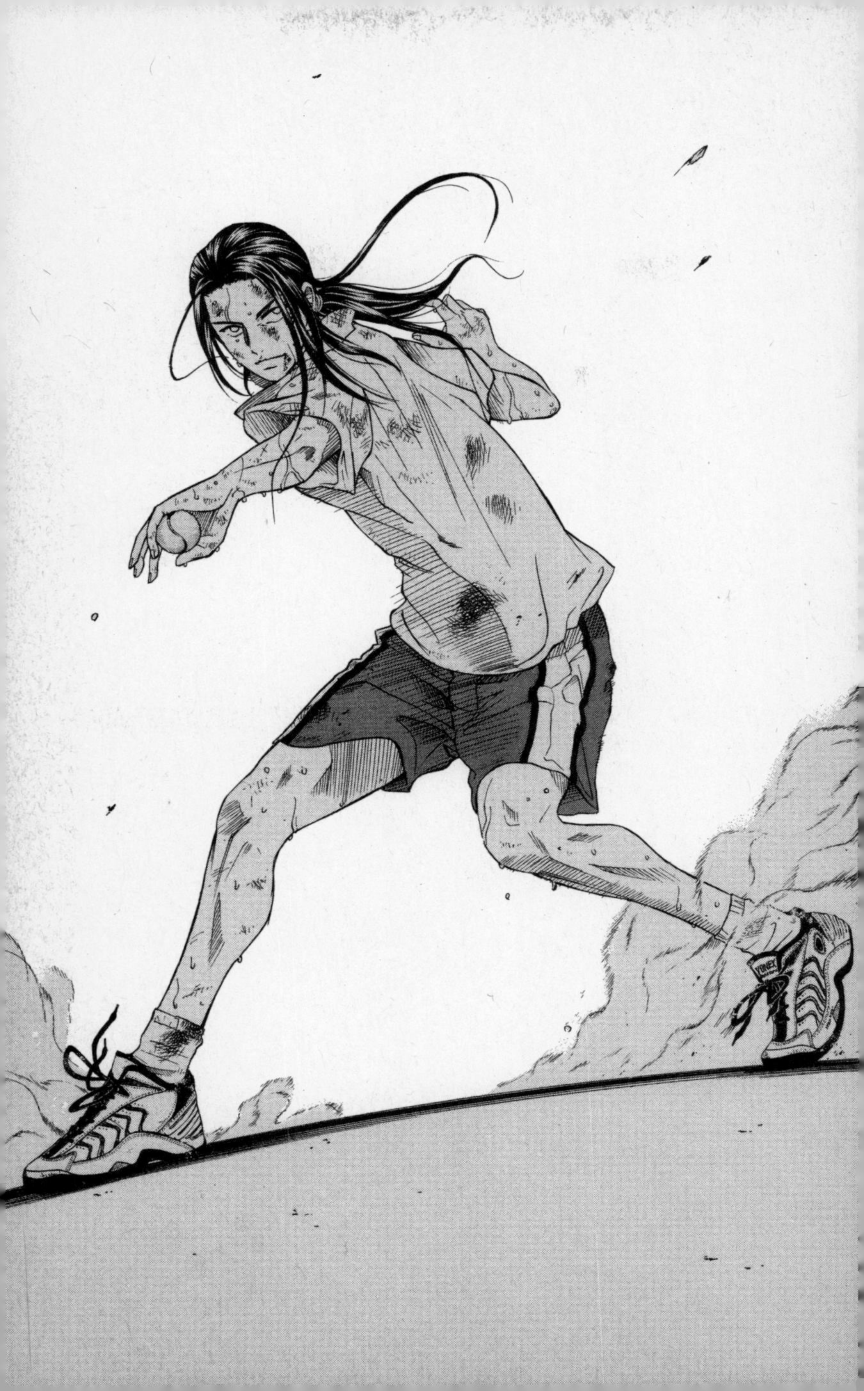

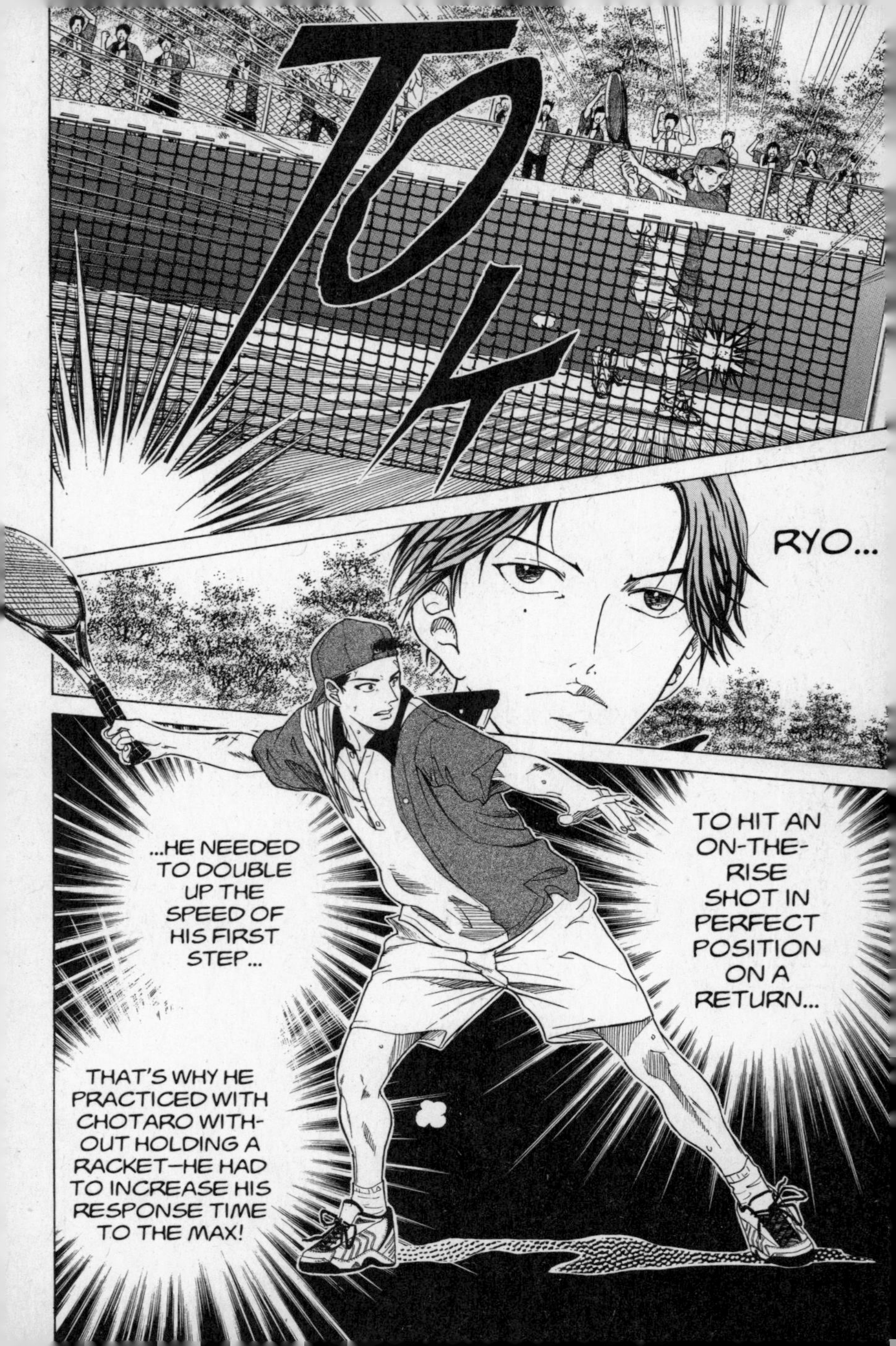
RYO...
TO HIT AN ON-THE-RISE SHOT IN PERFECT POSITION ON A RETURN...
...HE NEEDED TO DOUBLE UP THE SPEED OF HIS FIRST STEP...
THAT'S WHY HE PRACTICED WITH CHOTARO WITH-OUT HOLDING A RACKET—HE HAD TO INCREASE HIS RESPONSE TIME TO THE MAX!

READ THIS WAY

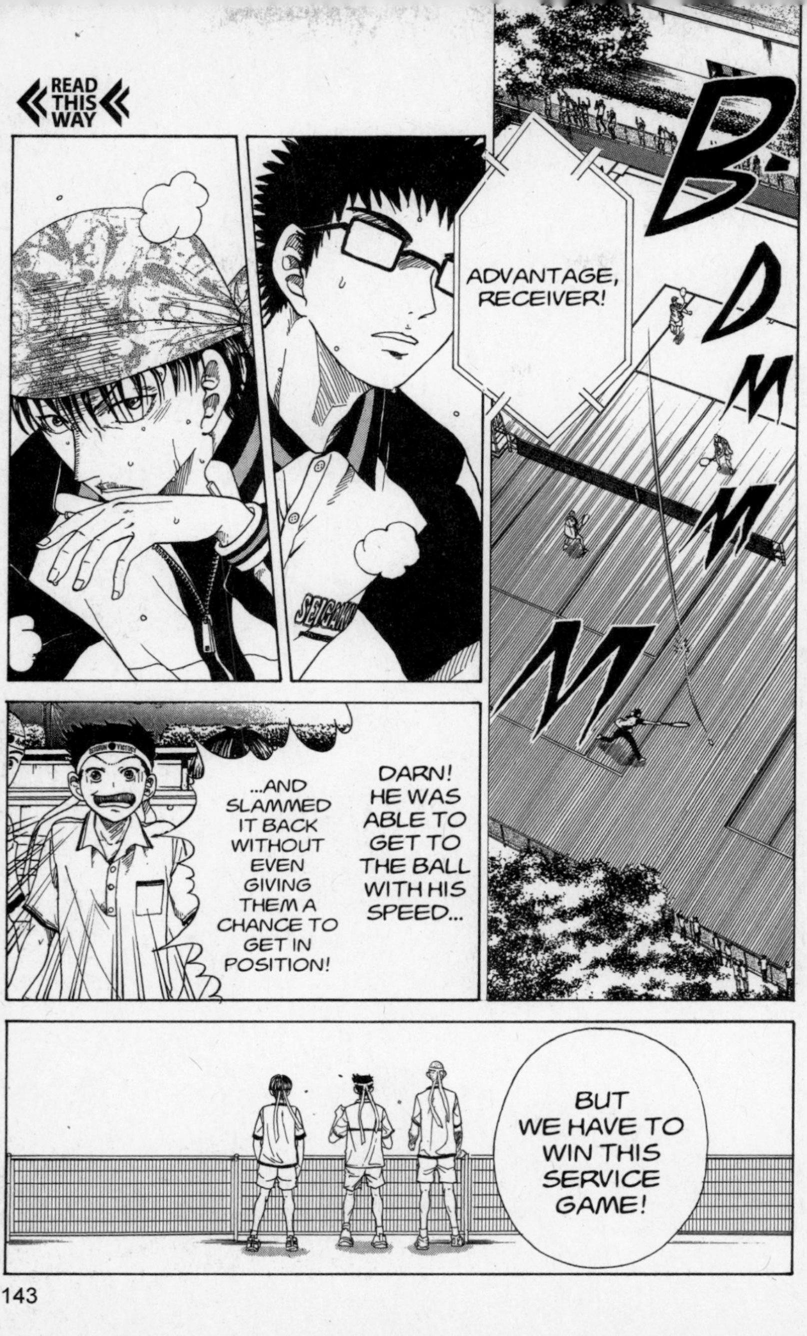
B-DMMM
ADVANTAGE, RECEIVER!
DARN! HE WAS ABLE TO GET TO THE BALL WITH HIS SPEED...
...AND SLAMMED IT BACK WITHOUT EVEN GIVING THEM A CHANCE TO GET IN POSITION!
BUT WE HAVE TO WIN THIS SERVICE GAME!

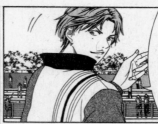

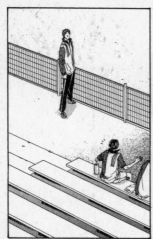

NO WONDER THEY BEAT YOU TWO AT DOUBLES!
NO!
TWITCH
WE JUST UNDER-ESTIMATED RYO, THAT'S ALL!
WE DIDN'T TAKE THEM SERIOUSLY...
UNDER-ESTIMATE? THAT'S EXACTLY WHY YOU LOST!
IDIOT!
GAME! HYOTEI LEADS 2 GAMES TO LOVE!
YEAH— HYOTEI! HYOTEI!

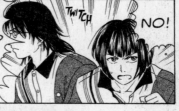

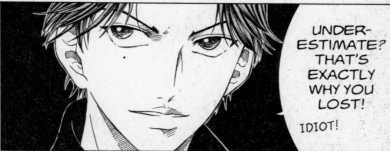

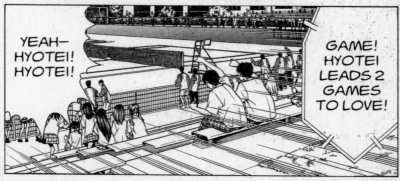

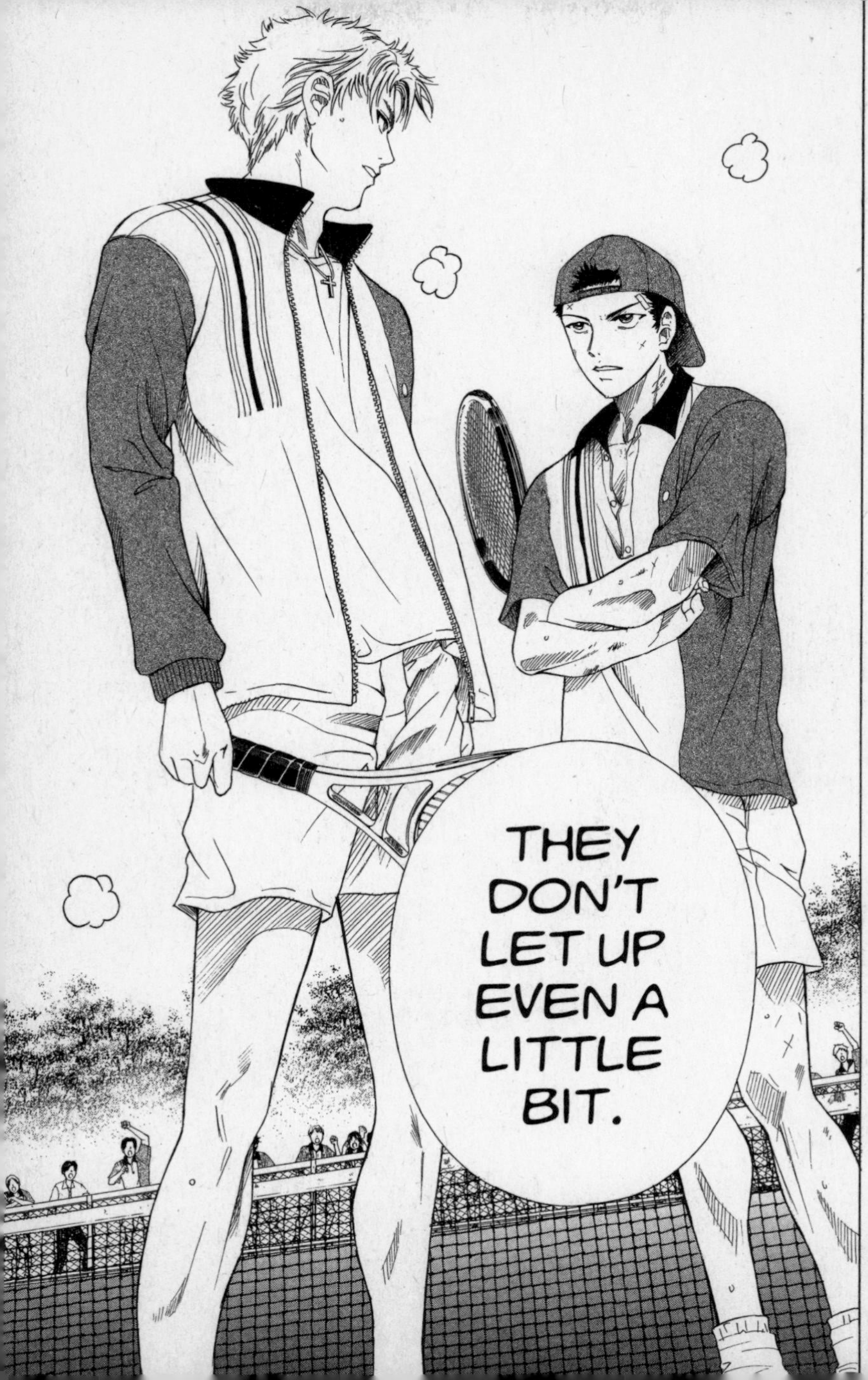
THEY DON'T LET UP EVEN A LITTLE BIT.

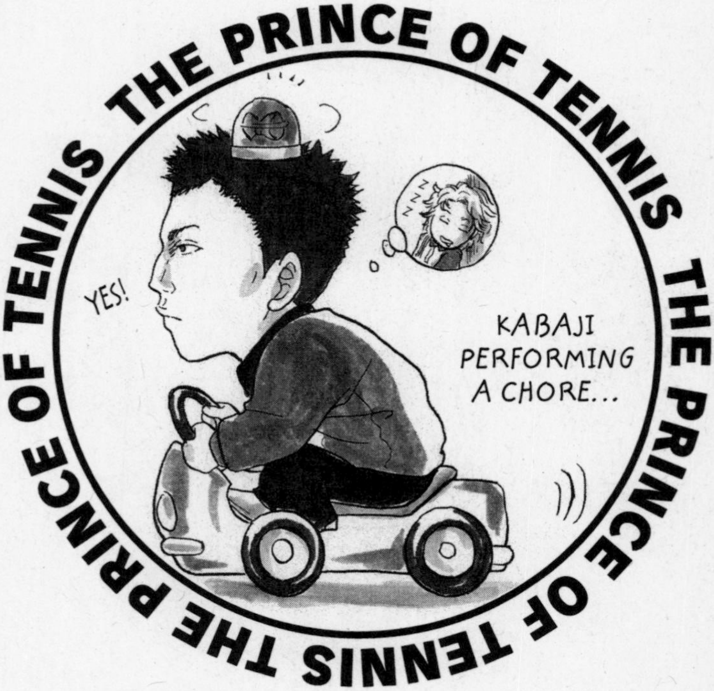
THE PRINCE OF TENNIS THE PRINCE OF TENNIS THE PRINCE OF TENNIS
YES!
KABAJI PERFORMING A CHORE...

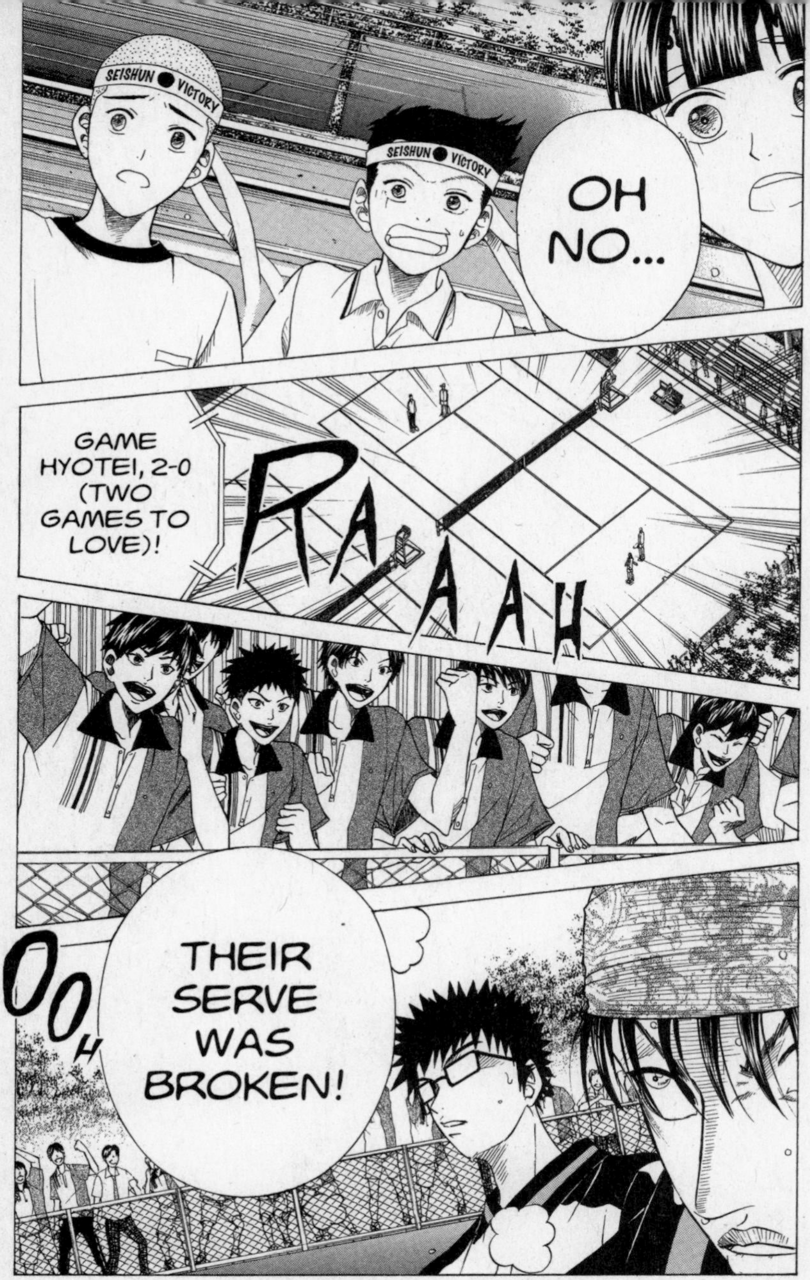
OH NO...
RAAAH
GAME HYOTEI, 2-0 (TWO GAMES TO LOVE)!
THEIR SERVE WAS BROKEN!
OOH

GENIUS 131: TRUST

GENIUS 131: TRUST

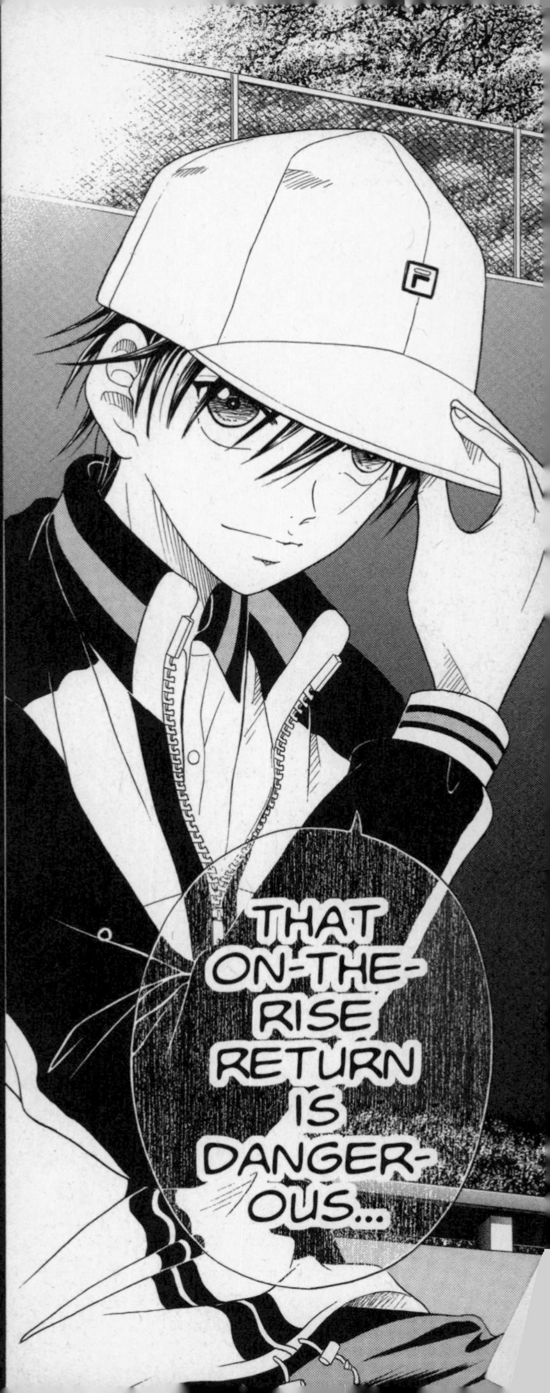
THAT ON-THE-RISE RETURN IS DANGER-OUS...

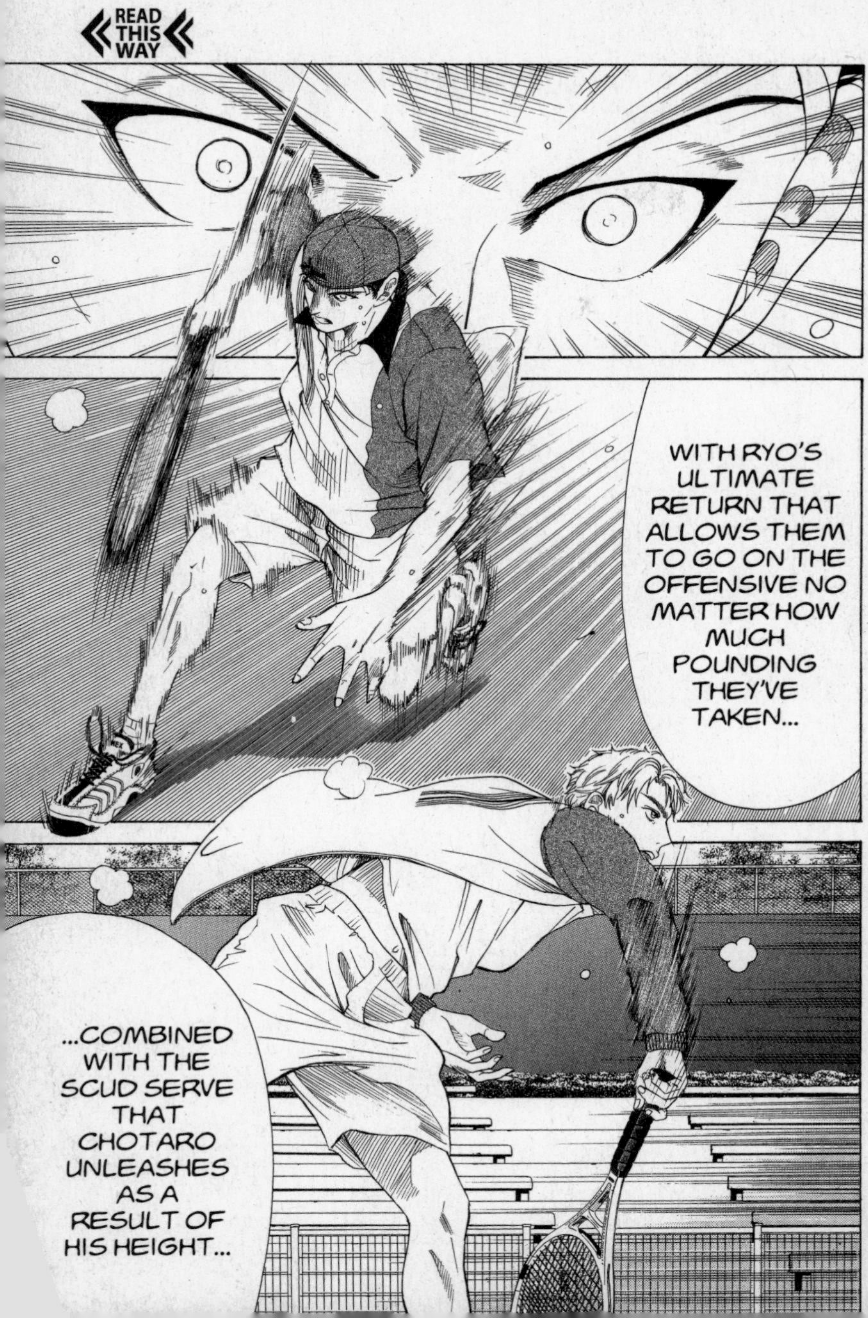
READ THIS WAY
WITH RYO'S ULTIMATE RETURN THAT ALLOWS THEM TO GO ON THE OFFENSIVE NO MATTER HOW MUCH POUNDING THEY'VE TAKEN...
...COMBINED WITH THE SCUD SERVE THAT CHOTARO UNLEASHES AS A RESULT OF HIS HEIGHT...

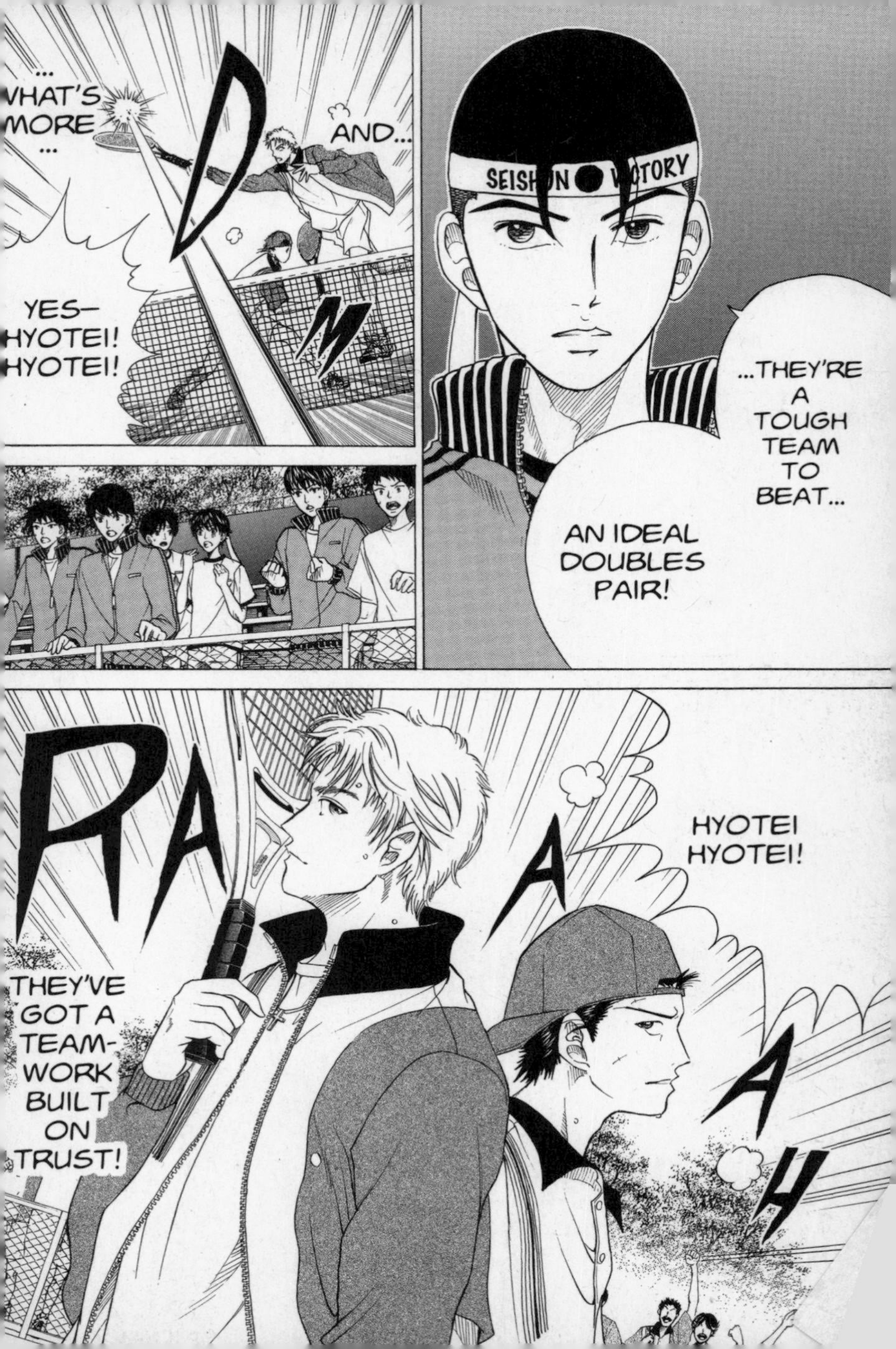
...THEY'RE A TOUGH TEAM TO BEAT...
AN IDEAL DOUBLES PAIR!
AND...
... WHAT'S MORE ...
DM
YES— HYOTEI! HYOTEI!
HYOTEI HYOTEI!
RAAAH
THEY'VE GOT A TEAM-WORK BUILT ON TRUST!

READ THIS WAY

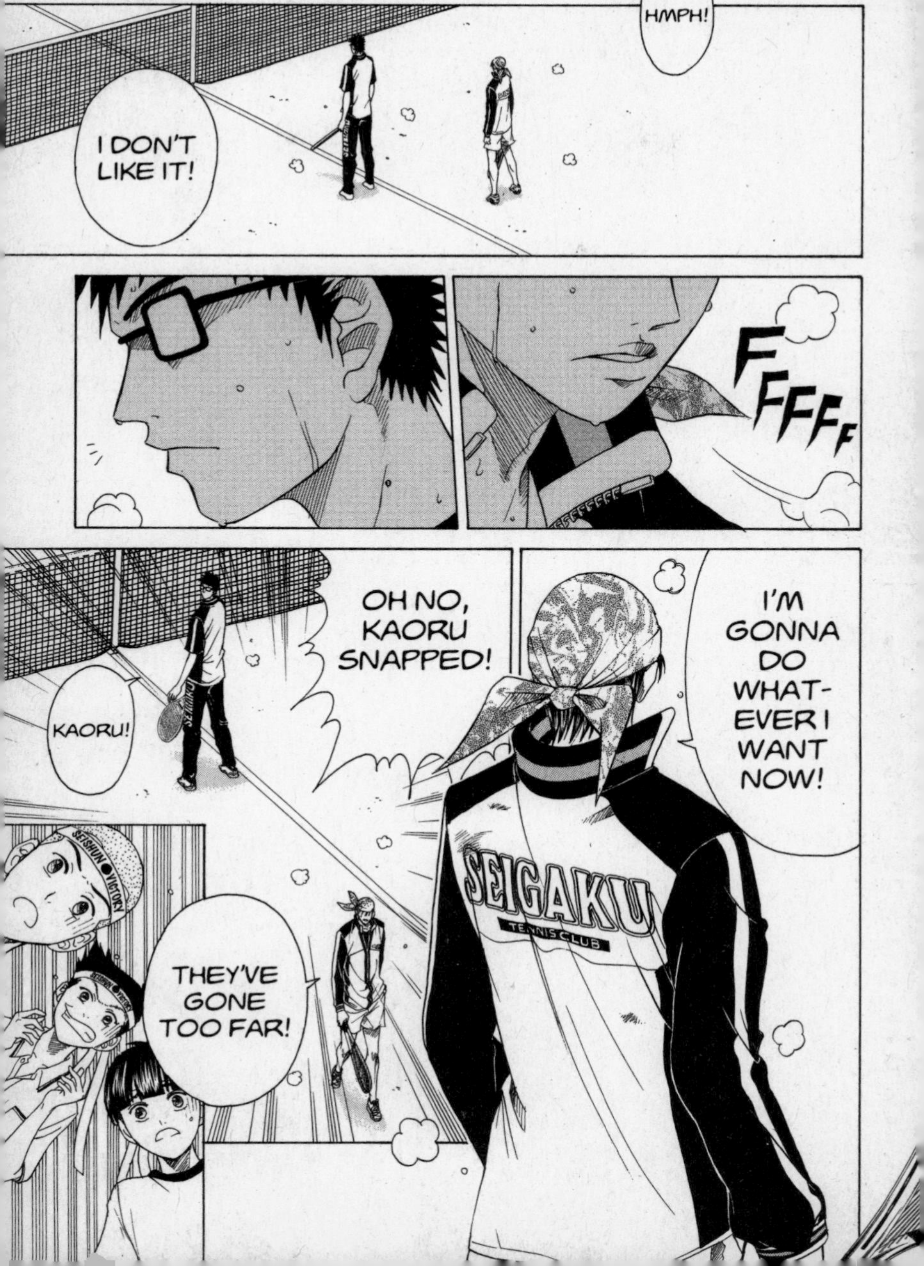
HMPH!
I DON'T LIKE IT!
FFFFF
I'M GONNA DO WHATEVER I WANT NOW!
OH NO, KAORU SNAPPED!
KAORU!
THEY'VE GONE TOO FAR!
SEIGAKU TENNIS CLUB

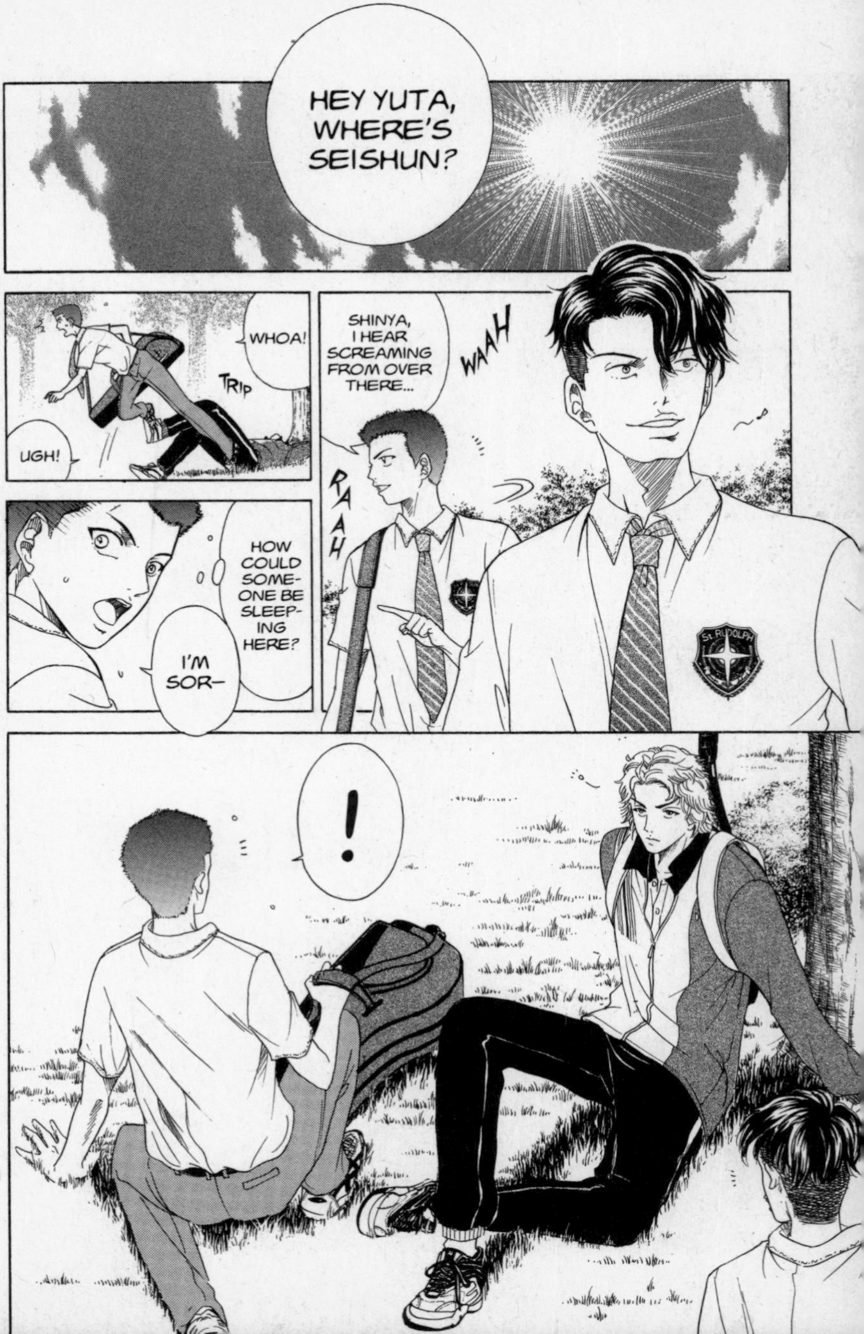
HEY YUTA, WHERE'S SEISHUN?
SHINYA, I HEAR SCREAMING FROM OVER THERE...
WAAH
RAAAH
WHOA!
TRIP
UGH!
HOW COULD SOMEONE BE SLEEPING HERE?
I'M SOR–
!

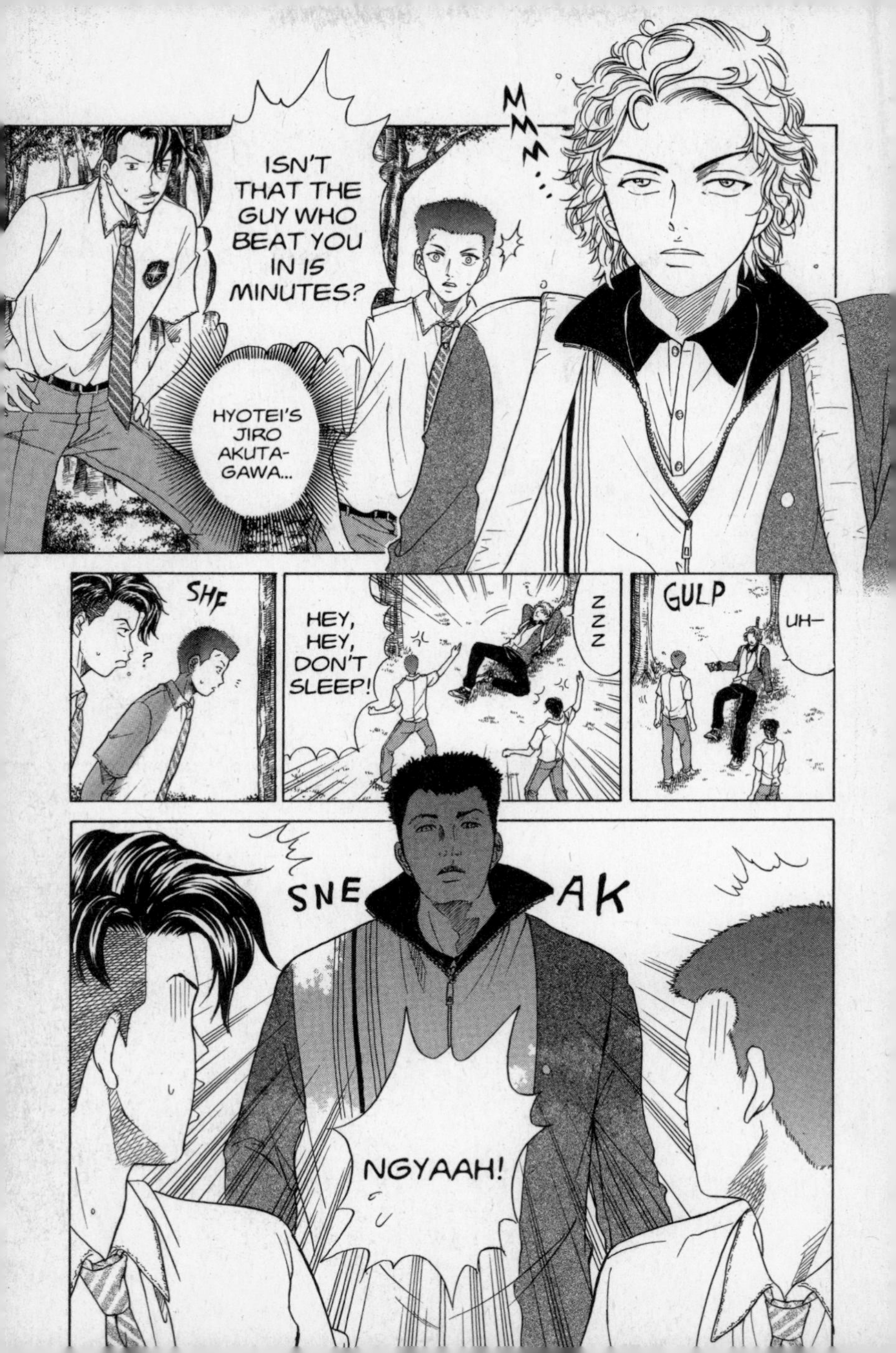
MMM...
ISN'T THAT THE GUY WHO BEAT YOU IN 15 MINUTES?
HYOTEI'S JIRO AKUTA-GAWA...
UH—
GULP
ZZZ
HEY, HEY, DON'T SLEEP!
SHF
SNEAK
NGYAAH!

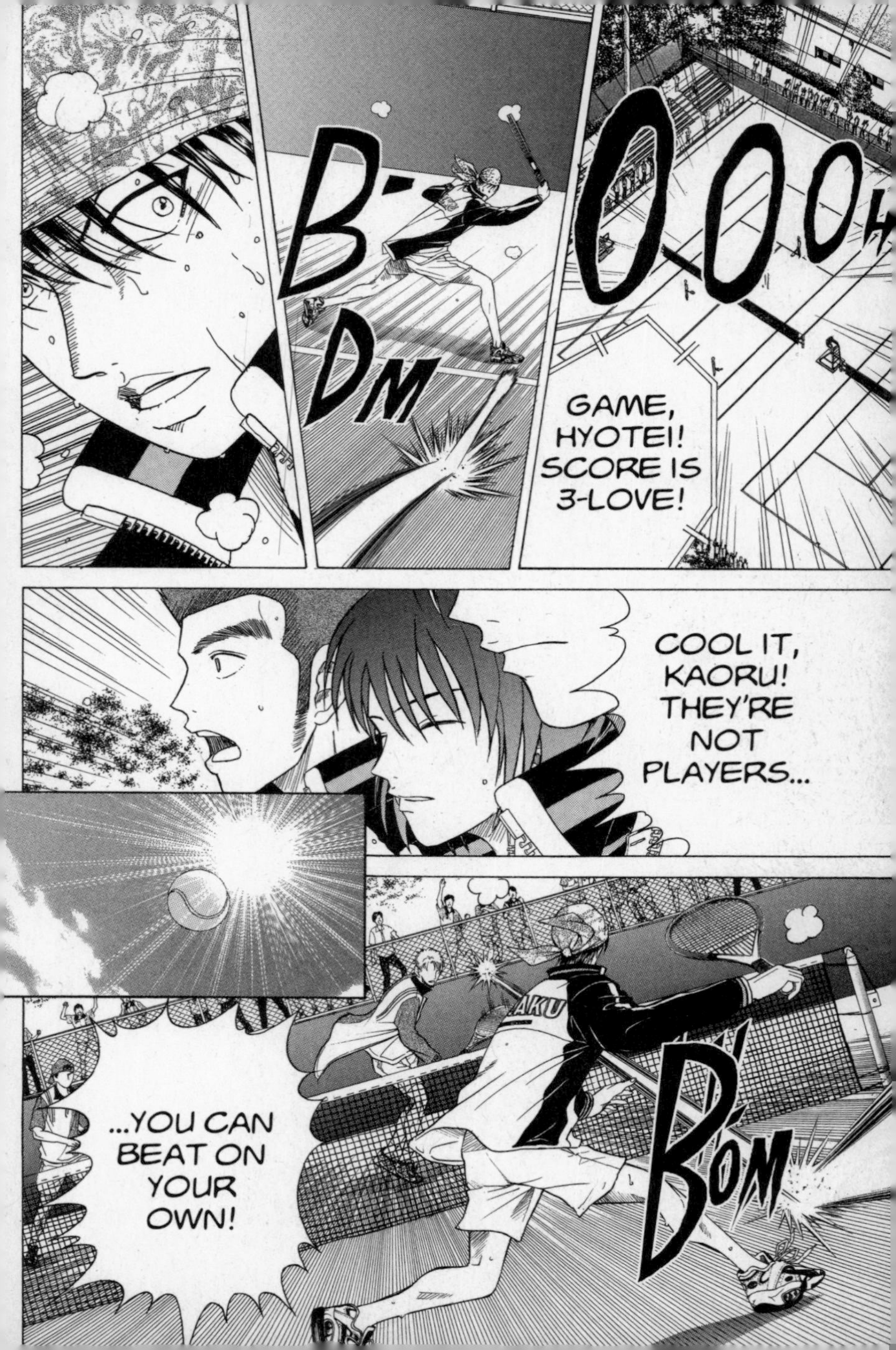
O-O-OOH
GAME, HYOTEI! SCORE IS 3-LOVE!
B-DM
COOL IT, KAORU! THEY'RE NOT PLAYERS...
BOM
...YOU CAN BEAT ON YOUR OWN!

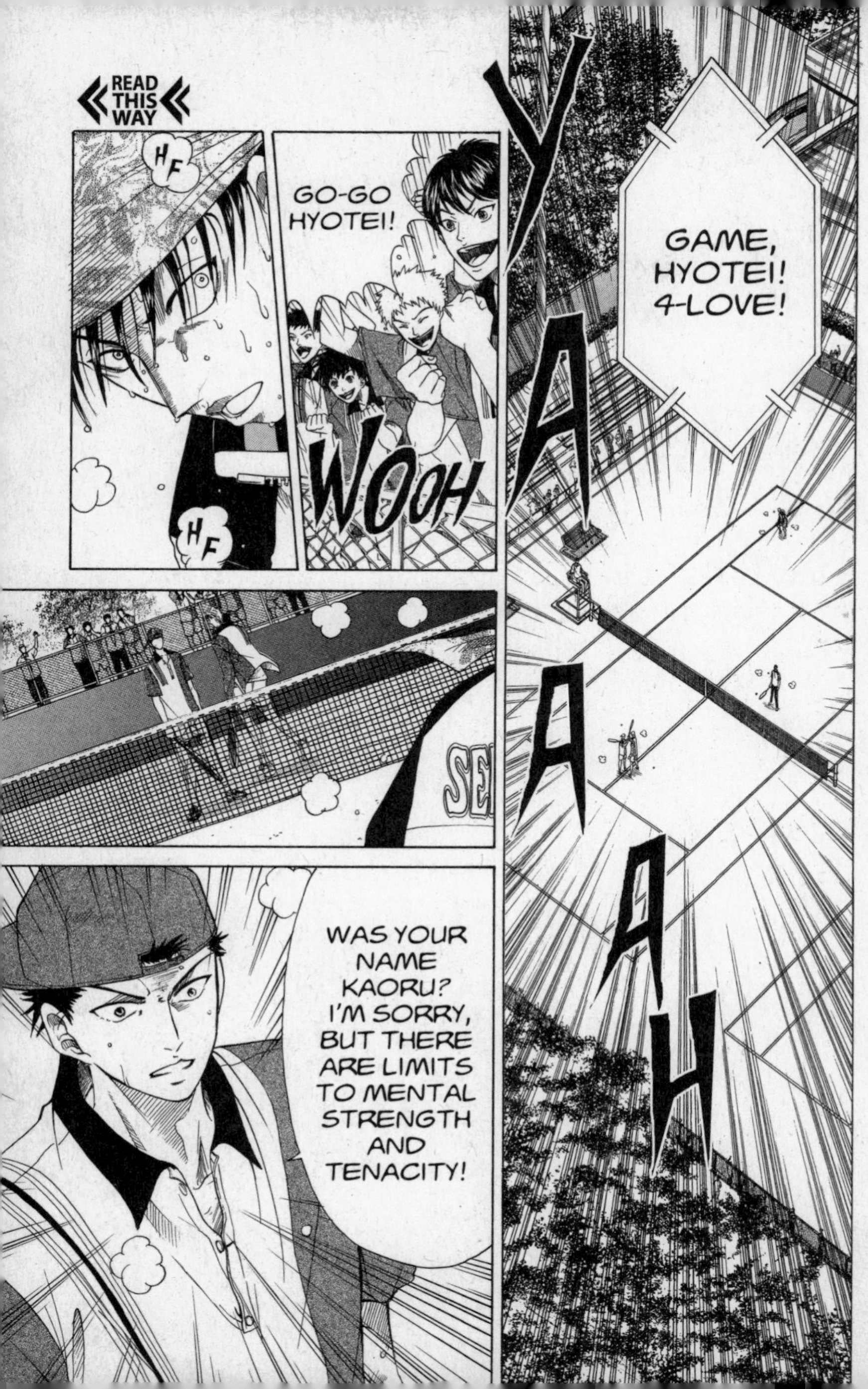
READ THIS WAY
YAAAAH
GAME, HYOTEI! 4-LOVE!
GO-GO HYOTEI!
WOOH
HF
HF
WAS YOUR NAME KAORU? I'M SORRY, BUT THERE ARE LIMITS TO MENTAL STRENGTH AND TENACITY!

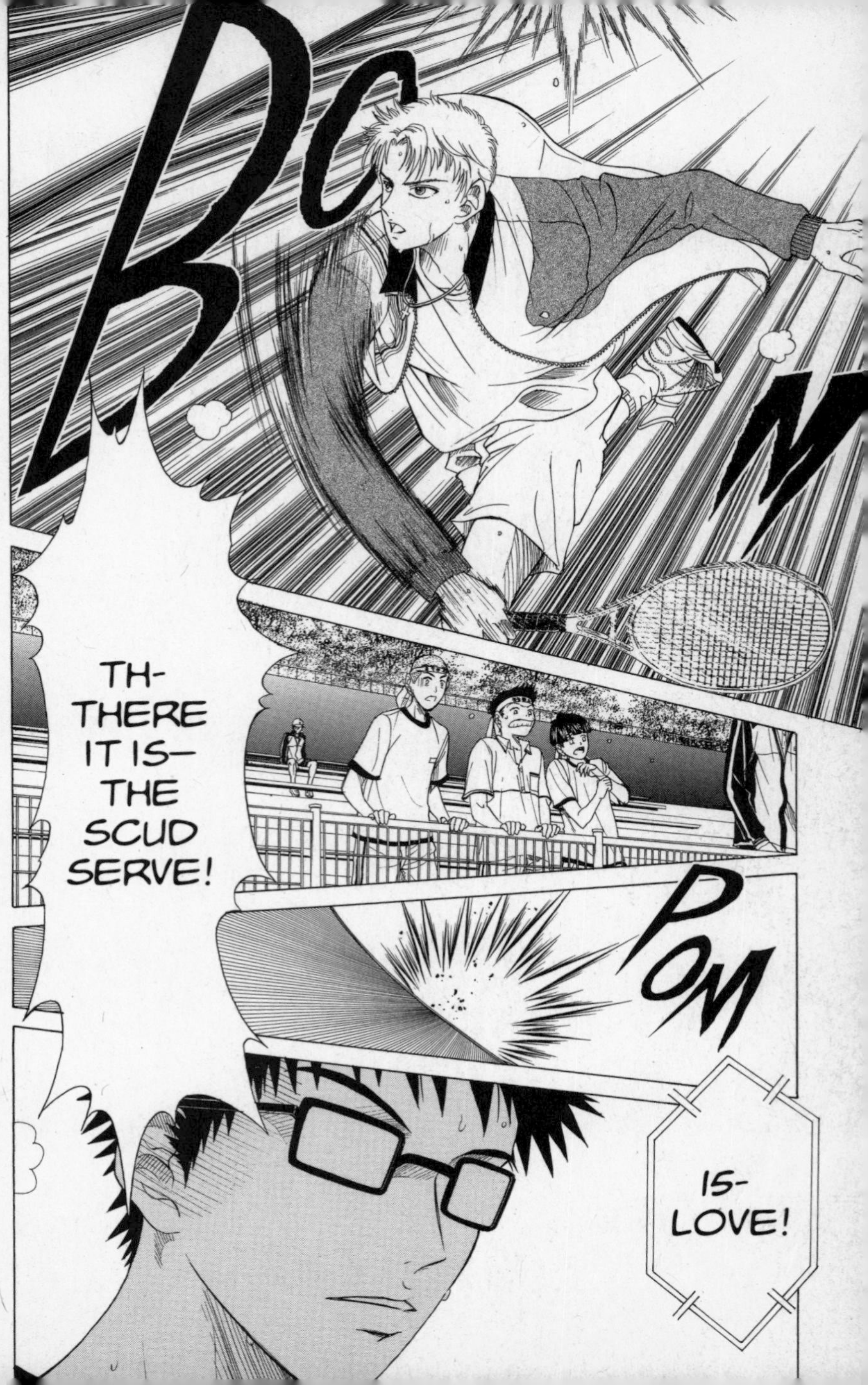
BOOM
TH-THERE IT IS—THE SCUD SERVE!
POM
15-LOVE!

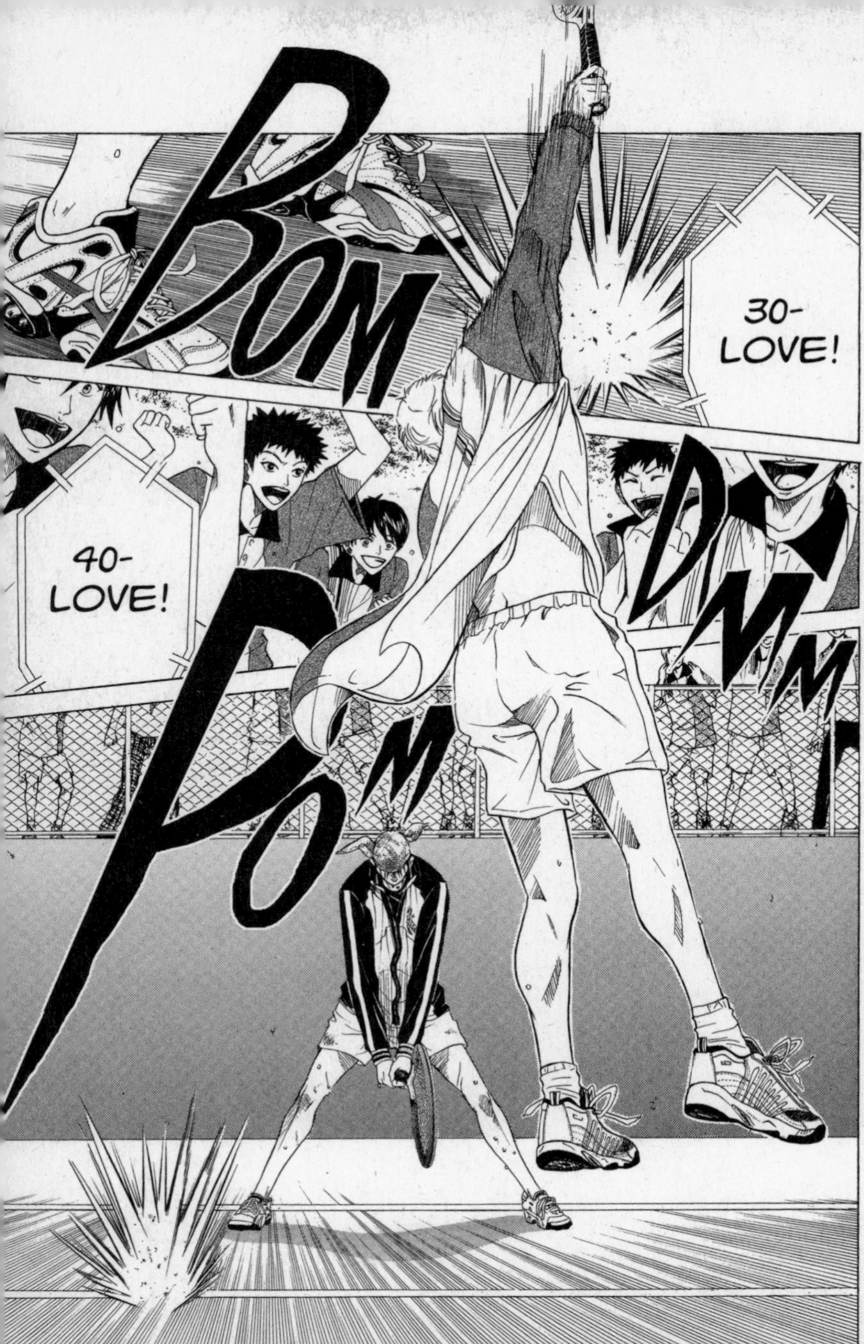
30-LOVE!
BOOM
DMMM
40-LOVE!
POMM

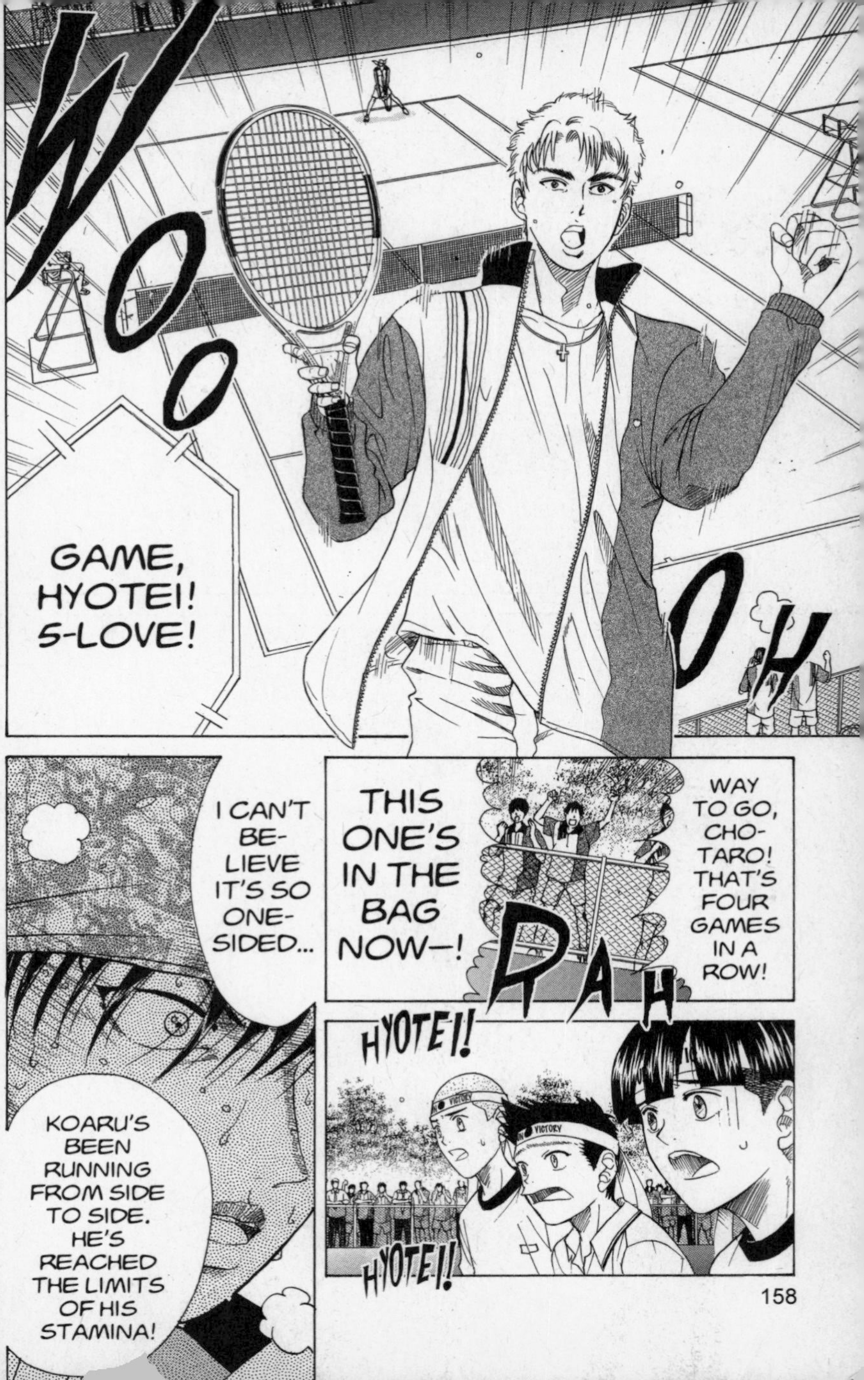
WOOOOH
GAME, HYOTEI! 5-LOVE!
WAY TO GO, CHO-TARO! THAT'S FOUR GAMES IN A ROW!
THIS ONE'S IN THE BAG NOW—!
DAH
HYOTEI!
HYOTEI!
I CAN'T BE-LIEVE IT'S SO ONE-SIDED...
KOARU'S BEEN RUNNING FROM SIDE TO SIDE. HE'S REACHED THE LIMITS OF HIS STAMINA!

READ THIS WAY

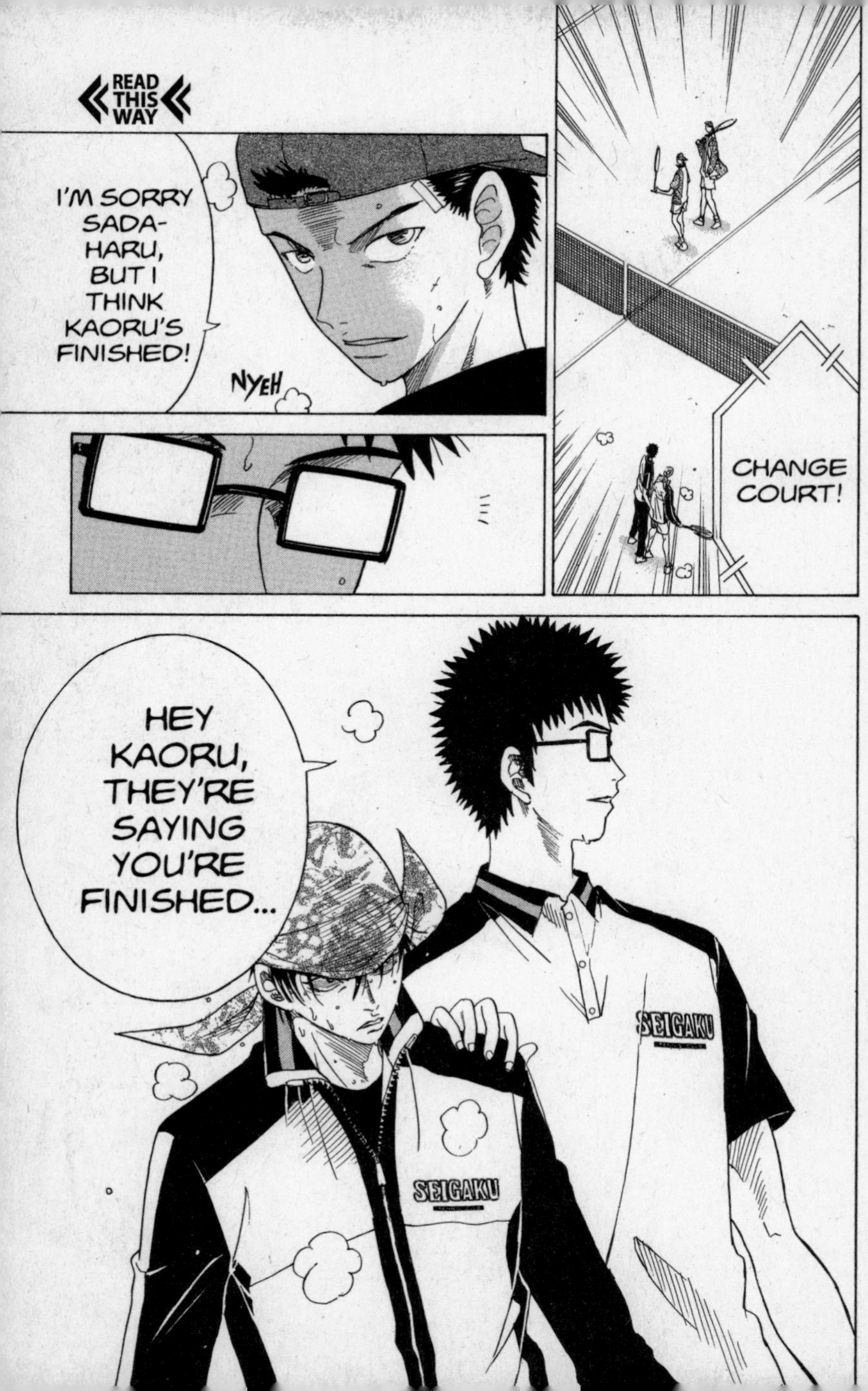

CHANGE COURT!
I'M SORRY SADAHARU, BUT I THINK KAORU'S FINISHED!
NYEH
HEY KAORU, THEY'RE SAYING YOU'RE FINISHED...

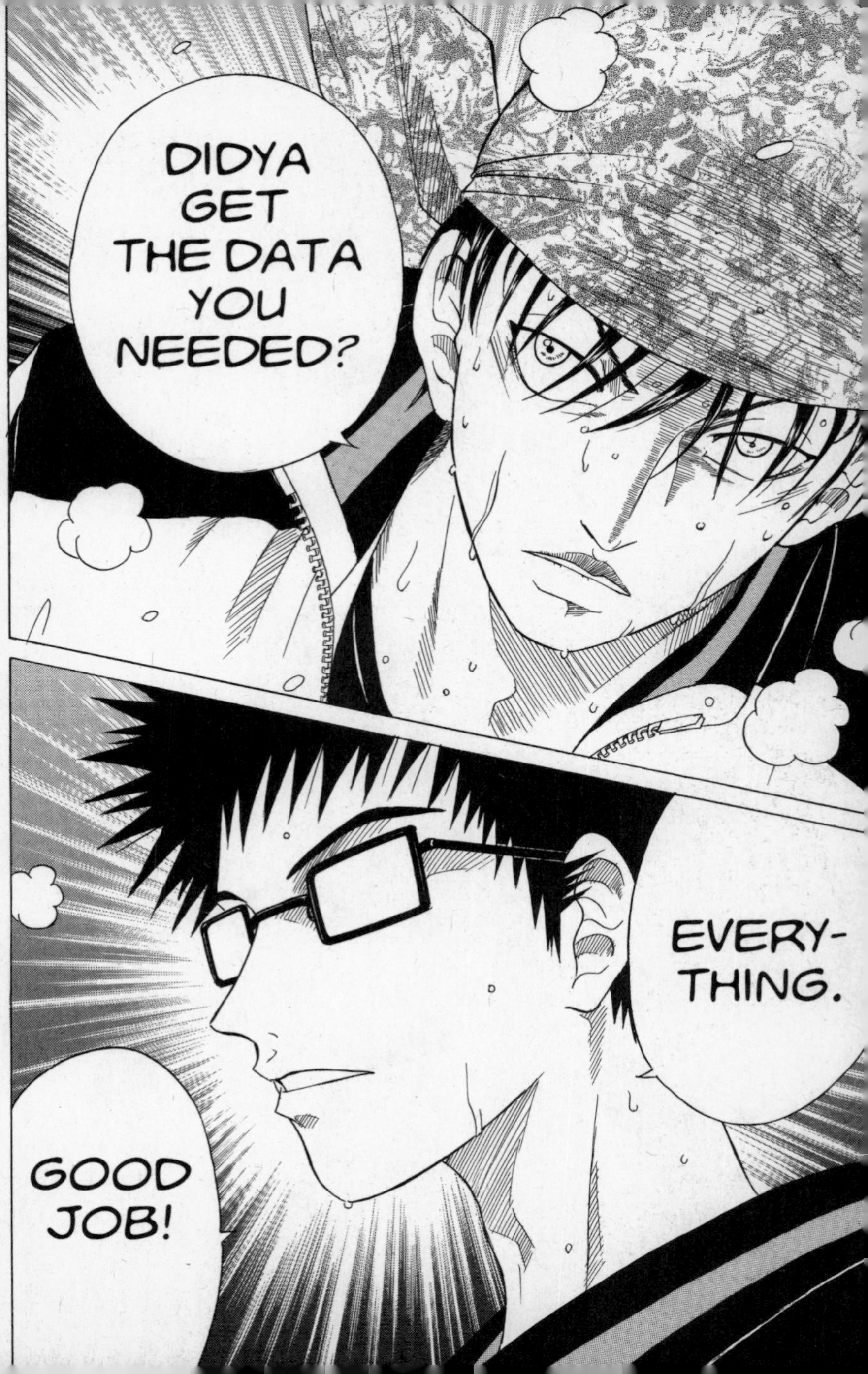
DIDYA GET THE DATA YOU NEEDED?
EVERY-THING.
GOOD JOB!

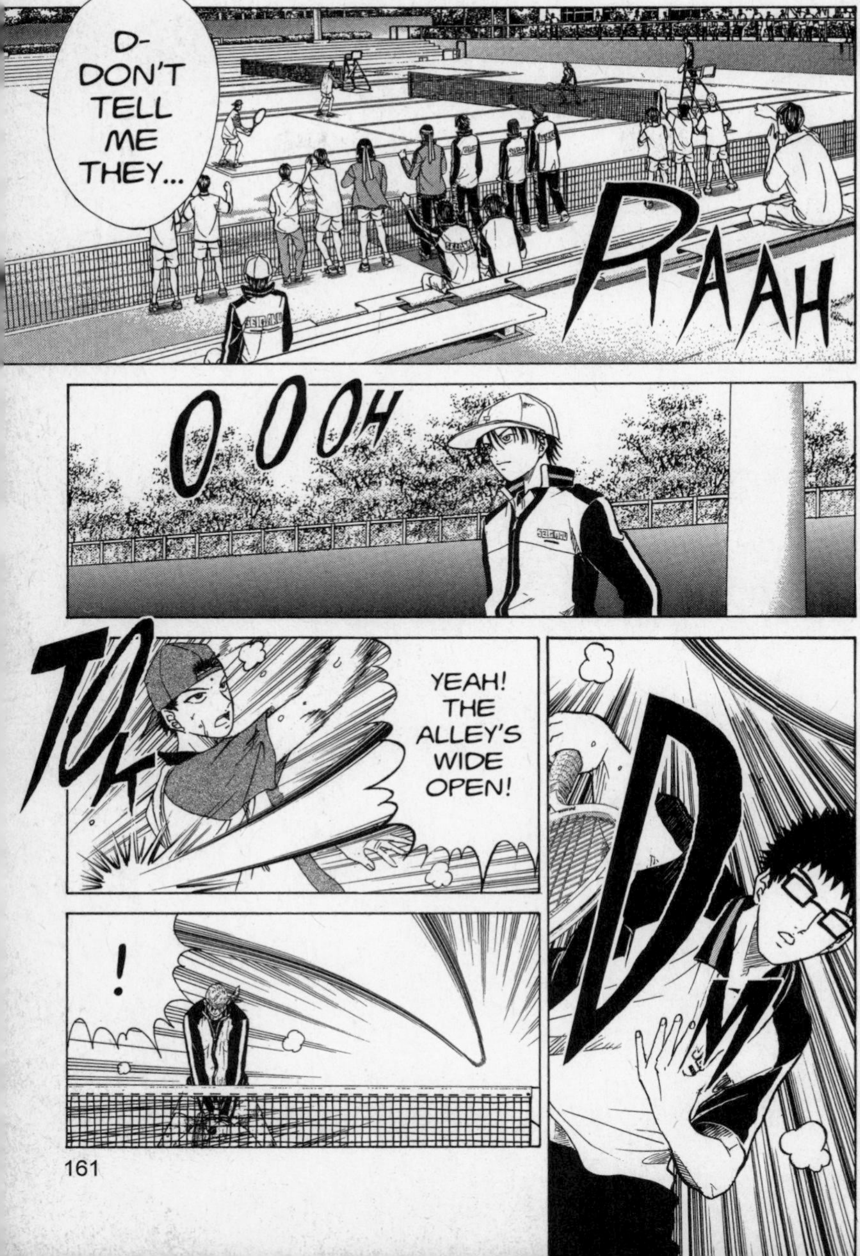
D-
DON'T
TELL
ME
THEY...
RAAH
OOOH
TOK
YEAH! THE ALLEY'S WIDE OPEN!
!

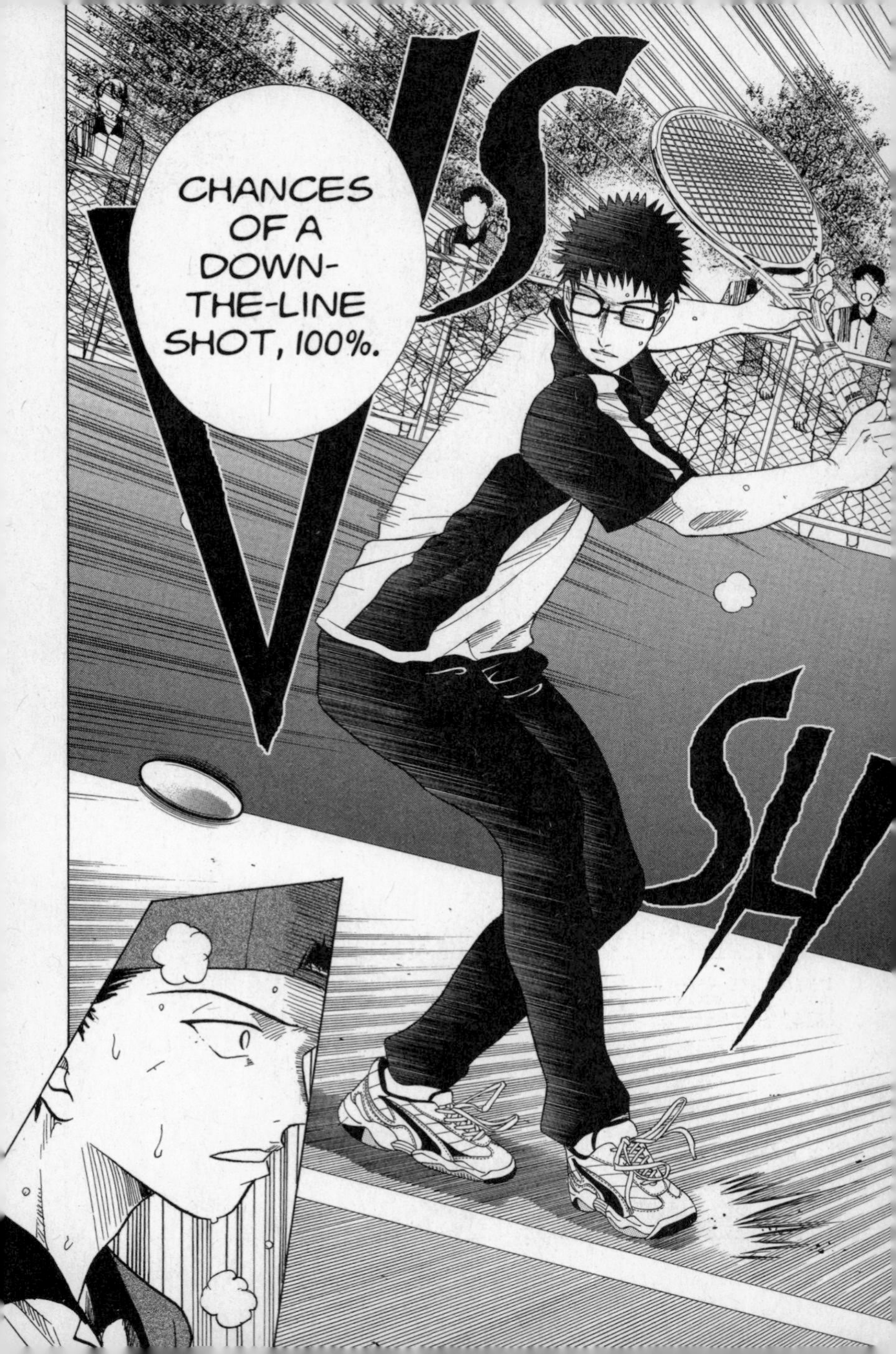
VS
CHANCES OF A DOWN-THE-LINE SHOT, 100%.
SH

READ THIS WAY

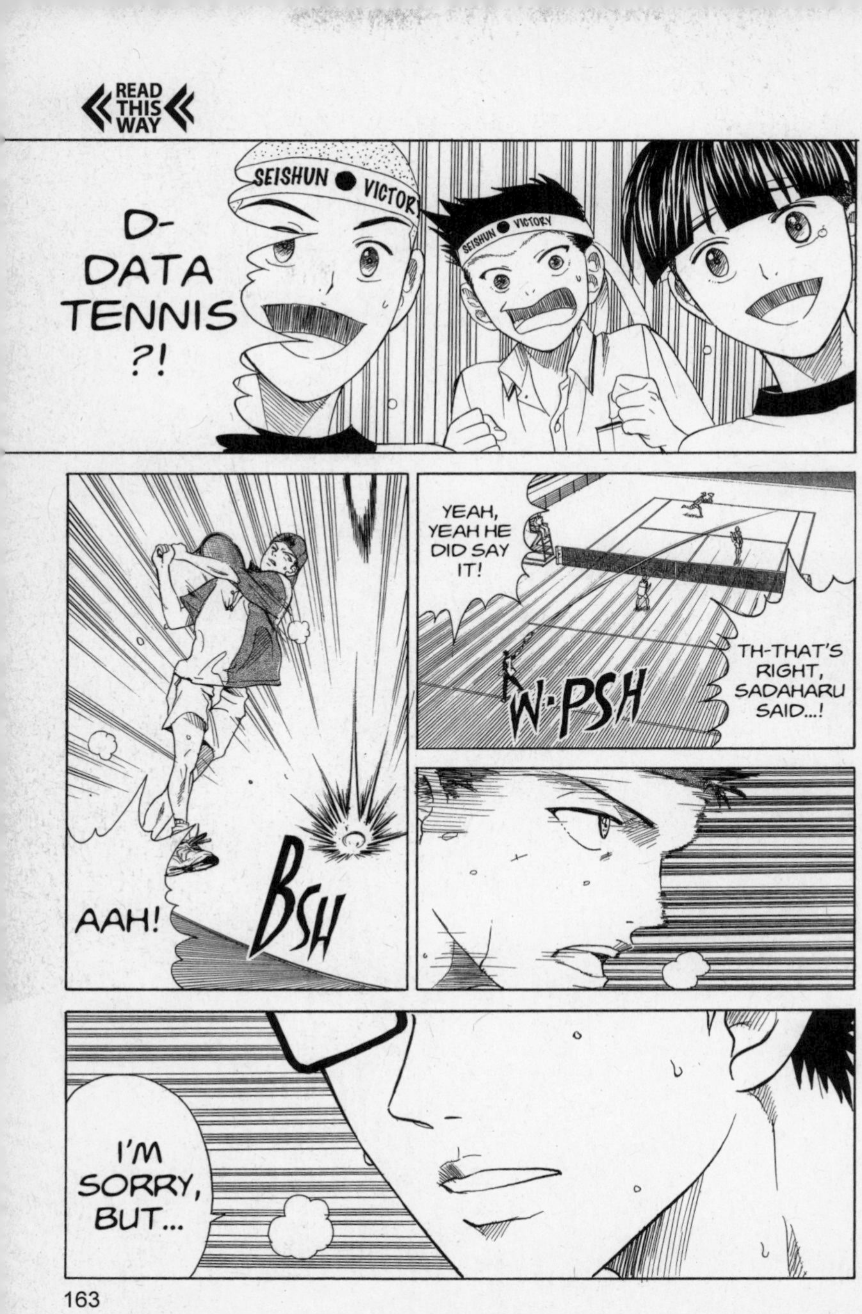
D-DATA TENNIS ?!
SEISHUN VICTORY
TH-THAT'S RIGHT, SADAHARU SAID...!
YEAH, YEAH HE DID SAY IT!
W-PSH
BSH
AAH!
I'M SORRY, BUT...

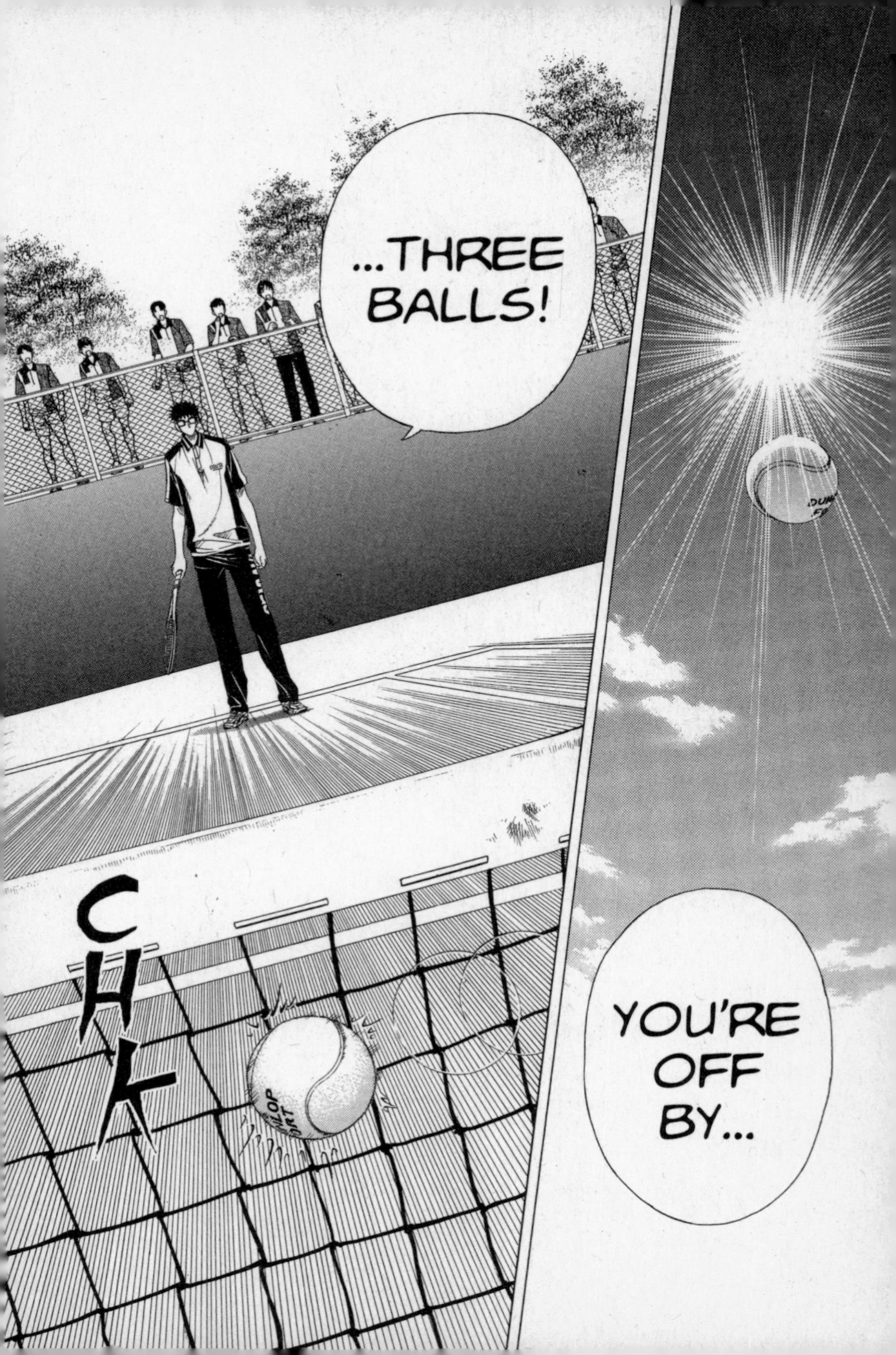
YOU'RE OFF BY...
...THREE BALLS!
CHK

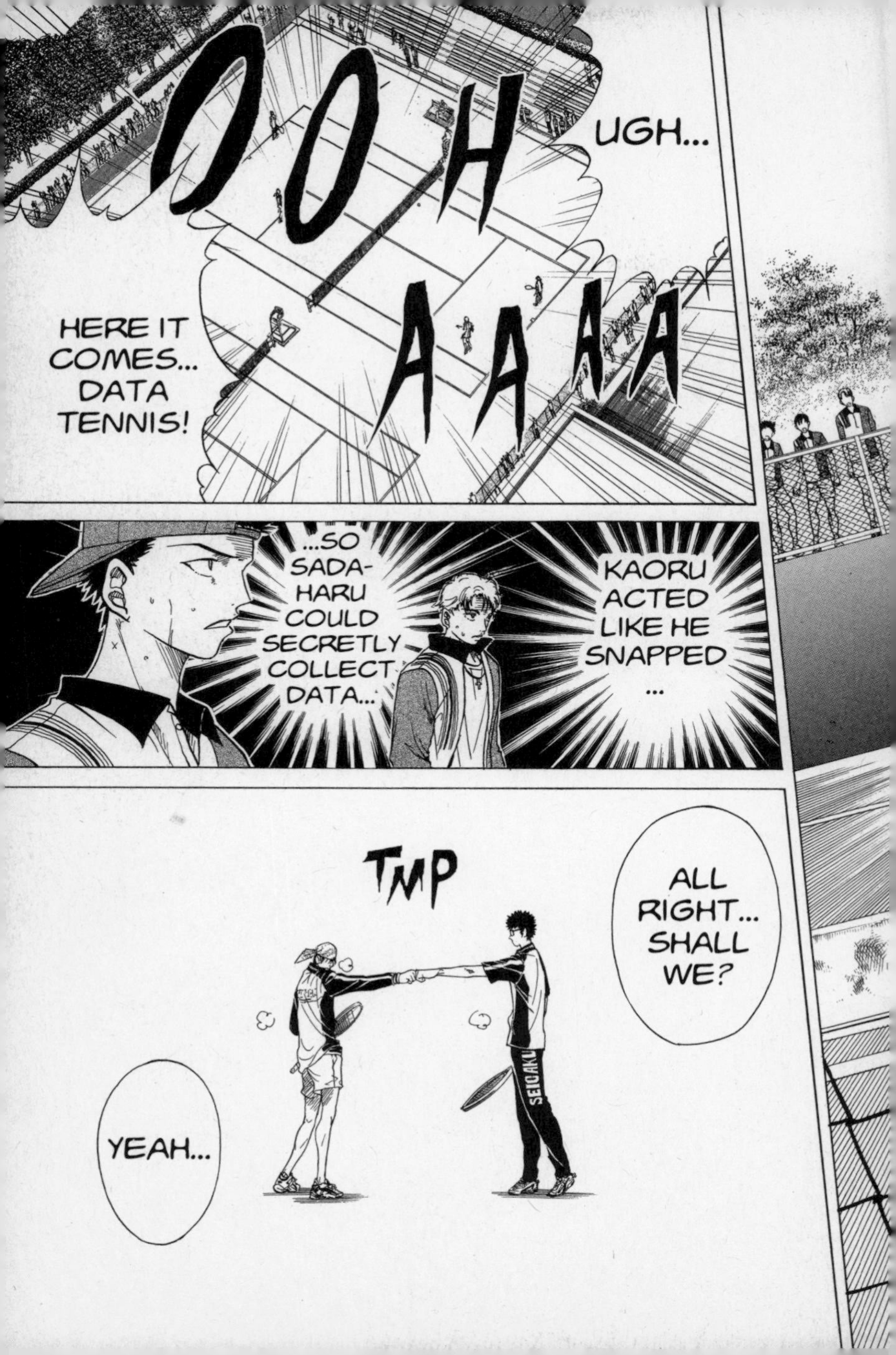
UGH...
OOH AAAA
HERE IT COMES... DATA TENNIS!
KAORU ACTED LIKE HE SNAPPED ...
...SO SADA-HARU COULD SECRETLY COLLECT DATA...
ALL RIGHT... SHALL WE?
TMP
YEAH...
SEIGAKU

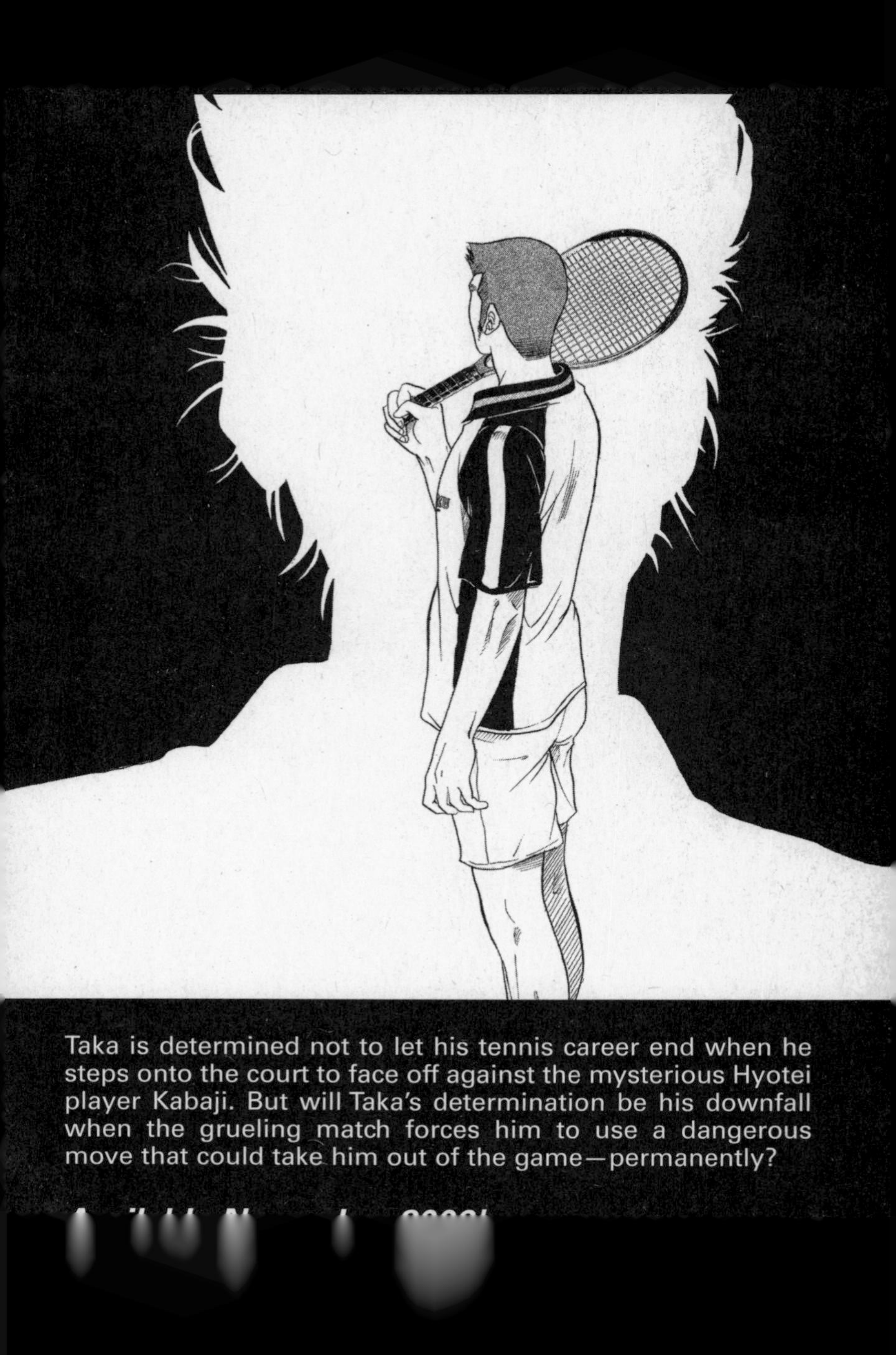

Taka is determined not to let his tennis career end when he steps onto the court to face off against the mysterious Hyotei player Kabaji. But will Taka's determination be his downfall when the grueling match forces him to use a dangerous move that could take him out of the game—permanently?

[redacted]

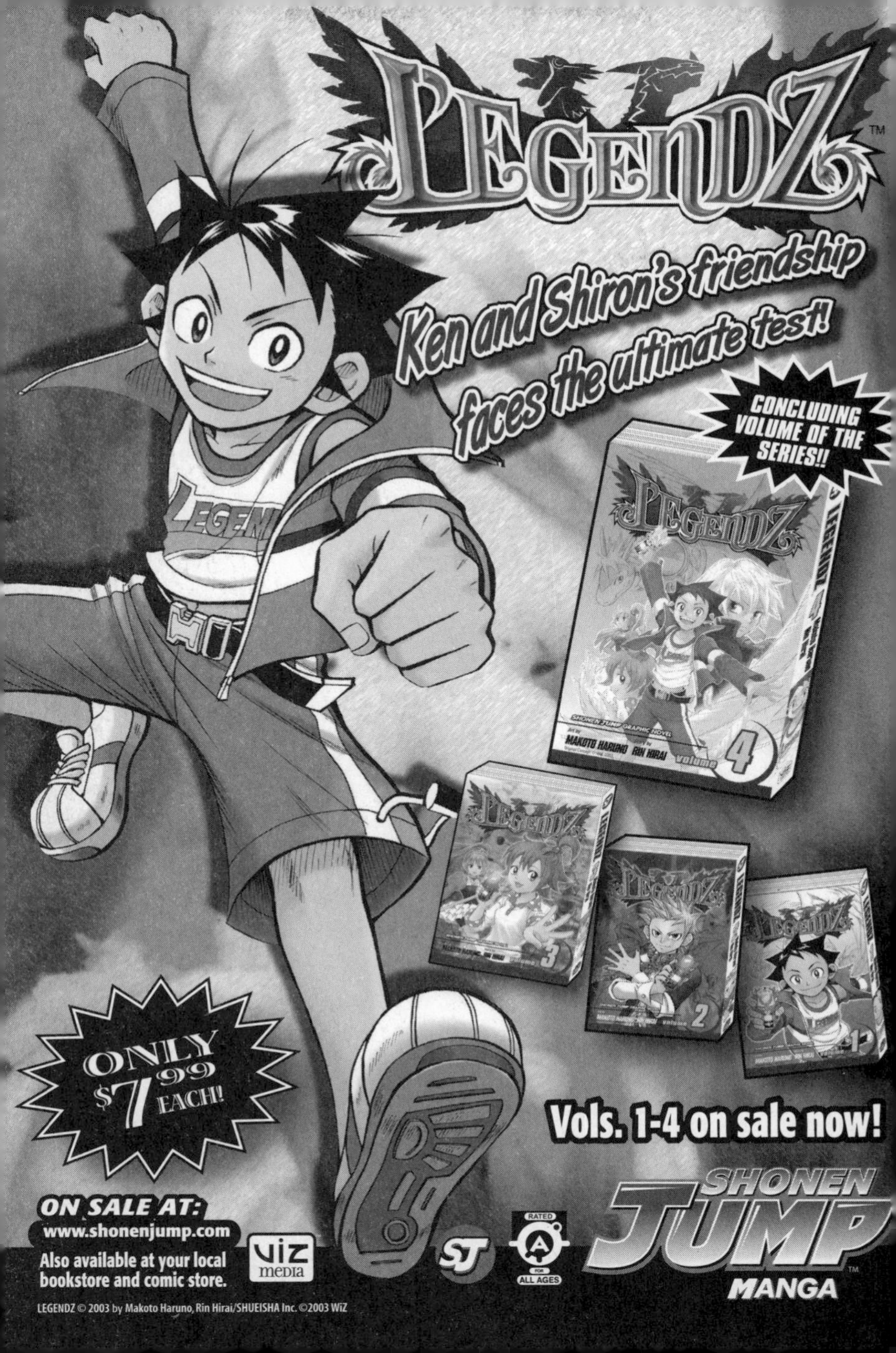
LEGENDZ™
Ken and Shiron's friendship faces the ultimate test!
CONCLUDING VOLUME OF THE SERIES!!
Vols. 1-4 on sale now!
ONLY $7 99 EACH!
ON SALE AT:
www.shonenjump.com
Also available at your local bookstore and comic store.
viz media
SJ
RATED A FOR ALL AGES
SHONEN JUMP™ MANGA
LEGENDZ © 2003 by Makoto Haruno, Rin Hirai/SHUEISHA Inc. ©2003 WiZ

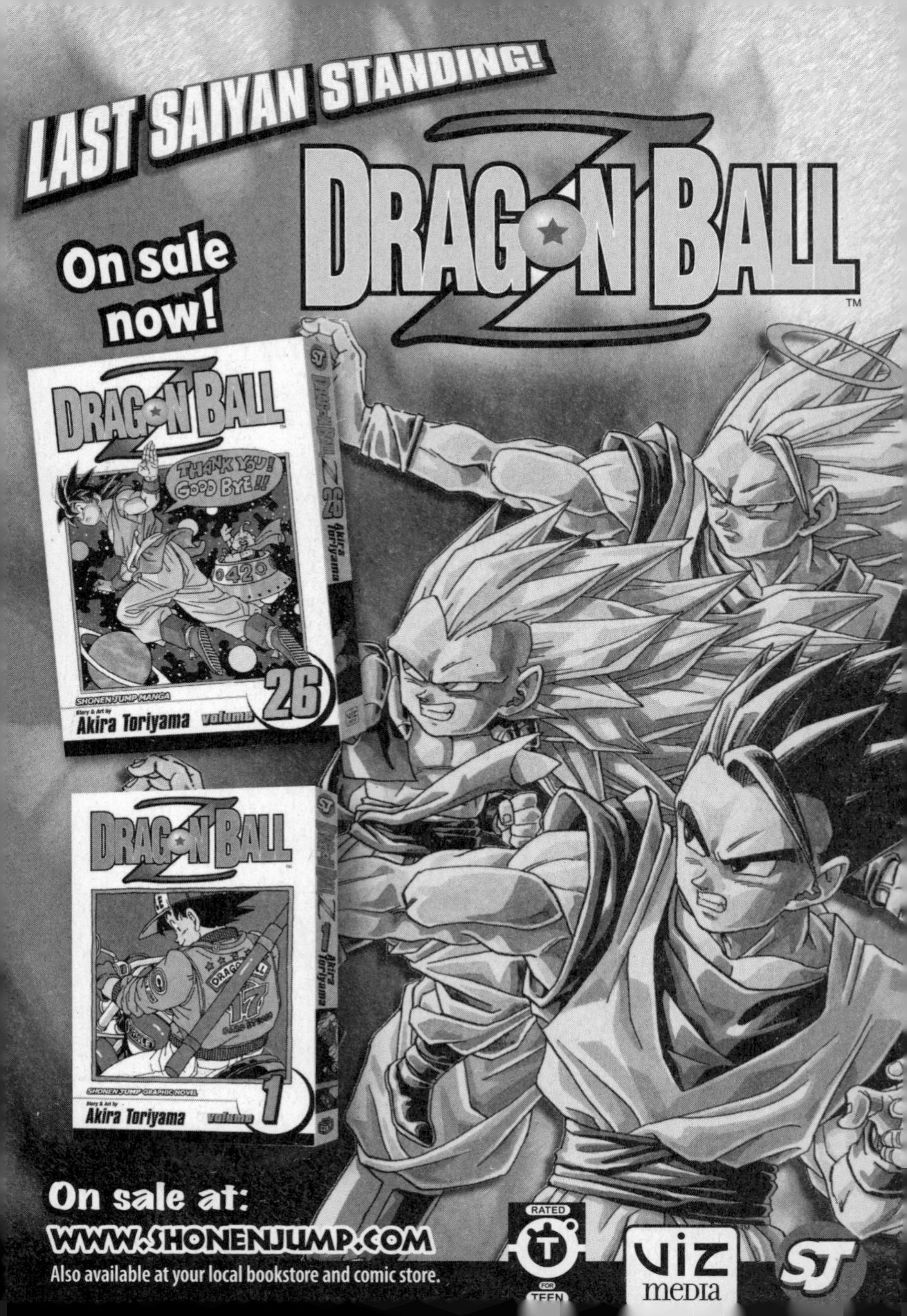
LAST SAIYAN STANDING!
DRAGON BALL Z
On sale now!
DRAGON BALL Z
THANK YOU! GOOD BYE!!
SHONEN JUMP MANGA
Akira Toriyama volume 26
DRAGON BALL Z
SHONEN JUMP GRAPHIC NOVEL
Akira Toriyama volume 1
On sale at:
WWW.SHONENJUMP.COM
Also available at your local bookstore and comic store.
RATED T FOR TEEN
viz media
SJ

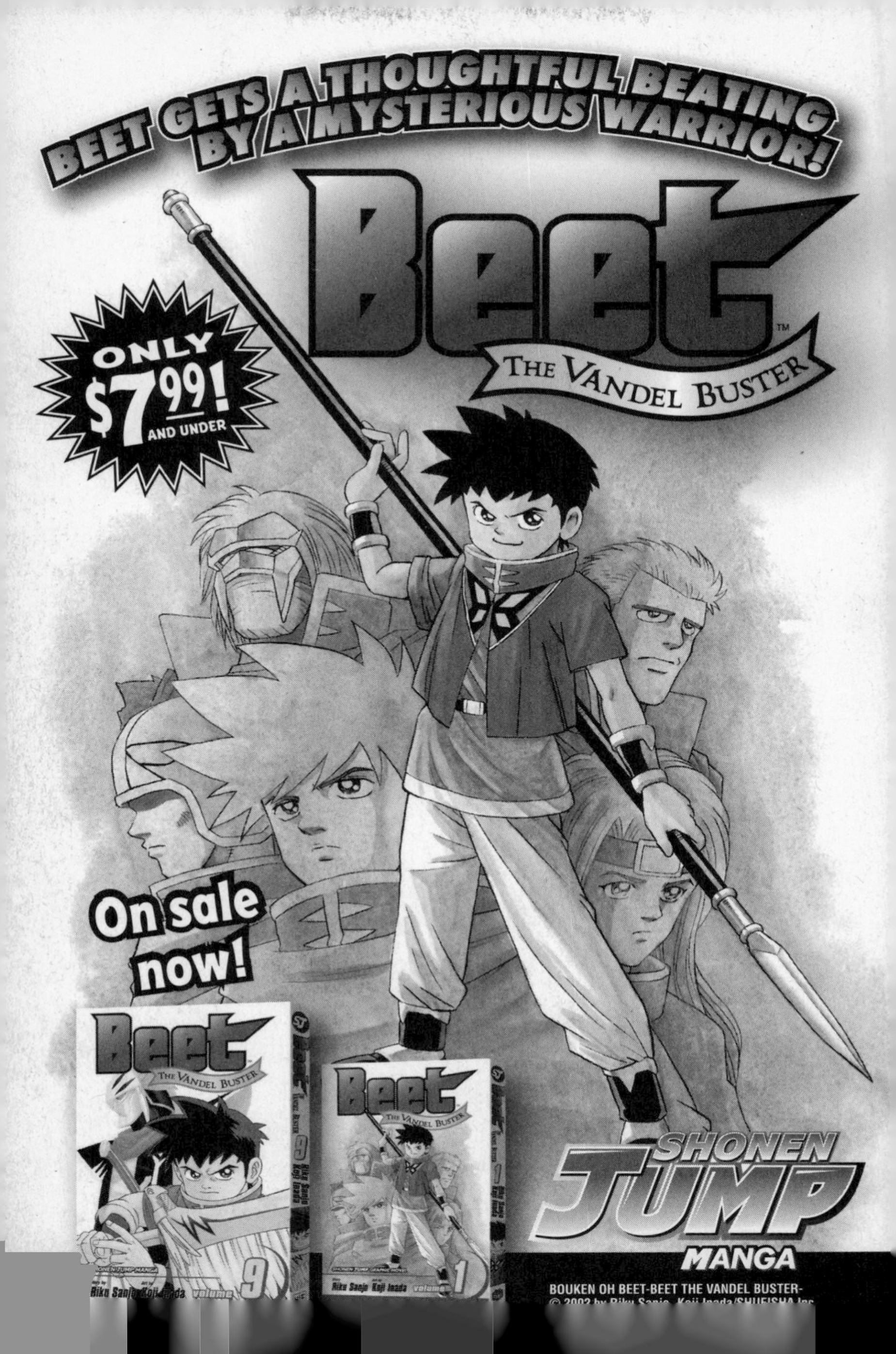
BEET GETS A THOUGHTFUL BEATING BY A MYSTERIOUS WARRIOR!
Beet™
THE VANDEL BUSTER
ONLY $7.99! AND UNDER
On sale now!
Beet
THE VANDEL BUSTER
9
Riku Sanjo Koji Inada
Beet
THE VANDEL BUSTER
1
Riku Sanjo Koji Inada
SHONEN JUMP
MANGA
BOUKEN OH BEET-BEET THE VANDEL BUSTER-
© 2002 by Riku Sanjo, Koji Inada/SHUEISHA Inc.

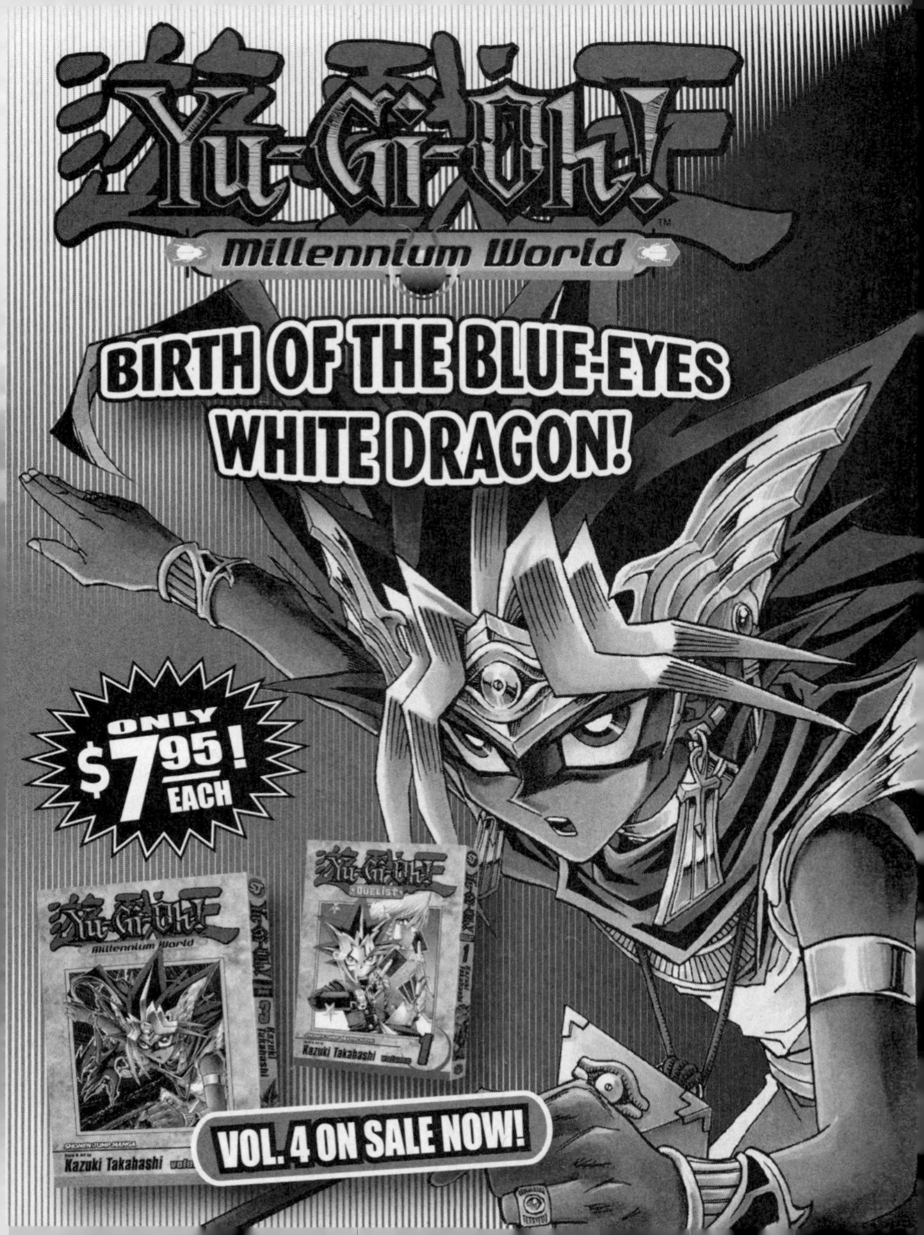
Yu-Gi-Oh!
Millennium World
BIRTH OF THE BLUE-EYES WHITE DRAGON!
ONLY $7.95! EACH
Yu-Gi-Oh! Millennium World
Kazuki Takahashi
Yu-Gi-Oh! Duelist
Kazuki Takahashi
VOL. 4 ON SALE NOW!

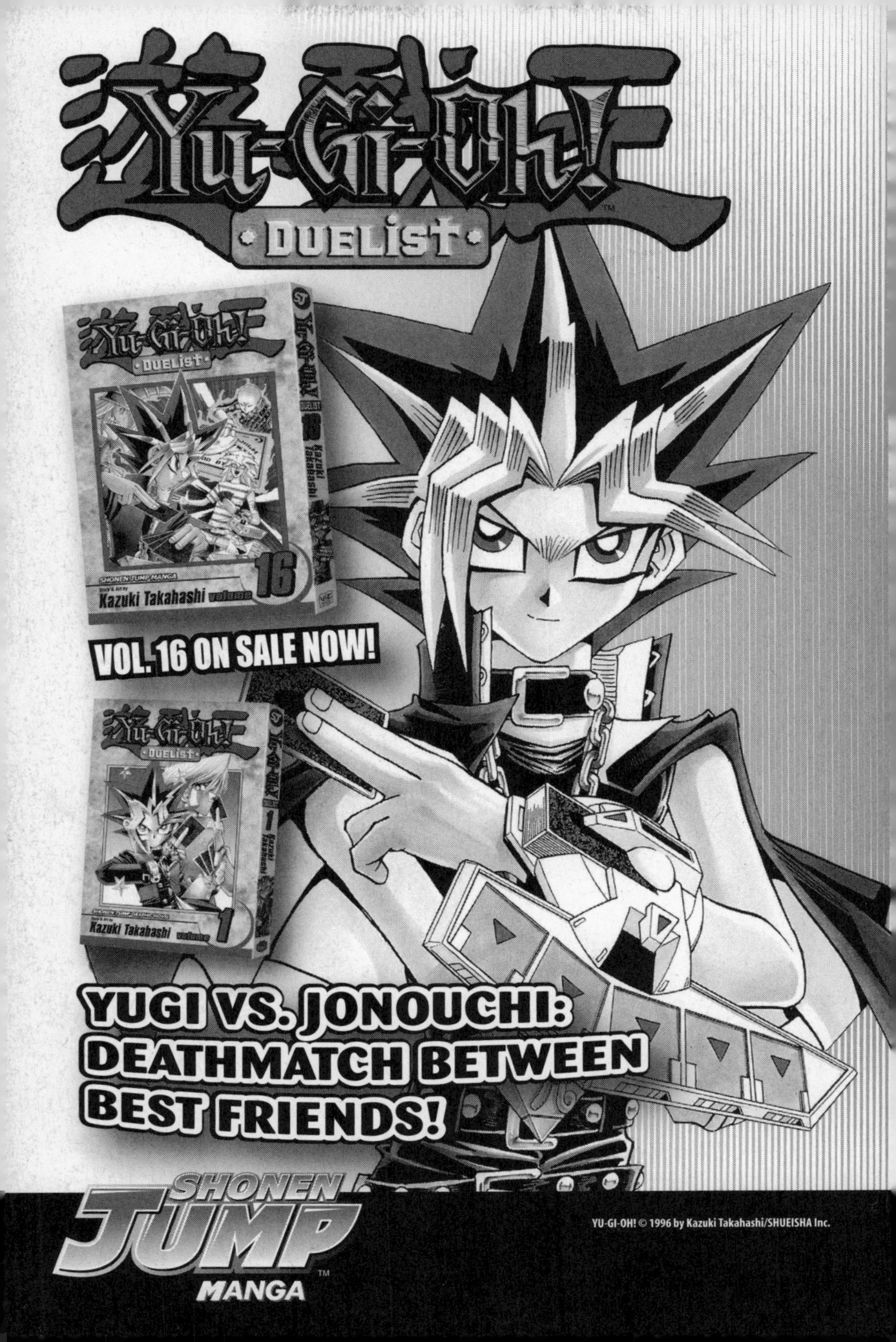
YU-GI-OH!™
DUELIST
VOL. 16 ON SALE NOW!
YUGI VS. JONOUCHI: DEATHMATCH BETWEEN BEST FRIENDS!
SHONEN JUMP™ MANGA
YU-GI-OH! © 1996 by Kazuki Takahashi/SHUEISHA Inc.

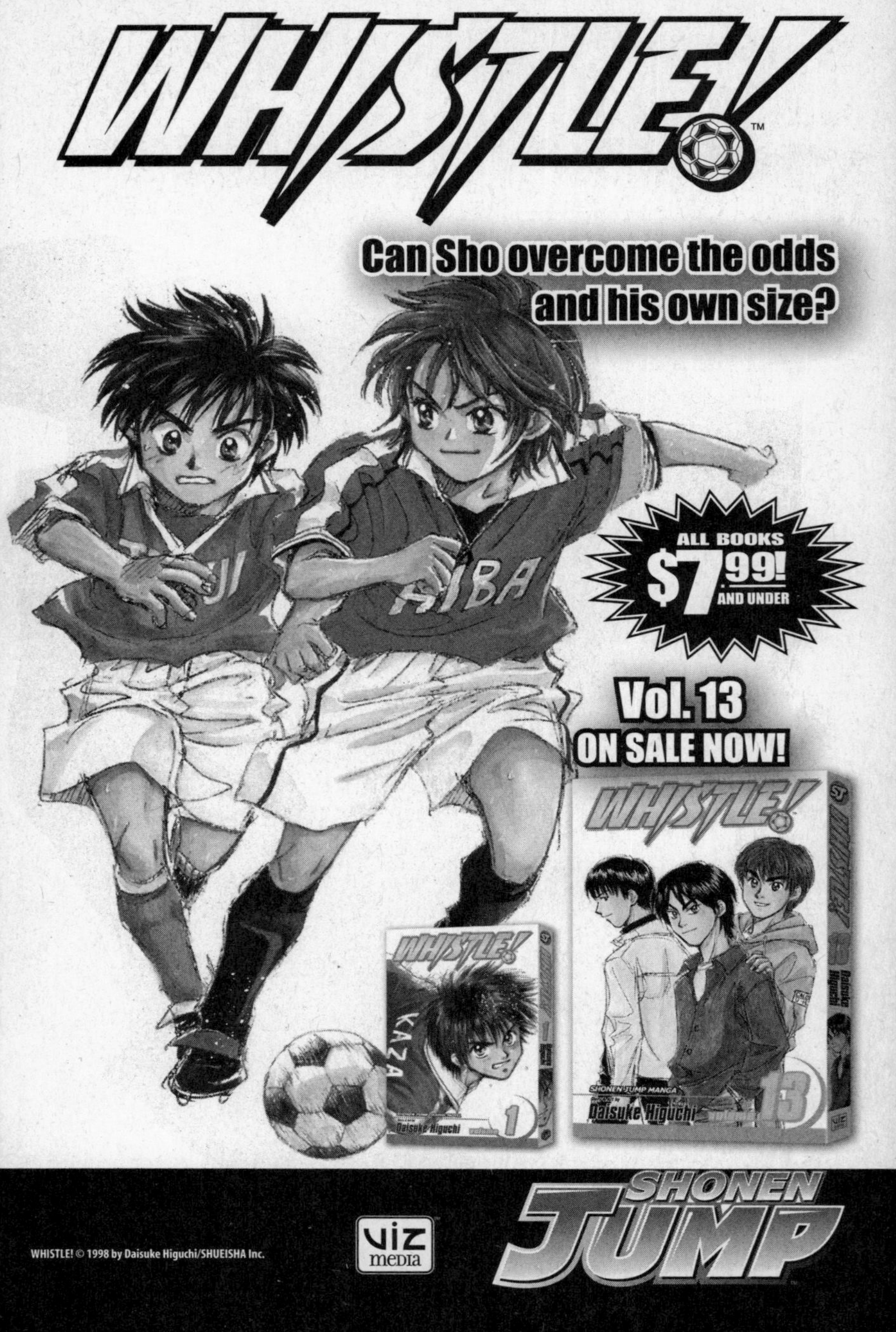
WHISTLE!™
Can Sho overcome the odds and his own size?
ALL BOOKS $7.99! AND UNDER
Vol. 13 ON SALE NOW!
WHISTLE!
Daisuke Higuchi
SHONEN JUMP MANGA
WHISTLE! © 1998 by Daisuke Higuchi/SHUEISHA Inc.
viz media
SHONEN JUMP

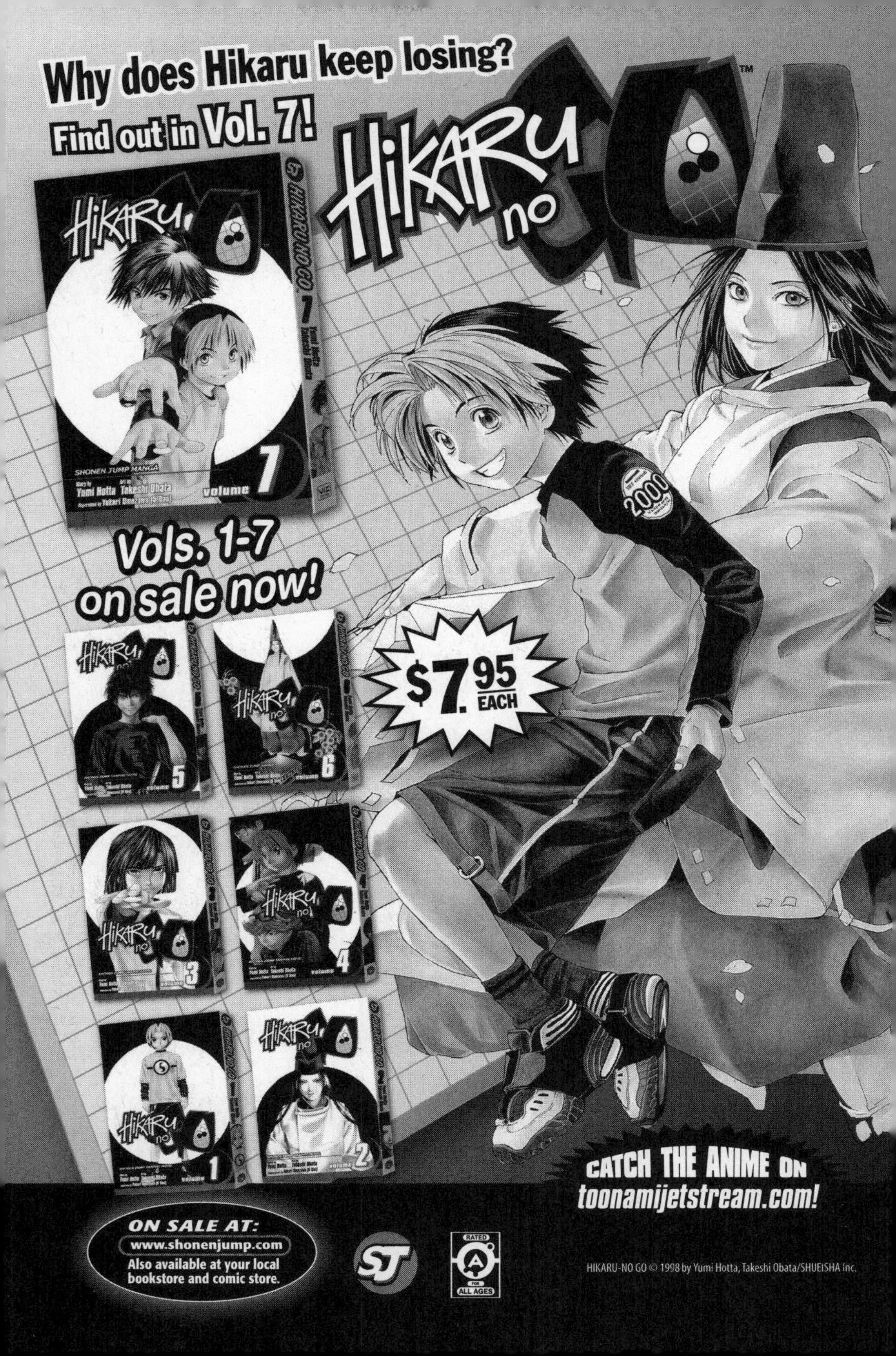

Why does Hikaru keep losing?
Find out in Vol. 7!
HIKARU no
Vols. 1-7 on sale now!
$7.95 EACH
CATCH THE ANIME ON
toonamijetstream.com!
ON SALE AT:
www.shonenjump.com
Also available at your local bookstore and comic store.
RATED A FOR ALL AGES
HIKARU-NO GO © 1998 by Yumi Hotta, Takeshi Obata/SHUEISHA Inc.

Tell us what you think about SHONEN JUMP manga!

Our survey is now available online.
Go to: www.**SHONENJUMP**.com/mangasurvey

Help us make our product offering better!